Warwick Studies in Industrial Relations
General Editors: Keith Sisson, Paul Edwards and Richard Hyman

Also available in this series

Government, Managers and Industrial Relations
Anthony Ferner

New Technology and Industrial Relations
Richard Hyman and Wolfgang Streeck

Farewell to Flexibility?
Edited by Anna Pollert

Training Matters
Helen Rainbird

Manufacturing Change, Industrial Relations and Restructuring
Edited by Stephanie Tailby and Colin Whitston

Legal Intervention in Industrial Relations
William McCarthy

Developments in the Management of Human Resources
John Storey

Developments in the Management of Human Resources

An Analytical Review

John Storey

BLACKWELL
Business

First published 1992
Reprinted 1992, 1993 (twice), 1994

Blackwell Publishers
108 Cowley Road
Oxford OX4 1JF
UK

238 Main Street
Cambridge, Massachusetts 02142
USA

British Library Cataloguing in Publication Data
A CIP catalogue record for this book is available from the British Library.

Library of Congress Cataloging-in-Publication Data
Storey, John.
   Developments in the Management of Human Resources / John Storey.
      p.   cm.
   Includes bibliographical references.
   ISBN 0–631–18398–1 (pbk.: acid-free paper)
   1. Personnel management.   I. Title.
HF5549.S877   1992
   658.3 – dc20   91–39200
                                                              CIP

Typeset in 11 on 13pt Times
by Graphicraft Typesetters Ltd., Hong Kong
Printed in Great Britain by TJ Press (Padstow) Ltd., Padstow, Cornwall

This book is printed on acid-free paper

Contents

List of figures   vii
Foreword   ix
Preface   xii
List of abbreviations   xv

 1 Transitions and Transformations?   1
 2 The HRM Phenomenon   23
 3 Mainstream Companies in Transition   48
 4 Managing Human Resources in Practice:
    A Thematic Analysis   80
 5 Managing the Process of Change   118
 6 The Part Played by Personnel Specialists in the
    Management of Human Resources   162
 7 The Part Played by Senior and Middle Line
    Managers in the Management of Human
    Resources   189
 8 The Part Played by First Line Managers in the
    Management of Human Resources   216
 9 Trade Unions and Industrial Relations   242
10 Conclusions   263

Appendix: Research Methods   280
Bibliography   286
Index   297

To Anne, Patricia, Pauline and Rebecca

Figures

Figure 2.1   HRM 'mapping' of various meanings   27

Figure 2.2   Twenty-seven points of difference   35

Figure 2.3   A model of the shift to human resource management   38

Figure 3.1   The case companies   49

Figure 3.2   A schematic outline of change in the case organizations   50

Figure 3.3   'Mission, Values and Guiding Principles', Ford Motor Company   57

Figure 4.1   Full summary of results   82

Figure 4.2   Employee Communications at Peugeot-Talbot Motor Company Ltd   102

Figure 4.3   Structure for employee communication and involvement at Jaguar   104

Figure 5.1   Types of managed-change process   123

Figure 5.2   Locational placings of selected case organizations on the managed-change map   124

Figure 5.3   Ford's EI eight-point implementation plan   141

Figure 6.1   Types of personnel management   168

Figure 7.1   A crucial fusion   195

Figure 7.2   Types of line manager   197

Figure 8.1   Types of supervisor   220

Foreword

The University of Warwick is the major centre in the United Kingdom for the study of industrial relations. Teaching of the subject began in 1966 in the School of Industrial and Business Studies, which now has one of the country's largest graduate programmes. Warwick became a national centre for research in industrial relations in 1970 when the Social Science Research Council (now the Economic and Social Research Council) established its Industrial Relations Research Unit at the University. In 1984 the Unit was reconstituted as a Designated Research Centre within the School of Industrial and Business Studies. It continues to be known as the Industrial Relations Research Unit, however, and it now embraces the research activities of all members of the School's industrial relations community.

The series of Warwick Studies in Industrial Relations was launched in 1972 by Hugh Clegg and George Bain as the main vehicle for the publication of the results of the Unit's research projects, as well as the research conducted by staff teaching industrial relations in the University and the work of graduate students. The first six titles were published by Heinemann Educational Books of London, and subsequent volumes have been published by Blackwell Publishers of Oxford.

This book contains the results of a project that was innovatory in many ways. Organizationally, it was a novelty for the Unit: in 1986 we began a system of two-year secondments, designed to permit senior staff in academia, government or industry to conduct full-time research. John Storey was one of the first colleagues to join us through this route. This book, together with a large number of related publications, demonstrates the value of the system.

The book's substantive novelty is that it is the first detailed research-based analysis of its subject matter. During the 1980s, there was extensive debate about 'human resource management', including such issues as how distinct it was from personnel management, its implications for line managers as well as personnel specialists, and how far it represented a new means of managing workers. There have been some valuable overviews and conceptual discussions, not least the volume *New Perspectives on Human Resource Management* which Storey himself edited. But thorough empirical exploration of HRM has been absent.

Developments in the Management of Human Resources looks in detail at 15 organizations, in the private and public sectors. A particular feature is that, as Storey notes in his preface, the great majority of interviewees were general or line managers, not personnel specialists. This is significant for the book's own themes, for one of the key arguments is that major initiatives often came from outside the personnel department and that line managers were willing to adopt the new style of 'people management' precisely because it was not a specifically personnel scheme but was embraced by their own superiors. It is also an illustration of the development of the Unit's research focus. Understanding industrial relations increasingly requires attention to issues outside the traditional area of collective bargaining and to actors other than personnel managers and trade-union officers. Our work has developed while retaining a central interest in the employment relationship.

This book illustrates continuity as well as development, for it stands in the Unit tradition of detailed, painstaking inquiry designed to study an issue in depth and to draw out analytical lessons. The reader will not find simple messages. Instead, John Storey explores the many facets of the HRM phenomenon, including how far it is an integrated practice, its links with other aspects of personnel management, its meaning for line managers, personnel specialists and supervisors and its implications for trade unions. The book will thus be invaluable to all those wishing to understand how human resource management operates in practice and how work in Britain was re-organized during the 1980s.

Keith Sisson
Paul Edwards
Richard Hyman

Preface

This book examines the changing contours of employment management. Using a unique database, it contributes to crucial debates about the change in employer-led initiatives; the extent to which these initiatives have a 'strategic' character; and the degree to which the combination of initiatives amount to a qualitative shift in the approach to the management of labour. In these and other regards the book is designed to be of interest to second and third year undergraduates and to MBA students.

The book also describes the welter of recent initiatives, their extent and their patterning. It analyses the meanings and significances of these initiatives and the changes which they have set in train. It also assesses their impact and ramifications. Information and analysis of this kind is likely to be of interest to many practitioners, certainly to personnel specialists, but also to line and general managers in all sectors.

The phenomenon of human resource management has evoked tremendous interest from practitioners and academics alike in recent years. *New Perspectives on Human Resource Management*, the book that I edited in 1989, went a long way towards meeting the demand for information and analysis of this controversial subject. However, as was emphasized in *New Perspectives* what was, and still is, needed is a solid research-based examination of recent changes. *Developments in the Management of Human Resources* is designed to meet that central requirement. It draws on 350 in-depth interviews with managers at all levels. These managers were located in 15 'core case' companies and in an additional 25 'panel' companies. Of particular note is that some 80 per cent of the interviewees were line and general managers rather than personnel specialists. This is critical given the thesis advanced in the book that many of the more far-reaching initiatives have been formulated *outside* the personnel function, and given the fact that most previous research has relied over-much on personnel specialist spokespersons for intelligence on what has been supposedly happening or not happening. This book may perhaps be truly described as the first full-length study of the part played by line and general managers in the conduct of the management of the human resource.

The study brings into focus those elements, such as organizational culture and restructuring, which although not traditionally regarded as central, or even perhaps part of, 'industrial relations' or 'personnel management' as traditionally conceived, can nonetheless be shown to be every bit as important to management-worker relations as pay and other effort-bargain elements normally seen as appropriately within the domain.

Another distinctive feature of this book is that real case names are used throughout and full use is also made of verbatim quotations from participants. These features add a further texture to the accounts.

A project of this size and complexity builds up more than the usual number of debts. The study was made possible in the first place because of funding from the Economic and Social Research Council. The Council paid my salary and allowed me to travel extensively to every corner of the country. I owe intellectual debts to many individuals. First and foremost I want to pay tribute to my colleague Keith Sisson. His profound ability to get quickly to the heart of complex issues and his unpretentious modest style are only but two of the qualities which won my admiration and respect. As a Research Unit Director he offers leadership and unstinting generous support to all of his staff. In this role one suspects he is unsurpassed.

I must also acknowledge the value of the critical reviews of earlier drafts of this work from the other Warwick Series Editors: Anthony Ferner, Richard Hyman and Paul Edwards. Practical support and assistance was also given by George Bain and Chris Voss – both now at the London Business School.

I was fortunate in being able to compare notes with many visiting academics to the University of Warwick from numerous overseas countries. Of particular help were the discussions and subsequent exchange of correspondence with Michael Beer from Harvard and Bob McKersie from MIT.

My final debt is to the 350 managers who cooperated with the data gathering. In a sense it is invidious to pick out particular names but certain individuals made an enduring impression on the study either because of the interpretive stamp they made or because of the enthusiastic assistance they afforded me. In these regards therefore I am pleased to thank: Bryan Cogger and John Hougham of the Ford Motor Company, Alan Hanslip of Whitbread, Mike Fenton of Eaton's, Jim George of Trent Regional Health Authority, Norman Haslam of Rover Group, Neil Fenwick of Bradford Metropolitan Council, Derek Bucknall of British Aerospace, David Herbert of Birds Eye Walls, Malcolm Boyd, Ken Beresford and Ivor Warburton of British Rail, Peter Boreham and Alan Kennedy of ICI, Mike Kinski at Jaguar, Alan Hurford and Nick Everest at Lucas, Geoff Armstrong of Metal Box, David Billingham and Ian Bonnar of Massey Ferguson, Mike Judge of Peugeot, Timothy Wood of Plessey, Roy Nicholson and Howell Parry of Smith & Nephew, and Ken Berry at Rolls Royce. Such is the pace of managerial job-change in British industry nowadays that nearly all of these individuals are now occupying different roles. Most of them have remained, however, in touch with the unfolding of this study. To them and the other participants: many thanks.

John Storey

Abbreviations

ACAS	Advisory, Conciliation and Arbitration Service
AEU	Amalgamated Engineering Union
ASLEF	Associated Society of Locomotive Engineers and Firemen
ASTMS	Association of Scientific, Technical and Managerial Staffs
BSC	British Steel Corporation
CBI	Confederation of British Industry
CMEAD	Council for Management Education and Development
CSEU	Confederation of Shipbuilding and Engineering Unions
DE	Department of Employment
EEF	Engineering Employers Federation
EETPU	Electrical, Electronic, Telecommunications and Plumbing Union
EI	Employee Involvement
ER	Employee Relations
ESRC	Economic and Social Research Council
FT	The Financial Times
GNP	Gross National Product
HMSO	Her Majesty's Stationery Office
HRD	Human Resource Development
HRM	Human Resource Management
IBM	International Business Machines
IDS	Incomes Data Services

IPM	Institute of Personnel Management
IR	Industrial Relations
IRRR	Industrial Relations Review and Report
JIT	Just-In-Time
JWC	Joint Works Council
MBA	Master of Business Administration
MCI	Management Charter Initiative
MIT	Massachusetts Institute of Technology
MRPII	Manufacturing Resource Planning
MSC	Manpower Services Commission
MSF	Manufacturing, Science and Finance Union
MVGP	Mission, Values and Guiding Principles
NEDO	National Economic Development Office
NHSTA	National Health Service Training Authority
NJIC	National Joint Industrial Council
NJNC	National Joint Negotiating Council
NSQC	National Society of Quality Circles
NUR	National Union of Railwaymen
OB	Organizational Behaviour
OD	Organizational Development
PBR	Payment by Results
QCs	Quality Circles
QWL	Quality of Working Life
SAYE	Save As You Earn
SBU	Small Business Unit
SWOT	Strengths, Weaknesses, Opportunities and Threats
TASS	Technical, Administrative and Supervisory Section (of the Amalgamated Union of Engineering Workers)
TGWU	Transport and General Workers Union
TSSA	Transport Salaried Staffs Association
TUC	Trades Union Congress
TVEI	Technical and Vocational Educational Initiative
WIRS1	Workplace Industrial Relations Survey, Number 1
WIRS2	Workplace Industrial Relations Survey, Number 2

1

Transitions and Transformations?

INTRODUCTION

From the United States and other advanced industrial countries have come reports of 'radical changes' in methods of management and work organization (Walton, 1987). These comprise part of a far-reaching response to intense international competition. The changes are said to go beyond 'adjustments' to the prevailing pattern deriving from concession bargaining on wages and work-rules. Innovations reportedly include changes across the whole band of ways in which human resources are deployed and managed. According to what is probably the most authoritative academic group in the USA (Kochan et al., 1986), the far-reaching changes in industrial relations amount to no less than a departure from the standard 'new deal' pattern forged over 50 years ago. The pattern of change has been seen also to impact on organizational structures and cultures: including, *inter alia*, fewer hierarchical levels, fewer job classifications, the use of work-teams, a step-change in commitment to training and an entirely new approach to quality (Walton, 1987; Altshuler et al., 1984; Beer, 1990; Pascale, 1990). A range of major cases in America tends to be cited by these authors: GM, Bethlehem Steel, AT&T, Digital, Ford, Hewlett-Packard, EXXON, Polaroid, Rockwell International and Xerox. Similar indicators, though certainly less dramatic, have been reported from many other parts of the world including Eastern as well as Western Europe, the Middle East and Australia.

But what, if anything, has been happening to management in Britain? More particularly, what changes are being wrought in the way employees are managed? One might imagine that after more than a decade of 'Thatcherism' there would be at least some broad measure of agreement about the answers to these questions; instead, there is massive controversy. According to one view just about everything has altered while according to another the pattern remains broadly the same.

The purpose of this book is to add an empirically-based analytical contribution to the debate. In large measure this has so far been missing. Discussion about 'human resource management' for example, of which there has been plenty, has been hampered by a lack of relevant information. There is widespread agreement that what is especially required is systematic case-based research. This book represents an extended report on a research project which set out to provide just this sort of data. The project focused on the mainstream employing organizations in Britain, that is, not the 'trail-blazers' or 'outliers' such as Rank Xerox or IBM. The journey of discovery began without any initial presumption of either transformation or stability.

The first real discovery was of the sheer welter of initiatives and 'programmes'. These were evidently on a scale which had not been encountered in my previous forays into management behaviour in the 1970s (Storey, 1980, 1983). Something was apparently going on. But what, and what depth did it have? The array of approaches found was almost bewildering. This was so not only for the outside observer but evidently for many of the participants themselves. From the researcher's perspective, the obvious first question concerned whether there was any underlying logic to this flurry of activity. In the background was the debate about HRM but it seemed to me that irrespective of whether these management-led initiatives were indicative of HRM or not they were important subjects for study in their own right. A range of different 'patterns', 'ideal types' and 'styles' of industrial relations has been mapped (Purcell and Sisson, 1983; Fox, 1974). Recent changes could be compared against any or all of these, in which case there would seem to be little reason to 'privilege' the human resource management model with special attention. It is notable in fact that neither of these sources even used the term. Yet by the mid-to-late 1980s, human resource management had become the dominant theme in attempts to 'make sense' of what was unfolding. While scepticism was as prevalent as conviction, the importance of the concept could not be doubted.

The approach taken in this book is to use the extensive body of data collected, not simply to 'test' the HRM model (though this will be part of the exercise) but to make a more definitive interpretation of what was going on in those cases where the model proved insufficient for the task. The central thrust of the analysis is thus the management of change. The degree to which some of this change has been cloaked in the rhetoric of HRM is in itself part of the research problem. How this came about, why it happened and with what consequences, are interesting and relevant issues.

FORMS OF EXPLANATION

In addition to describing what was happening in these organizations, this book is intended to go a step further, and that is to interpret and 'make sense' of developments found. In the social sciences it is well recognized that there are different ways in which an 'explanation' can be constructed. For example, social behaviour can be 'accounted for' using rational cause-and-effect explanations; alternatively, 'functionalist' explanations can be used to trace the 'reason' for social action back to certain positive outcomes for the 'system' irrespective of the rationales offered by participants. In contrast, interpretive and phenomenological accounts give primacy to actors' own meaning systems; structural accounts delve into deep-seated material interests of conflicting groups which may pattern behaviour at the unconscious level; micro-political explanations call attention to the vested interests of organizational and occupational coalitions. (See Hopper, Storey and Willmott, 1987, for a discussion of the application of these diverse frameworks to the study of management behaviour.) The phenomenon of human resource management could conceivably be examined and 'explained' using most, if not all, of these perspectives, though obviously with varying degrees of successful insight. Given the nature of HRM as an evocative rhetoric, the potentialities of the symbolic, interpretive perspective seem to cry out for particular attention.

Analysis of organizational behaviour, drawing upon the significance of the 'symbolic', came to the fore in organizational studies in the early 1980s (Pondy et al., 1983; Dandridge et al., 1980; Pfeffer, 1981). These writers drew, in turn, upon an earlier generation of anthropologists and social psychologists (Malinowski, 1955; Eliade, 1963) who delved into the deeper layers of meaning, which are part of all human interaction and organization. The insights afforded by attending to these 'hidden' aspects of behaviour have more recently been recognized and applied by analysts working on strategic change management (Johnson, 1990) and industrial relations (Ahlstrand, 1990) as well as in organizational analysis itself (Turner, 1990). Johnson's work, which stresses the importance of 'cognitive shifts' in bringing about strategic change in business organizations, is redolent with implications for our attempt here to understand changing paradigms in the management of labour. As he suggests, organizational change needs to be understood 'in cognitive, cultural, and political terms; and also in terms of political symbols and symbolic action' (Johnson, 1990: 183). In similar vein, Ahlstrand explains the persistent attachment to productivity bargaining at Fawley, in the face of repeated failure at the rational level, as deriving from the deeper symbolic significance of this approach on the Fawley site. This analysis also is powerfully suggestive of a possible way to account for the HRM phenomenon. However, attractive as the 'symbolic approach' may appear to be, it would be too simplistic to purport to 'explain' attachment to, or changes to, managerial recipes for labour management purely in these terms.

There are two key problems in applying the Ahlstrand account to human resource management. The first problem is one which in my view is a contradiction even in the original study. In essence, Ahlstrand's argument is that by attending to the 'symbolic' one can access the 'hidden reasons behind the continued use of productivity bargaining at Fawley', that is the 'deeper set of meanings' which 'make sense' of what was happening (p. 211). Ahlstrand argues that productivity bargaining can be investigated at a deeper level if one attends to the 'underlying symbolic basis' of it – 'that is, in terms of its function as "myth", "ritual" and "rhetoric"' (p. 212). Now, the problem is that if one appeals to these supposed 'hidden', 'deeper' and 'unconscious' aspects of social life, then it is surely awkward if the vast bulk of the data is constituted by the accounts of interviewees who, far from being ensnared by 'myth', are patently worldly-wise about the whole thing. Seemingly, all Ahlstrand's informants, from senior managers and supervisors to shop stewards, 'explained' the 'meaning' of productivity bargaining precisely in the terms of 'I gave them what they wanted to hear' (p. 218). Other informants talked of trading on the 'productivity mystique' (p. 223). And at the height of the fad there were even articles in national newspapers publicly assessing productivity bargaining in precisely these terms. It is therefore hard to argue from a basis of 'deep hidden meanings' when these self-same meanings are so manifestly traded. It hardly suggests 'an unquestioned belief about the practical benefits of certain techniques and behaviours that is not supported by demonstrated facts', which is how Trice and Beyer (1984: 655) actually define 'myth'. None of the informants quoted by Ahlstrand gives the remotest hint of holding an 'unquestioned belief' about the phenomenon; on the contrary they all adopt a quite opposite view. This discrepancy is clearly a problem for the symbolic approach.

A second problem, and this one arises not in connection with Ahlstrand but directly out of the 15 mainstream cases, is that many of the managers in the study were clearly all too aware of the possible 'symbolic' appurtenances of HRM and were, in consequence, cautious about simply adopting the rhetoric. Hence, even those who were quite heavily involved in driving forward major initiatives, were often chary about donning the garb of HRM. The implication is that analysts should not expect to be able simply to borrow concepts and methods devised by anthropologists for studying non-literate cultures and apply these unproblematically to complex and sophisticated formal organizations.

Accordingly, while the explanatory approach used in this study has recourse to 'symbolic management activities' in its attempt to interpret recent management initiatives, it does not imply by this a simplistic adoption of a 'new phrase' by managers as if this might 'explain' the take-up of human resource management. The reality was much more complex and much more subtle. If 'symbolic action' is taken to denote 'signs which express much more than their intrinsic content' (Pondy et al., 1983: 5), then many of the actions taken by management and workers could be seen as carrying symbolic aspects. For example, the importance accorded to having a certain number of quality circles operating, stemmed not so much from what these circles delivered but from the implied message that part of the shopfloor could be persuaded to engage in job-related problem solving and therefore, by extension, that the effort bargain was more open-ended than a labour contract approach would suggest.

Many of the elements, separately and accumulatively, of the management initiatives explored in this book carried this latent message, that is that there were viable alternatives to the closely argued 'proceduralist' route to labour management. It was possible but not necessary, to bundle up these initiatives into a coherent package or programme. Some managers saw tactical advantage in so doing; others divined it otherwise. But, separately or together, the initiatives represented symbolic action in the Pondy sense in that they carried meanings which extended beyond their 'intrinsic content'.

The point that is worthy of note, even in these introductory remarks, is that the majority of the participants did not dress up their accounts in terms of human resource management, although the underlying logic often revealed key elements of that frame of reference. Thus for example, appeals to 'consistency', 'set procedures', 'compromise', 'rule and regulation' (all of which figured prominently in my 1970s research) were very, very rare in this late 1980s project. References to 'competitive markets', 'needs of the business', 'our organizational culture', 'mission', 'customer requirements', and 'commitment' were, however, routine. These phrases and their associated outlooks were embedded in the managerial consciousness at just about all levels of the hierarchy. To this degree at least, there seemed to be some evidence of a paradigm shift.

This in itself was of interest. The next problem became how to trace and interpret the extent and depth of change to actual practice and behaviour. In addition, what alteration to employee meaning systems had occurred? This project opened up the opportunity to advance debate in these matters. It was necessary to proceed in logical steps in order to make this advance. First, as indicated, it was evident that managerial language and frames of reference had changed. This then raised a second issue: had these been translated into concrete initiatives, and if so, of what nature and significance? The third issue concerned impact, that is, to what extent had any new policies and practices in labour management actually made any difference?

Answers to some of these questions were more easily obtainable than others. There were signs of a plethora of managerial initiatives. This in itself should not be underestimated. It stands in contrast to the situation in the 1960s and 1970s when fads and fashions such as 'quality of working life' (QWL), 'organizational development' (OD), job enrichment and task level participation were being hyped in the journals but rarely translated into much of substance in the workplace. It soon became evident in this project that the critical aspects concerned not so much whether an organization had 'tried' say, quality circles, team briefing or whatever, but the extent of their application, whether they constituted the new main approach to labour management replacing pre-existing policies and practices, whether the initiatives were integrated with each other and with the business strategy, what durability they had, and what impact.

As I have already pointed out, the debate had been cast in fairly simplistic terms. Transformation had been pitched against continuity (or more strictly speaking the other way around because while continuity theorists were in the main reacting to writers who were proselytizing transformation, these latter have rarely even acknowledged the existence of their critics). Evidence to substantiate the rival positions has been rather flimsy. On the transformation side much of it has been anecdotal whereas on the continuity side the measures such as the persistence of bargaining machinery clearly cannot in themselves refute the possibility that other, arguably more significant changes, have meanwhile been occurring.

If one brings a social action perspective to bear, these rival positions open up rather more fruitfully. First, to take the sceptical stance, one can attend closely to the reactions of shopfloor workers to the new initiatives. At this point in the argument just one case will serve to illustrate. In the company in question a series of measures had been taken to 'promote excellence' over the immediately preceding three-year period. Changes to working practices had been driven through, everyone had attended culture change courses and service engineers and others who had occasion to meet customers were encouraged to start selling products and services. Cash commissions were initially paid but these have since been replaced with a system of 'points' which can be traded for consumer items listed in a colour catalogue. Additional points can be accumulated by correctly answering questions pertaining to the change programme materials. Then, towards the end of the period during which this case was studied, a 'total quality' programme was introduced. Further training days in local hotels were arranged. I asked one of the engineering craftsmen what it all meant to him. He replied:

> It's indoctrination isn't it? Nobody wants to go on all these courses, people find them very boring. We go because we have to, there's no choice. They are just something you have to get through. Even the trainers are bored. They go through the same lines time after time, using the same scripts and even the same jokes. What a waste of time! They gave us little lapel badges with 'TC' on them and told us that anyone wearing one of these would be approached by interesting people in the pub.

> *Well, what did you do with yours? Did you wear it?*

> [Laughs] No! I threw it away. It's not just me either. There are 20 in my team. Not one of them has started wearing the badge. They'd be too embarrassed to now.

> *So what is going on? What is the meaning of total quality to you and all of the other changes we've been talking about?*

> As far as I'm concerned it's about getting us all to work harder. It means sacking half the blokes and getting the other half to work twice as hard.

There is evidently little sign of the 'winning of commitment' here. Yet behind the impasse on attitudes, there had been, even in this case, substantial changes in work patterns and behaviour. Productivity was higher, the range of responsibilities shouldered was much wider. What seemed to need looking at was the possibility that the way in which management has moved since the mid-1980s has been of a different order. The nature of that movement seems complex. There has been no sign of a concerted change of direction. But, through experimentation, the use of consultants, an unusual willingness to learn from other cases – and through a whole set of other means which are discussed in detail in chapter 5, many British organizations in the late 1980s did appear to begin to alter their 'recipes' relating to labour management.

Whether this change in direction merits the vaunted title of HRM is hardly the main point. Far more interesting is the exploration of the actual nature of that change. What were its main ingredients, how was it brought about, and to what extent was it applied through organizational levels and across functions, departments and divisions? These are the kind of questions tackled in this book. In contrast to the 'little change' thesis there is the possibility that labour management was changing in a qualitative way. The main initiatives impacting on labour during this period arguably derived not from amendments to personnel policy manuals but from extensive investment in operations and material-handling techniques and philosophy such as manufacturing requirements planning (MRPII) examined in chapter 4, from total quality initiatives and from redistributions of power in managerial organizations which put line managers to the fore. If this last was, as I suspect, critical, then the continuance of personnel policy in the background may well have occurred but with a reduced significance. This point raises interesting questions, of course, about intra-managerial competition and this is an aspect raised in chapters 6–8.

There is, then, the distinct possibility that change has crept upon us under an unusual guise. The intricacies of the people-management dimensions in major programmes of organizational change were such that two aspects needed to be considered. First, the familiar categories of what represented 'industrial relations' or 'personnel management' or 'manufacturing management' may have begun to dissolve. They have become unreliable guides to the actuality of change. Second, it seems that under these circumstances the initiatives which have had most significant impacts upon working arrangements and 'rules' (informal as well as formal) were conjured from outside the traditional categories. Structural, cultural and operational changes were all rife at the time of this study. It was not unusual to find that industrial relations' specialists and personnel managers were on the periphery or even completely outside these forms of change. They were often among the most reluctant of participants. In consequence, surveys which rely on personnel managers as the sole informants on change are open to considerable question.

Unpicking the 'personnel', 'human resource', or 'industrial relations' aspects from the groundswell of change is fraught with difficulty. One even has to contemplate the possibility that the very basis of our understanding on these matters has to alter. Programmes of organizational change which carry far-reaching alterations into the very basis of the work experience (and of course there are many which do not) are subject not merely to industrial relations 'repercussions' or 'aspects'. They may alter the total conceptual 'map' such that the apparent 'IR consequences' (e.g. a change in payment system or work-time patterns) only touch the surface of what has occurred. To take just one case example, in one of the process companies, supervisors and section heads had been completely removed, operatives had been obliged to 'apply' for newly designed posts and only a certain proportion of them had been accepted. Those who had were then reorganized into cross-functional teams where the work process (schedules, products and specifications) became governed by the computer-based MRPII 'recipe'. Here, in what was, and on the surface still is, a highly unionized workforce, on a North of England site with a legacy of highly formalized procedures, the operatives, technicians and graduate engineers are participating in problem-solving task forces and are tuned to management communication channels on a regular basis. The potential enormity of what has happened in just a three year period is hard to fathom. After waves of interconnected change programmes (the interconnection between them was, however, somewhat above average among the range of cases which will be reviewed later) the workforce remained highly unionized and in a formal sense many of the procedures had survived. But in terms of what work was like, how things got done, productivity and quality and the degree of attention paid to investment decisions (the company had locations in a number of countries), then the scale of change was very extensive. How to assess these sorts of change certainly presents a problem. The analysis pursued in this book may be regarded as an exploration of that problem.

TRANSFORMATION OR 'REMARKABLE CONTINUITY'?

The transformations traced in the United States have come up against a number of structural limitations in the British context (Storey and Sisson, 1990). Nonetheless, the British scene itself has been subject to some considerable change with political, legal, economic and social dimensions all being affected. These have, in the main, all been widely discussed and there is little need to rehearse them here. Rather less well known outside specialist industrial relations circles, will be the analyses arising out of a number of large-scale surveys. Far from revealing a pattern of change, it is argued that the surveys demonstrate remarkable continuity. (See Legge's 1988 summary.) The number of shop stewards has not fallen disproportionately to the size of the workforce – indeed in some parts of the public sector in particular, their absolute numbers have increased. When put in historic context, it is suggested, even the incidence of strikes is not out of line with previous decades. The institutional machinery – union and shop steward recognition, collective bargaining arrangements, consultation, grievance procedures and the like are reported to have remained remarkably intact. And the much-vaunted productivity miracle is a hotly-debated issue among labour economists. In sum, instead of a picture of massive changes in the management of labour, a number of academic observers have stressed that on almost all aspects of procedure, 'things have stayed pretty much the same' (MacInnes, 1987: 98).

The evidence used to support these markedly contrasting depictions of management in the 1980s will be examined more closely later in the book. And without disentangling the various strands, it is not possible glibly to come down at this point in support of one account rather than the other. However, the new data which are presented in this monograph will help the reader to formulate a more considered view on this area of debate.

Whatever may, or may not, have been happening on the industrial relations machinery front it would be misleading to infer that somehow, by extension, the total picture on labour management had remained unchanged. The management of organizations – accomplished through a constellation of measures which all, ultimately, impact on labour management – has responded, and is continuing to respond, to a number of marked environmental changes. It is too frequently assumed that because the common soubriquet of 'Thatcherism' has been applied to the whole decade of the 1980s this signified a homogeneous phenomenon and relatively constant set of conditions. In fact, the environmental conditions underwent considerable alteration even during the period – one clear example would be the turnaround in the demographic pattern and the related labour market situation. The concentration on employment-support measures in the early part of the decade gave way to an almost reverse concentration on the implications of the 'demographic dip' as the end of the decade approached.

An important source of change was wrought by the increasing globalization of markets. One or two examples may serve to indicate the magnitude of changes here. In 1975 only three of the world's ten largest banks were Japanese, by 1987 the number was seven. When Toyota announced its decision to locate a manufacturing facility in Derby it was the hundredth Japanese manufacturing company to invest in this way in the UK. It took a fifteen-year period, from 1972–87 for the first 50 to arrive; the next 50, however, were rapidly established in the following two years. Or to take a further example: between 1965–87 Britain's indigenous car-manufacturing capacity experienced a decline in its domestic market share from 45 per cent to 12 per cent.[1]

There is *prima facie* evidence concerning the way that organizations have responded to the changing context. Senior managers have, for instance, become more acutely aware of their markets. The mind-set of many has been under direct assault: their organizations, they have been chided, must be redirected from traditional, production-oriented practices to a market-oriented stance. This kind of analysis and admonition has become familiar stuff. It has found expression across the range from banks to factories, to railways and to many other settings. In British Rail, as we will see, the intent found expression in a massive political struggle. A whole new organizational structure was created in order to further it and simultaneously this was underpinned by other measures to amend values, style and behaviour. In other words, both cultural and structural changes have been notable features.

The concentration on product-market conditions and corporate 'positioning' has entailed but a short step for many managers into considerations of corporate strategy. The analysis of their organization's strengths and weakness in the kaleidoscope of opportunities and threats has become a more familiar exercise than heretofore. The 'SWOT matrix' on management courses and in management meetings has become a commonplace. This is not necessarily to say that this has yet worked through into the routine practices of the corporate echelons[2] but it is suggestive of the possibility that the potential, and perhaps even the nascent practice, of adopting a more strategic approach to the management of resources – including, vitally, human resources – is now beginning to happen. What is remarkable is that academic analysis has signally failed to keep pace. This is so in terms of the adequacy – or, perhaps more accurately, the inadequacy of empirical research – and a similar state of affairs obtains on the theoretical front. In the latter sphere, commentators on 'strategic human resource management' and 'the management of change' have failed to take any account, for example, of the established body of analysis on the varying means of management control (Edwards, 1979; Storey, 1983, 1985; Salaman, 1979; Littler and Salaman, 1982). Yet a more fruitful and incisive review could surely be made if the control theme as well as the 'involvement' was to be attended to.

The need for subtle analysis of managerial action has never been greater than now. The reason for this is that the combination of circumstances in the economic, political and social environment, allied with the (at least, rudimentary) forms of strategic business planning, appears to have prompted a range of relatively novel organizational measures. Widely noted have been certain structural changes including devolved organization, expanded role definitions for line managers, new forms of control system and new forms of production system.

Accompanying these structural changes there appear to have been certain 'cultural' changes such as new management styles designed to give renewed emphasis to customer orientation, innovation, enterprise and competitive edge. Developments of this kind have been in part a product, and in part a stimulus, to an influential literature on 'excellence' and corporate culture. Indeed, apart from all else, the near ubiquity in management circles of the idea of 'managing a culture change' is surely one of the most remarkable features of management thinking in the 1980s and the early 1990s.

Management selection decisions, training and development programmes, redesigned appraisal and report systems, management 'outflow' or redundancy decisions . . . and a number of other occurrences are regularly explained nowadays, by practitioners themselves, as impelled by the recognized need to effect a change in the 'culture' of the organization. Some of these accounts will no doubt be cliches, but that is not the main point: the sheer degree of penetration of this mode of thinking seems likely, in itself, to have some real consequences in behaviour.

Integral to most of the above changes in organizational culture and structure are developments in the way employees are managed. A key tendency appears to be the increased emphasis upon 'individual' as opposed to 'collective' relations with employees. Accordingly, there has been an upsurge of interest in direct forms of communication and involvement: team briefings by each line manager, the use of quality circles, problem-solving teams and the like. Commensurate with this are the developments in integrated reward systems and the linking, in one form or another, of remuneration to performance rather than to 'rate for the job'. The renewed interest in harmonization can also be seen as a logical extension of such initiatives. So too, the explosion of interest in more systematic selection techniques so as to control for the 'type' of individual who will be joining the organization. The use of psychometric tests for employees (at all levels) which appear to be occurring falls into this pattern also.

Since the now famous indictments of Britain's training record in well-publicized reports such as *Challenge to Complacency* (MSC/NEDO, 1986) and *Competence and Competition* (NEDO/MSC, 1984), there would seem to have been a flurry of activity on the training and development front. The subsequent reports on managerial education training and development (Constable and McCormick, 1987; Handy, 1987) served to intensify that concern. The establishment of the Council for Management Education and Development (CMEAD) and the Management Charter Initiative has put the issue high on the agenda. It is true that one does not have to be unduly cynical to wonder what measure of real impact all of this concern for training and development will have. On the other hand, the issue is now being discussed at a far higher level in managerial hierarchies than hitherto. Moreover, there are already signs of considerable increases in the amount of training activity.

Appraisal and performance-report systems have also been brushed-down and relaunched in many organizations. The level of awareness of how these interlink with objective-setting on the one hand (often now talked of as itself emanating cascade-fashion from the corporate plan) and to reward on the other, would seem also to have increased.

Then there has been the massive amount of attention paid to the notion of 'flexibility'. So well publicized has been the idea, that along with the concept of the 'enterprise culture' it could almost stand as a leitmotif for the decade of the 1980s. Managers at all levels appear familiar with the idea and seem, moreover, to believe that they and their colleagues are, in one form and another, driving it forward. Scrutiny of hard evidence may reveal this belief to be something of a conceit, but the widely-held character of the belief makes it unlikely to be entirely without consequence.

In sum, there would appear to be ample *prima facie* evidence of considerable change in the overall approach to the management of labour. In a number of organizations these kinds of developments or aspirations in their direction have been symbolized by the change in terminology from 'industrial relations' to 'employee relations' and from 'personnel management' to 'human resource management'. In a few, as yet rare cases, IR/ER has itself been integrated with HRM so that the traditional division which still exists in most large British organizations between a specialist group to handle collective relations with the 'works' and a separate specialist staff to handle individual relations with managers and senior white collar/technical 'staffs' has been removed.

It has to be recognized, however, that there are a number of marked exceptions to this implicit model. Some organizations have evidently not pursued these kinds of policies. It cannot necessarily be said that they are accordingly simply 'laggardly'. There may be some situational reasons – such as technological circumstances – for the adaption of an alternative approach. Some senior managers whom I interviewed, reported that they had looked at various aspects of the model and decided that, at least for the present time, they were not going to invest in this type of change. Nonetheless, there are clearly other organizations which have pursued practices of this type.

The most notable examples of change in the human resource management direction have become very familiar: British Airways, Toshiba, Nissan and Rank Xerox. In many managerial accounts these now tend to be routinely classified alongside IBM,

Hewlett Packard and Marks and Spencers. But of course such instances can be too easily sidelined as 'special cases'. Since the earliest days of the industrial revolution there have always been exceptions to the norm. Cases such as Rowntrees at York, Cadbury in Bourneville, Wedgwoods in the Potteries or Lever Brothers at Port Sunlight, have been benignly tolerated as rather quirky exceptions to the norm. The norm was rarely viewed as seriously threatened by any extensive contamination from these instances where employers, fired by religious conviction such as Quakerism, or prompted by some other unusual circumstance, had steered their particular ships in a moderately deviant path from the main convoy.

There is clearly a possibility that the flurry of interest in contemporary 'unusual cases' (Wickens, 1987; Tse, 1985; Bassett, 1986; Trevor, 1988) may be similarly catalogued as marginal. In consequence this alone would be reason enough to now place the focus of analysis outside this coterie of *atypical* cases. Bassett, for example, in his study of the 'new industrial relations' (comprised of no-strike agreements, single unionism and pendulum arbitration) suggests that they cover only a fraction of the total workforce – perhaps merely 9000 employees in total.

Because there have always been these kinds of exceptional cases, the recent phenomenal interest in the notion of HRM cannot be explained by such latter-day variants. The inference to be drawn is that there is a lurking suspicion that new departures have also now been made across the traditional heartland of British employment. It was indeed in order to examine this possibility that the central thrust of the research project upon which this book is based was largely conducted in a sample of *mainstream organizations* such as Austin Rover, British Rail, Ford and the NHS. If evidence of new forms of human resource management could be educed in these, rather more severe test conditions, then it may be more safely assumed that something of real significance was occurring.

In the main, the literature to date has not proved to be very helpful in unravelling the nature of what has been happening. In part, this reflects the predominant bias in most of the personnel management literature towards idealized, prescriptive models with little hard information about actual practices in real contexts (Sisson, 1989, makes this point forcefully). Even where the personnel journals are leavened with 'case studies', these tend to exaggerate the degree of change. They bestow upon it a coherence and neatness which distorts reality. Moreover, they rarely give details of the real difficulties encountered. Where problems in implementation are acknowledged, they are normally quickly dismissed as 'teething troubles' which, when participants have had time to 'understand' fully the innovations, are apparently overcome.

As a result, on more than one occasion, I visited companies which had happened to feature in the managerial literature because of some new 'package' or other, only to discover that the 'breakthrough' was viewed as a peripheral trial, was hardly recognizable to the participants on the ground, or had been abandoned altogether. Such experiences on research visits soon induce caution, not to say scepticism, in one's approach.

In seeking to unravel the plethora of managerial initiatives, the 'human resource management' model can prove to be both a helpful guide yet a dangerous travelling companion. The advantageous side of its character derives from its potentiality in acting as a yardstick, or template, against which to compare found practices and patterns. The downside is that the seductive power of the concept means that it is all too easy to fall into the trap of distorting reality by reifying the often incomplete and indeed amorphous character of everyday managerial practice by attributing to it a spurious coherence. The question of how to work around these elements accordingly brings us to the final sections of this chapter – an outline of the aims and methods of the research reported in this book.

Aims

The basic aim of this book, and of the research project on which it is based, is to shed descriptive and analytical light on the nature of the developments in the way the contemporary employment relationship is managed. More particularly, it seeks to illuminate what, if anything, has been taking place in the mainstream as a result of the kind of environmental changes noted above, and consequent to the ideational compilations which have been widely diffused.

A distinguishing feature of the research was that it sought to gain purchase on these issues by focusing, in particular, on line managers. In part, this was because a number of informed observers had frequently made elliptic references to their growing importance[3]. But additionally, this focus was chosen because it was becoming increasingly apparent that the success or failure of many of the publicized initiatives would depend critically upon such managers. The line manager's role has long been held to be important but many senior managers now appear to believe it has become especially crucial. Despite these points, the line manager's role in influencing the nature of the employment relationship has remained largely neglected in previous research.

An elaboration of these aims can be made by posing them in the form of a series of questions. The issues highlighted have theoretical and practical significance. It is somewhat artificial to separate the two but, in recognition of the needs of the various audiences for this book, some broad distinctions are drawn below.

The practical questions are as follows:

- In what precise ways is the role of the 'line' manager (senior as well as junior) changing at the present time?

- What implications are organizations drawing for the recruitment and selection of line managers?

- What kinds of management development and training are organizations providing to equip line managers to handle these changes?

- Is the relationship between line managers and specialist personnel managers changing and, if so, in what ways?

Stated in a rather more abstract way the central questions are thus:

- What range of patterns exists within the new forms of human resource management? What choices are available?

- To which contexts do particular models seem best fitted?

- What internal conditions and factors influence the successful transition to the new modes?

This means addressing: what has been done (the content of change); why it has been done (contextual and perceptual aspects of change) and how it has been done (the process).

Putting much of this together, the research focused on how 'people management' was being integrated within the context of management as a whole. Hence, the research gives insight both on aspects of strategic management and on the processes of implementation. This encompasses an exploration of who deals with human resource management and to what extent developed policies on HRM have been devised. It also entails an examination of the ways in which HRM initiatives sit alongside, or are part and parcel of, traditional IR and personnel.[4]

METHODS

In order to address these issues the book draws upon a rich body of new research data born out of two solid years of field work. By far, the greatest resources were directed towards examining 15 major organizations between 1986–8. These cases included high-ranking private sector organizations such as Ford, Whitbread, Smith & Nephew and Plessey as well as key public sector employers such as the NHS and British Rail.

Interviews were conducted with a vertical slice of, mainly, line managers. These were drawn from corporate level, through MDs of various businesses, works managers and so on down through the operational structure to first line management. A total of 350 interviews were conducted and these ranged in duration from around an hour to as many as four hours each. Some managers were interviewed on more than one occasion. Nearly half of the total number of interviews were recorded on a pocket-sized tape cassette and were then transcribed.

The case organizations differed in market structure and technology; but they also shared certain important characteristics. They are all large, complex organizations: multi-site and, typically, multi-divisional. Each of them is unionized, has elaborate personnel and industrial relations procedures and is staffed with personnel specialists. Most of them have, in the past, been not altogether unfamiliar with turbulent industrial relations. In many respects, therefore, they would seem to fit broadly with the 'pragmatic' or 'constitutional' categories identified by Purcell and Sisson (1983). To put this another way; rather than representing the exceptional, greenfield-site, Japanese-owned, late arrivals, they are more typical of the mainstream of British employment.

Despite procedure-based legacies, they nevertheless each seemed to be taking some steps to readjust its employment management approach. The research objective was to get close to these situations in order to examine objectives, methods, perceptions and actual practices and to locate these within their contexts.

It is intended in this report to capture something of the reality of recent initiatives in a 'warts and all' fashion – thus avoiding the superficial, celebratory tone of most of the ubiquitous 'excellence' literature.

A list of the 15 core cases is given below:

The core cases

 1 Austin Rover
 2 British Rail
 3 Bradford Metropolitan Council
 4 Eaton Ltd
 5 Ford Motor Company
 6 ICI
 7 Jaguar
 8 Lucas
 9 Massey Ferguson
10 NHS
11 Peugeot-Talbot
12 Plessey (Naval Systems)
13 Rolls-Royce
14 Smith & Nephew
15 Whitbread Breweries

In addition to these core case studies, a wider programme of visits was made to organizations where significant new management initiatives were seemingly taking place. Examples included Birds Eye Walls, where a new teamworking system has been introduced; Golden Wonder, where a whole package of change was being implemented; and Metal Box (now MB) which was moving rapidly towards building up its strategic business units.

Other 'panel' companies included: British Aerospace, Corah, CWS, GEC, IBM, Ingersoll and Stanton. Illustrations from both sets of cases are used extensively throughout the book.

THE PLAN OF THE BOOK

The central themes which have been identified in this introductory chapter find more detailed expression in the remainder of the book. Chapter 2 elaborates and critically examines the predominant model of 'human resource management'. Chapters 3 and 4 interrogate the data gleaned from the research by slicing through it in two different ways. The first of these introduces the cases and summarizes the key changes on a case-by-case basis. The purpose is to reveal the interconnections between initiatives and their relative weights when viewed in context. The second of these chapters adopts the alternative approach by undertaking a thematic analysis, drawing upon the case material by way of illustration. In chapter 5 the perspective switches to an examination of the process whereby managerial initiatives were managed.

In order to assess the apparently crucial role increasingly played by line managers in steering the new departures in labour management, chapters 6 to 8 focus on different types and levels of management. Then, chapter 9 takes up the issue of what implications the new departures have carried for the way in which managers approach trade unions and collective bargaining. The concluding chapter brings together the main findings of the study and makes an assessment of trends and future prospects.

Notes

1 Financial Times, 13 March 1989.
2 The report prepared by McKinsey & Co. for NEDO on Performance and Competitive Success (1988) in the UK electronics industry, illustrates the lack of strategic vision in major UK companies.
3 Among a very wide range of possible references see, for example, from the practitioner perspective, Nicholas Cowan (1986) of the London Clearing Banks, and from the academic perspective, Edgar Schein (1987).
4 It is notable that as the 1990s approached, the emphasis in the literature

began to switch from 'how-to' manage success towards an identification of *dilemmas*. Richard Pascale (1990) in *Managing on the Edge* talks of 'vectors of contention' such as elitist versus pluralist structures; Charles Hampden-Turner's (1990) analysis of corporate cultures is built on the concept of dilemmas (he sees the function of corporate culture as being to mediate these); while Schuler (1988) also focuses on dilemmas in the shape of 31 'human resource practice choices'. The certainties and nostrums with which the 1980s began had evidently been greatly dissipated as it came to a close.

2

The HRM Phenomenon

As stated in the introduction to chapter 1, the purpose of this book is to trace recent reconfigurations in the management of the employment relationship. Also noted was the point that one particular 'model' became central to the debate about change. It is accordingly necessary to scrutinize that model with special care in order to weigh its possible contribution to our analysis of change. Irrespective of the intellectual coherence which HRM may be found or not be found to carry, the sheer level of interest which the idea has generated is itself a matter of some significance. The aim of this chapter is to examine HRM at the conceptual and theoretical levels so it may serve as one critical benchmark against which to interpret the fieldwork data. It is organized into four sections:

- the first looks at the meanings of HRM
- the second traces its antecedents
- the third examines it in terms of social science modelling
- the fourth explores the hypothesized conditions which are seen to be favourable for its development.

MEANINGS OF HRM

The very idea of HRM is controversial. This is so for a variety of reasons: ideological, empirical, theoretical and not least, the micro-politics of professional vested interests. An important distinction that needs to be made, for example, is whether HRM is being depicted in a normative or a descriptive manner. We will cover each of these in the course of this chapter but a useful place to start is with a listing of the variety of meanings that the term carries.

First, it is sometimes used as a synonym of personnel management. There are two subcategories of this loose usage. The first is when no particular connotation is implied: that is it is merely a guileless substitution for a range of other possibles – including for example, 'employee relations', 'people management' and the like. The other subcategory is when this term is preferred simply because it has a more modern ring; thus one can find second and third edition versions of personnel management textbooks being given a title switch so as to capture the prevailing mood though with no evident alteration in subject content.

Second, it may also signal that the various techniques of personnel management (e.g. selection, appraisal and reward devices) are being/ought to be used in a more integrated way. The clearest expression of this position is found in Devanna, Fombrun and Tichy's (1984) discussion of the concept of 'strategic human resource management'. They suggest that human resource managers perform four 'generic functions' of selection, appraisal, reward and development. Performance is the dependent variable; it is influenced by a 'cycle' of human resource interventions which 'represents, sequential managerial tasks' (p. 41).

Third, it is sometimes used to signal a more business-oriented and business-integrated approach guiding the management of labour; the emphasis is placed on the concept of 'resource', it puts employees alongside other factors of production such as capital, technology, energy and materials. In consequence, it suggests the potential of gaining added value through the sophisticated use of this factor rather than simply viewing it as a problematical arena in which the best that might be hoped for is quiescence. (The thrust of Winkler's (1974) famous article characterizing the way in which boards of directors traditionally regarded industrial relations, provides a graphic counterpoint to what is being suggested here.)

So, according to this view, HRM is only fully present when the levers of selection, reward and so on are being pulled in an integrated way and that this 'system' is itself fully attuned and integrated, in turn, with a wider business strategy. This usage is essentially that of Beer et al., (1985) in their Harvard Business School text, *Human Resource Management: A General Manager's Perspective*. This text does not explicitly prescribe a set of distinguishing factors beyond these two elements, though in their abstract model and in their selection of illustrative cases, the authors signal an implicit set of characteristics. They say they 'choose the term because it reflects what companies who choose it are trying to do: integrate' (1985: xi). A whole range of approaches which differ markedly could of course nevertheless show the characteristic of being 'integrated'. So if this is all, or even mainly, what HRM means then there would seem to be little that is truly distinctive about it. Moreover, many commentators have urged an integrated approach to IR at the prescriptive level for some years (Cuthbert, 1973; Anthony, 1977; and, see Legge, 1989).

A fourth position, and one which involves a more severe test, is the desideratum that not only ought both types of integration be in evidence but, in addition, if the HRM appellation is to apply there needs to be some extra qualifying factor such as an underlying logic in pursuit of employee 'commitment' or some similar characteristic feature (e.g. Walton, 1985). Hence, under this interpretation, HRM is not simply a question of having some systematic linkage between personnel interventions, there must also be something qualitatively different about those interventions. This 'difference' is seen as relating to the aims of those interventions (i.e. something more ambitious than securing 'mere compliance', maintaining order, or simply securing behaviour in according with rules). The difference in aims also implies something about the content of these interventions: they are not just better interrelated but they look and feel different in themselves. Associated with this 'stronger' version of HRM is the idea that there is a philosophical underpinning to it which sharply marks it off from Taylorism and indeed from the pluralistic conventions of industrial relations orthodoxy.

The above four positions may be thought of as points on a continuum: with the very weak or loosely attributed meaning being at one end, and the more demanding, meaning-full version being at the other. The problem with this metaphor is that it implies a single axis of meaning whereas HRM in different hands may carry varied connotations. Thus, as I have already indicated (Storey, 1987), human resource management has its 'hard' and its 'soft' versions. The hard version puts the stress on the idea of 'resource', that is something to be used dispassionately and in a formally rational manner. The soft usage lays stress on the term 'human', thus conjuring up echoes of the human relations movement. What is striking is that the same term is thus capable of signalling diametrically opposite sets of assumptions. Hence, some observers are found objecting to the term 'human resource management' because it smacks of an 'instrumental' treatment of people, while other critics are inclined to dismiss it for a very different reason, namely, that it suggests a wishy-washy, liberal approach which, they say, however much we may lament the fact, is simply inappropriate to the harsh realities of business.

These various positions may be located as Guest (1989) also has suggested, on a matrix. My version of this is shown in figure 2.1. As is suggested by this figure, much of the interest must inevitably turn on the 'stronger' versions: those which carry a particular distinctiveness. Of paramount concern is what is seen to constitute the nature of this distinctiveness: is it, for example, one particular quality, or is it a package? If the latter, must all parts of the package be present or are some elements optional while perhaps leaving an irreduceable minimum? In order to give a better 'feel' for the character of the 'stronger' version of HRM it will be found worthwhile to sketch a synoptic view.

Four key elements express the essence of the concept. The first is the view that, fundamentally, it is the human resource which 'makes the difference'. It is human capability and commitment which, in the final analysis, distinguishes successful organizations from the rest. It follows from this premise that the human resource ought to be nurtured. This in turn, means making decisions in respect of it, not as though it was an unfortunate 'cost' to be minimized but as a valued 'resource'.

This leads to the second key feature of the HRM approach, namely, that the making of such decisions is, in consequence, an organizational matter of strategic importance. This has a number of aspects. Chief among them is the view that people-management decisions ought not to be treated as incidental operational matters or be sidelined into the hands of personnel officers. On the contrary, the HRM 'message' is that decisions about what kind of

Figure 2.1 HRM 'mapping' of various meanings

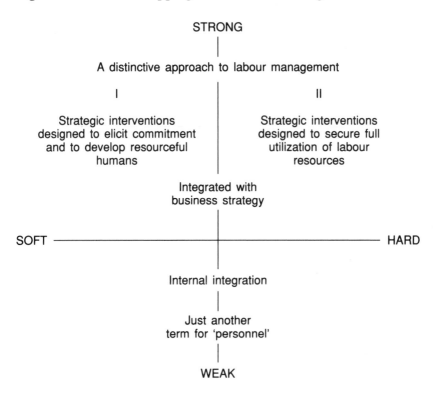

STRONG

A distinctive approach to labour management

| I | | II |

Strategic interventions
designed to elicit commitment
and to develop resourceful
humans

Strategic interventions
designed to secure full
utilization of labour
resources

Integrated with
business strategy

SOFT ———————————————————————— HARD

Internal integration

Just another
term for 'personnel'

WEAK

employee 'stock' one is going to aspire towards, how much is to
be invested in it and so on, are issues of crucial top management
importance and ought not only to be seen to derive explicitly
from the corporate plan, but to constitute a key set of considerations which feed into that plan.

Third, HRM is, therefore, seen to have long-term implications
and to be integral to the core performance of the business or
public sector organization. In other words, it must be the intimate
concern of line managers. They will be the key figures in implementing the human resource policies or the top managerial
team; they must 'own' it, understand it and be capable of acting
in accordance with it.

The final feature, or set of features, concerns the key levers
which are used to activate the HRM approach. These relate to a
systematic and integrated approach to managing certain critical

events: the inflow into the organization; the clear communication of objectives; the calculated deployment of the human resource; the evaluating of its performance and the rewarding of it accordingly. The tools are to be used to seek not merely compliance but commitment.

As is evident from the above summary of the human resource management approach, it relies, in the main, upon 'individualistic' rather than 'collectivistic' means to relate to labour. Therefore, the tools of its craft revolve around, for example, direct communication via briefing groups, rather than indirect communication via joint consultation or collective bargaining. It is a moot point, however, whether HRM necessarily must eschew collective procedures. The fact that these, so far, have carried little emphasis in the way HRM has been espoused, practised and analysed may simply reflect its pedigree in sophisticated American, often non-union companies rather than any inherent incompatibility with trade unions and collective bargaining. Indeed, this vital, but so far unexplored, issue is a central feature in the analysis which follows.

THE INTELLECTUAL ANTECEDENTS OF HRM

It is instructive to consider how the ideas about 'human resource management' can be located within already available theoretical frameworks. One reason for attempting this is that it is important to consider the theoretical antecedents of the constituent ideas. To an extent, the underlying ideas and assumptions of HRM would seem to be traceable to the human relations movement dating from the 1930s onwards. The familiar ingredients of releasing human potential through effective managerial leadership and good communications are present. So too, the measured forms of 'participation' which were associated with the neo-human relations school of McGregor, Likert, Blake, Herzberg and other managerial writers and consultants. The standard criticisms of this line of work – that, for example, it is simplistic and fails to give appropriate attention to structured, cultural and contextual factors – remain valid.

But there is also a second set of antecedents to HRM. This emerges from the 'corporate strategy' and 'business policy' lineage.

It places emphasis less on the 'motivational', 'participative' or 'leadership' elements but gives weight instead to the importance of environmental scanning, forward planning and the integrating of all aspects of managerial action (including of course the management of the human resource) with the business plan. It thus fosters the strategic and calculative approach to human resource management. The emphasis arising from this strand is not so much the 'human' but the compelling idea of 'resource'. To this extent at least, therefore, the 'hard' and 'soft' versions of HRM derive from different intellectual traditions. The 'hard' version stresses the quantitative, calculative and business-strategic aspects of managing the 'headcount resource' in as 'rational' a way as for any other factor of production.

One way of enacting this, though not the only way, is through the use of human asset accountancy. The influence of this approach is particularly evident in the work of Odiorne (1985). Strategic human resource management for Odiorne means building on 'human capital' theory. His central line of argument is worth quoting at some length:

> Conventional wisdom in management as well as economics has viewed the employee as one of the three factors of production: land, labour and capital. In such a paradigm labour is an expense item and its contribution to value-added lies in its cost being minimised. This concept has produced the effect of the employee being treated as an expense item on the profit and loss statement. The new human capital theory on the other hand sees the employee as an asset that should be valued in much the same way that other assets – such as factories, computers or inventories – are valued. Far from being mere word chopping this new paradigm has enormous implications for the human use of human beings. It also has major implications for the professional field of personnel and employee relations because the treatment of human assets and their valuation, acquisition and disposal call for new rules and strategies. (Odiorne 1985: 4–5)

The actual practice of human asset accountancy in the form originally envisaged has not so far developed, but, the influence of the ideas which underpin it continues to be felt (Benjamin and Benson, 1986; Flamholz, 1974; Giles and Robinson, 1972; Jauch and Skigen, 1977). Indeed, according to Odiorne (1985: 3) resistance to it is reducing because 'coyness about treating employees as assets has diminished in this century especially in the past twenty five years.'

HRM AS A MODEL

To ask whether recent changes in employment management exemplify human resource management in action clearly begs the question as to which of these meanings of HRM is to be adopted as the referent. If some real substantive change is being looked for then our attention is inevitably drawn to the more demanding versions sketched above. Much of the debate, to date, has been at cross-purposes because it is often not made clear whether:

- a prescriptive model is being used – that is one which, in effect, instructs practitioners on how they ought to proceed; or

- a descriptive model is being presented which reports on actual developments in the field; or

- a conceptual model is being offered which affects neither to describe what exists nor to recommend what should exist.

Some discussions became hopelessly confused because unsignalled switching occurs between all three.

Now, the first approach, prescriptive or normative modelling, which purports to tell how employment management should be conducted, we can deal with fairly quickly. As noted earlier, personnel management as a field of study has been dominated by prescription with little concern given either to the validity of the basis from which the confident prescriptions arise, or with how actual personnel management is conducted in the real world. Nonetheless, even at this level, it is worth asking whether the prescriptive models of HRM contain anything distinctive when compared with the prescriptive accounts of personnel management. This kind of comparison has been adroitly made by Legge (1989) and she concludes, on the basis of a series of formal definitions of the two (drawn from the available texts), that there is, on this measure, not a lot of difference between personnel management and human resource management. In other words, recommended 'best practice' appears to have remained, in essence, broadly the same.

Nonetheless, even Legge, who takes a sceptical view, detects some differences between the two and these would seem not to be of a trivial nature. Three key shifts of emphasis are noted:

- whereas personnel management is oriented almost totally to the management of subordinate, non-managerial employees, HRM, at the normative level, gives emphasis to the development of the management team
- the role attributed to line managers differs: in the personnel management normative models it tends to be merely the 'implementation' of specialist personnel procedures, whereas under HRM line managers are centrally responsible for devising and driving an integrated business-management and people-management strategy
- HRM normative models, unlike personnel, posit the management of the organizational culture as a central activity for the most senior management.

These are not unimportant shifts of emphasis; if acted upon they might be expected to result in rather significant differences in employment management approaches. Of note also is that two of these distinctive points of emphasis would apparently not be confined to just one or other of the 'hard' or 'soft' versions. Thus, the focus on the management of managerial employees as a key constituency and the emphasis on line managers as crucial players in assuming responsibility for human resource management would be factors which could embrace both versions. The third one, which postulates organization 'culture', tends to imply, in most hands, a leaning towards the 'resourceful humans' version but it is logically not necessarily tied to this approach.

Nonetheless, all three characteristics so identified are derived, it should be remembered, from a normative modelling and they are therefore open to the challenge that these characteristics do not necessarily have any experience in practice.

This brings into view the second class of model – the descriptive variety. To date, there has not been sufficient systematic field work to permit confident statements to be made under this heading. As a method, however, it points the way forward for research. Case studies could allow the progressive refinement of a model in an inductive fashion so as to produce what Hughes (1976: 125) calls 'an interpretation that begins to look more promising than others . . . an account of what is going on'. This indeed is the aim of the fieldwork-based chapters which follow. But even to begin isolating the kind of variables upon which study should be concentrated, and on which data should be collected, requires some initial framework of analysis. That is, if the research is not purely exploratory but aims, if only in part, to contribute to ongoing debate, then some kind of conceptual framework of analysis is required. This directs attention to the third category of models: that of the conceptual variety.

If human resource management is to be shown to have made an appearance in Britain – or indeed be shown not to have done so – then it is necessary first of all to set out carefully the elemental features which would make it distinctive from other approaches to labour management. Such an exercise should help in making choices between the positions shown on figure 2.1 and help further in filling out these analytical positions.

But from where can a conceptual model of HRM be produced? As Guest (1989a) has noted, there are a number of options. One is to distil the practices of companies claiming to practise HRM. But, if mere retitling has taken place this will prove fruitless. Another approach is to extract the essence from studies of successful companies. This has been the celebrated path of the 'excellence literature' which has sought to codify the winning formula. However, the research base of this genre is of doubtful quality and much of it sails uncomfortably close therefore to the prescriptive modelling discussed above. A final alternative, and one chosen by Guest, is to 'develop theory by "borrowing" from the social sciences' (1989a: 49).

Now, conceptual modelling in the social sciences has a rich heritage but it does not in itself offer a singular, let alone unproblematical, path. There are, for example, different types of conceptual models. One key distinction turns on the origin or source of the model – whether, for example, the model is derived from a process of hypothetico-deductive reasoning or from inductive reasoning. In the former instance the key concepts and their interconnections are derived from deductions based on previously-established 'knowledge', whereas, using the inductive method, generalizations are constructed from observation and fresh 'data'. This 'inductive modelling' is a process of formulating and re-formulating ideas in order to reach an account of 'what is going on'.

In the case of most current accounts of what HRM 'is', it is not clear how they have been arrived at. They seem simply to have been asserted.

Additionally, apart from how the model has been arrived at, it is also necessary to enquire what purpose the proffered conceptual model of 'HRM' is to serve. Is it to be classificatory so that actual cases can be attributed as members of that class (or 'not members' as the case may be)? Or, more ambitiously, does the HRM model purport to reveal connections between variables? In the latter instance, though not the former, it would be possible to talk of a 'theory of human resource management'. The hypo-thesized connections between say, worker 'involvement' and 'commitment', and 'commitment' and 'productivity', might be ex-pected to reveal testable propositions for the social scientist and to promise guides-to-action for the practitioner.

The dominant approach to conceptualizing HRM, in Britain at least, has been to pursue the classificatory path – that is to define it by contrasting its features with those of personnel management. The logic is that if HRM really is new and distinctive, it ought to be possible to understand it by locating its elemental features in relation to the more familiar profile of personnel managers.

This approach offers some potential in clarifying the meaning of human resource management. But the main problem with it is the danger of contrasting an idealized version of HRM with a practical lived-in account of the messy reality of personnel management. However, depending upon how one wishes to use the model, this may not necessarily be a problem. For example, Walton's (1987) purpose in constructing a model of work trans-formation is to utilize it as a 'guide'; that is it serves as a marker of the path to follow. The fact that it represents an as-yet-to-be-achieved desirable state as opposed to a less desired current one is its very point. For Walton, 'a model is a general concept of the future organisation and evolves from an understanding of the limitations of traditional organisation and experimentation with alternatives' (1987: 15).

If used in an informed and aware way this approach towards modelling HRM would be permissable and potentially fruitful. What needs to be clarified, however, is that the 'idealized' future state constructed here is not a prescription devised by the author but a representation made by reconstructing the implicit models of the managers interviewed.

To take advantage of this approach to concept-use it is necessary to be clear about the sociological device of the 'ideal type'. Max Weber's classic usage, as in his discussion of 'bureaucracy', was to regard it purely as an instrument, that is as an analytical construct. He wrote:

> An ideal type is formed by the one-sided accentuation of one or more points of view and by the synthesis of a great many diffuse, discrete ... phenomena which are arranged according to those one-sidedly emphasised viewpoints into a unified analytical construct. In its conceptual purity, this mental construct cannot be found anywhere in reality.   (Weber, 1949: 90)

The abstraction produced does not therefore represent any actual state of affairs. Its purpose is to simplify by highlighting the essential features in an exaggerated way. An 'ideal type' of this sort is not constructed for 'testing' empirically in the sense of confirming or disconfirming its existence; rather its purpose is heuristic.

In contrast, there are 'ideal types' of a different kind which denote achievable states at the end of a continuum. In certain cases these can exist if the appropriate conditions are present. The purpose of this approach to constructing ideal types is primarily to facilitate classification. It is on the basis of the classifications reached that linkages can be traced between different phenomena and varieties of conditions.

Working from this premise, the way forward is to elaborate the dimensions which express the aspirations of British managers. Whether the states in the right-hand column of figure 2.2 are achievable in an empirical sense is another matter and is one which is addressed in the ensuing chapter. Inspiration for this type of summary was drawn from Guest (1987).

The elements are categorized following the four-part basic outline of:

Figure 2.2 Twenty-seven points of difference

DIMENSION	PERSONNEL AND IR	HRM
Beliefs and assumptions		
1 Contract	Careful delineation of written contracts	Aim to go 'beyond contract'
2 Rules	Importance of devising clear rules/mutuality	'Can-do' outlook; impatience with 'rule'
3 Guide to management action	Procedures	'Business-need'
4 Behaviour referent	Norms/custom and practice	Values/mission
5 Managerial task vis-à-vis labour	Monitoring	Nurturing
6 Nature of relations	Pluralist	Unitarist
7 Conflict	Institutionalized	De-emphasized
Strategic aspects		
8 Key relations	Labour-management	Customer
9 Initiatives	Piecemeal	Integrated
10 Corporate plan	Marginal to	Central to
11 Speed of decision	Slow	Fast
Line management		
12 Management role	Transactional	Transformational leadership
13 Key managers	Personnel/IR specialists	General/business/line managers
14 Communication	Indirect	Direct
15 Standardization	High (e.g. 'parity' an issue)	Low (e.g. 'parity' not seen as relevant)
16 Prized management skills	Negotiation	Facilitation
Key levers		
17 Selection	Separate, marginal task	Integrated, key task
18 Pay	Job evaluation (fixed grades)	Performance-related
19 Conditions	Separately negotiated	Harmonization
20 Labour-management	Collective bargaining contracts	Towards individual contracts
21 Thrust of relations with stewards	Regularized through facilities and training	Marginalized (with exception of some bargaining for change models)
22 Job categories and grades	Many	Few
23 Communication	Restricted flow	Increased flow
24 Job design	Division of labour	Teamwork
25 Conflict handling	Reach temporary truces	Manage climate and culture
26 Training and development	Controlled access to courses	Learning companies
27 Foci of attention for interventions	Personnel procedures	Wide ranging cultural, structural and personnel strategies

- beliefs and assumptions

- strategic aspects

- line management

- key levers

It must be re-emphasized that this classification is an abstraction built around managerial depictions of the 'was', and their preferred path. The fact that it caricatures the personnel and IR approach and is normative with regard to HRM, is part of the nature of the model. It is not vulnerable to criticism on these grounds. Where there is, however, considerable room for debate is upon the summary depictions of the items comprising the 27 dimensions. The HRM 'vision' would seem to have a certain skeletal shape but this leaves, as we have already observed, scope for variation on a number of points. For example, the role of trade unions is by no means clear: some managerial depictions of the future seem to justify well the 'marginalized' tag given to this dimension in the figure. But other versions would seem to allow and indeed to envisage a new order of 'cooperative relations' with unions. Indeed, the 'paradigm shift' chronicled in the United States by Kochan et al. (1986) and Walton (1987) is built around just such an enhanced level of corporate-level employee and union involvement. Ford, in the UK and in Europe, seem to believe that the 'new industrial relations' will entail relationship-building with the unions. Whether it is fair therefore, to characterize HRM as 'unitarist' on dimension number 6 is debatable. Nonetheless, even bearing in mind these sorts of variants, the general tenor of the depictions – such as an aspiration to attain 'transformational leadership', to see behaviour spring from a common set of values, and to effect a more strategic and integrated approach to labour management – would seem broadly to express what managers in the study were saying.

Whether particular end-states can be attained, or will be attained, is perhaps not the main point. The 'HRM model' has been conceived and diffused at a time when considerable change is being sought. The battery of ideas revolving around competences (hence the renewed interest in training, development and flexibility) and attitudes (hence the attention given to communications and 'leadership') gain their significance, even now, as signposts for multitudinous line and general managers who know they are expected to gear their workforces for change but who also know that the precise ways in which they are supposed to proceed are unlikely to be spelled out from corporate levels.

This schema makes explicit a set of assumptions and notions which are implicitly held by many managers across a range of industries and sectors. A *theoretical* model, however, would go further by indicating possible connections between key variables.

Just such a model is shown in figure 2.3. This is a fairly typical abstract depiction of assumed or hypothesized connections between the market environment and the sequence of 'responses' within economic organizations. In this particular model, the four key elements used in figure 2.3 (strategy, beliefs and assumptions, assertive line managers and change in key levers) are shown in their relative positions at the heart of the hypothesized 'shift'.

The trigger element in the model (the competitive environment) has been highlighted by a number of observers as probably the key 'causal' factor in the whole process. Such an account, however, can smack of economic determinism. It is likely that other factors will be found also to have a bearing. For example, there is the question of how ideas about appropriate ways to respond to 'heightened competition' are transmitted and diffused. One influential conduit is undoubtedly furnished by management consultants. Under the pressure points of the early 1980s, even large, erstwhile insular corporations reduced the size of their in-house personnel specialist staffs and at the same time became more open to the possibility that external ideas and ways might carry some import. On both counts the opportunities for management consultants rapidly expanded. Although it is an extreme case, an indication of the massive scale of consultant use in the human resource area may be glimpsed by referring to one large organization known to the author. Here group personnel has used around 250 different consultant groups in the two-year period up to 1989. These ranged from a series of separate contracts with the major consulting firms to contracts with individual consultants. The figure does not include 150 specialist recruitment agencies which were also used.

Diffusion of new work practices within and between companies and indeed countries is not entirely dependent, however, on

Figure 2.3 A model of the shift to human resource management

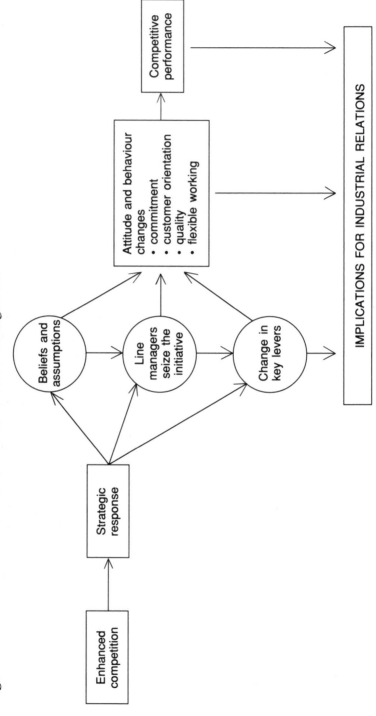

external consultants. Some companies take active and positive steps to transmit findings from pilot projects from one location to another. An outstanding example among the panel of cases represented in this book is that of Ford Motor Company which consciously planned, in a formal way (using a specially prepared 'package'), to diffuse the Employee Involvement (EI) programme from its home base in the United States to its various locations overseas. In a less formal way, there is also a constant stream of information passing between the European countries which constitute the Ford regional empire.

Economic pressures, although vital factors in explaining a great deal of organizational change and human resource management change, cannot, in themselves, serve as the only point of reference. The 'messages' coming from the environment have to be given meaning by social actors within the organization. (This is apart from the mediation of economic factors which occurs at the state level – via interventions in the form of subsidy or market protection, sector planning, or indeed, studied non-intervention.)

The mediation occurring at company level is influenced by prevailing logics or 'recipes' which reflect ingrained and distilled wisdom derived from habituation to a given set of rules and familiar conditions. These logics may even find expression in a conventional wisdom which extends across whole sectors (Smith and Child, 1987). At company level, the process whereby a break is made away from accepted ways of doing has been described as a 'debate between mental constructs'. Thus, in their account of the process of transformation at Cadbury's, Smith and Child describe it as taking place around simple, yet symbolic watchwords such as 'decentralization', 'core-businesses', 'rationalization' and, of course, 'flexibility' (pp. 586–7).

Establishing agreement about the appropriate diagnosis of the problem, let alone the prognosis or prescription, even among the management group, is not to be viewed as something accomplished unproblematically. 'Management' despite the collective noun is not a uniform entity. Contestation between different managerial specialisms is to be expected (Armstrong, 1984, 1989). A detailed exploration of these and other key aspects involved in the management of change process is made in chapter 5.

Assuming sufficient mobilization of opinion has occurred to legitimize and allow some change in direction, a theoretical model would indicate that human resource decisions may then emerge either as a result of strategic integration with the corporate plan, or, in spite of the fact that this logical step may be bypassed. Although a prescriptive model would almost certainly fail to countenance this, it has to be recogized that, not infrequently, the policies stem not from corporate business strategy but from *a priori* assumptions about the best way to manage labour.

A similar point needs to be noted concerning HR practices themselves. Prescriptive models invariably portray the range of HR practices, be it selection, appraisal, reward systems or whatever, as rational products of the chosen set of HR policies. In reality, the actual practices as opposed to the espoused policies are, in Britain at least, just as likely, if not indeed more likely, to result not from explicit policies but from *ad hoc* or customary ways of doing.

One key part of the 'theory' of HRM (and the fact that it is only one part is a crucial problem which we will return to) is that it is possible to 'predict' a set of outcomes from a set of HR practices. In other words, this is the heartland of the theoretical modelling of the cause-and-effect variety. Contributions of this sort have been relatively few in number and skeletal in form (Beer et al., 1985; Walton and Lawrence (eds) 1985; Fombrun, Tichy and Devanna 1984; Walton, 1987; Guest 1989 (a)). In a more implicit way, rather than in the explicit way exemplified by the references just given, there is a much wider range of texts which suggest that a certain set of policy options will result in a given set of HR outcomes (Peters and Waterman 1982; Peters and Austin, 1985; Peters, 1989; Bradford and Cohen, 1984; to cite just a few examples).

Beer et al., (1985) led the way with their hypothesized connection between sets of HR policy choices and an associated set of HR outcomes (commitment, competence and cost effectiveness). This set of desirable outcomes is postulated as causally connected with a wider set of long-term consequences (individual well-being, organizational effectiveness and societal well-being). But the demonstration of a causal linkage between different human resource practices and business performance is fraught with immense difficulty because of the vast range of confounding variables. It was not a task attempted in this current research. Rather, the critical questions addressed are the way in which, and the extent to which, the methods of labour management have been in transition. Explanations for the found patterns are also sought. In subsequent chapters, where the empirical data is presented and interpreted, the conceptual categories used in this present chapter (most notably those used in figures 2.1 and 2.3) will be used to structure the data and to form the basis for data analysis.

CONDITIONS FAVOURABLE AND UNFAVOURABLE TO HRM

In this section, examination is made of the conditions hypothesized to be propitious (and conversely inimical) for HRM. The focus of the analysis here is upon organizational-level conditions rather than the societal-level conditions which may or may not prompt a general predisposition towards HRM-type policy options. The task is to probe those organizational conditions whose presence, or absence, may help explain the differential take-up of HRM. Hypotheses derived from the already existing literature and from the abstract models presented earlier in this chapter can then be compared with the findings emerging from the case-study reports which follow.

Where are we likely to find HRM in practice? Those stances in HRM which proselytize it as of universal applicability, and as the acme of current practice, offer little in the way of an answer to this kind of question. But a contingency approach (e.g. Sisson and Scullion, 1985) suggests some possibilities.

Thus, one might expect human resource management will be influenced by corporate strategy and structure. For example, a single-product strategy should normally be associated with a functional organization structure. This in turn can be hypothesized as likely to favour what is usually known as a 'strong culture'. Conversely, companies which have grown by a strategy of acquisition of unrelated businesses will probably not have a uniform human resource management philosophy and approach. Multi-divisional companies, however, which have emerged through a strategy of internal growth may be hypothesized as representing a third category of HR practice. For example, they can be expected to treat at least their managerial staff as a corporate-wide resource and to develop these staff cross-divisionally as well as cross-functionally.

This kind of case has been argued most forcefully by Purcell (1989). He sees the trend toward diversification and decentralization, along with the use of portfolio planning techniques, as a major inhibitor of HRM. Under these conditions of corporate strategy and structure, the implication is that the enterprise will be viewed not holistically, but in a fragmented way, that is as a mere aggregation of separate businesses. The use of portfolio planning techniques simply exacerbates the inherent problem: the techniques are said to discourage commitment to the long term and to, in effect, ignore one of the key concepts of HRM – the idea of corporate culture. The essential logic of having strategic business units (SBUs) is that all forms of corporate influence and control other than those of a financial control character will be removed. Managers of SBUs are encouraged to find their own way and their own solutions; the aim of a consistent human resource strategy across the corporation is abandoned. By implication, for Purcell, SBUs and corporate HRM are, in effect, incompatibles. He writes: 'This pessimistic conclusion is difficult to avoid . . . current trends in corporate strategy in many large diversified companies render the ideals of human resource management . . . unobtainable' (1989: 46).

But this is rather too deterministic an argument. Purcell's pessimism derives from being too ready to accept that there are inevitable logical outcomes of particular organizational structures. The multi-divisional structural form cannot necessarily be viewed as an organizational condition inimical to strategic human resource management. If some diversified corporations employ less HRM than others, the implication is that one needs to look beyond the structural conditions in order to locate the factors which are influencing managerial behaviour. This is a further example of an area where there is a pressing need for fieldwork data.

Another aspect concerning organization structure is the possibility that strategic business units are developing their own human resource management approaches – with, or without, assistance from higher organizational levels. There is an implication in the arguments of those who stress the structural constraints, that such a process is likely to be heavily impeded by the short-term financial performance horizons imposed by corporate head office. But as some of our cases will reveal, inter-plant and inter-business competition for investment funds may rest on more subtle aspects – including demonstrable progress on employee relations.

A set of factors which is seen as favourable for the growth of HRM revolves around the stance taken by top management. The argument, in simplistic terms, is that senior management commitment to the idea is vital. With it, the scepticism at lower levels can be eventually surmounted; without it, even the most well-intentioned initiatives will soon wither. The weight of a committed 'founder' is seen as an especially powerful instance but the exceptional nature of this phenomenon is such that the point tends to marginalize HRM to the special-case, residual category outside the normal band. This will not therefore be a hypothesis that we can test with the body of data gathered for this project.

The hypothesized importance of mobilization around a unifying idea or 'change programme', returns us to the mainstream. There have, in recent years, been major instances of considerable investment by companies in programmes such as 'Total Quality Management' at BT, 'Harmonization' at Johnson and Johnson, and 'Customer First' at British Airways. One can see how such programmes furnish a shared vision and thus provide a clear sense of direction; they can also assist progress towards the goal by giving everyone a common language. Moreover, programmes such as these typically involve the planning of 'milestones' which, when reached, give a sense of achievement and momentum. Heavy investment in a programme with HRM implications can also send such powerful symbolic signals to all concerned that it is necessary to 'fall in' with this initiative. In these circumstances it would be politically damaging to be seen to oppose it or even to fail to support it. One might hypothesize therefore that another favourable condition for HRM would be the existence of some sort of programme of this kind.

But Beer (1988) usefully warns of the false seduction of the 'programme' approach to achieving corporate transformation. The problems associated with programmes are that:

- they tend to be top down in character and so employees lack a sense of 'ownership'
- they are often viewed as gimmickry at operational levels

- they tend not to engage with the key problems of sub-units

- they may even be 'fads' borrowed without adequate diagnosis of the real problems facing the company

- corporate programmes also usually suffer from being 'uni-dimensional' – that is, they cannot engage with the diverse aspects of real organizational problems involving structure as well as systems, politics as well as style.

Additionally, programmes are rarely sufficiently targeted at be-haviour but attend instead to glossy presentation. Despite these problems they tend to be used because they are an easy way to give an impression of managerial action in respect of problems which, in truth, require more fundamental measures.

In Britain, a key factor which might be expected to play a part in the employment or non-employment of a human resource management approach, is trade unionism. Again this is another vital issue which is usually ignored or marginalized by the OD/OB literature. But if HRM is primarily pursued on an individu-alistic plane the reaction from trade union representatives and union members might be expected to play a not inconsiderable part in the success or otherwise of such an approach. It might be predicted that, in broad terms, HRM will have made less progress in highly unionized, public sector organizations – especially in conditions where multi-unionism is still a factor. A related point concerns the prevailing state of industrial relations: where these are antagonistic one would hypothesize that the conditions would be unpropitious for HRM. Similarly, where managerial style is assertive and adversarial one would not expect to find much advance for human resource management policies and practices.

On the other hand, it has been suggested that post-crisis conditions are unusually opportune for transformative techniques. The conflagration at Eaton's Manchester factory has often been cited as a turning point. Relations before the fire in 1981 were fractious, but, given the trauma over whether reinvestment would be made, and then the eventual rebuild with computer-controlled machine tools, a new set of approaches and a new set of relations were established. Traumas of an economic and employment nature have also been noted in many other cases as the cue for radical change. The crisis response to extreme situations such as factory closures or major redundancies has been said to be the trigger which releases forces to counteract inertia. In the light of this hypothesis some senior managers have been known to talk of it being the corporate manager's duty to 'create' periodic crises or even, more extremely, to seek to maintain conditions of continual crisis. Whether these are, in fact, the sorts of conditions which are conducive to commitment and to other related aspects of human resource management must be open to some doubt. One might indeed put forward the converse hypothesis – namely that human resource management will have advanced further in those situations where there is perceived security.

This point leads to the next: HRM, one might expect, will primarily be directed at core employees and not at the so-called 'peripheral' groups such as part-timers, short-term contract workers and temporary staff. Further, it is possible that in Britain, to date, HRM will be found to be largely confined to managerial staff.

A final hypothesis would be that HRM is likely to be associated with particular technologies. Where jobs are arranged in ways which give little opportunity for the exercise of discretion and autonomy, it seems likely that managers will invest little in methods which would either countermand 'technological control' (Edwards, 1979) or would be dissipated in the face of it. An associated question is the extent to which companies in Britain which have launched organizational change programmes with an HRM component, have also taken steps to engage in job redesign. This, along with the wider series of questions and hypotheses which have constituted the main part of this chapter, will form the core issues in terms of which the data presented in the ensuing chapters will be examined.

CONCLUSIONS

This chapter began by explicating the meanings that the HRM model can carry and it then moved on to trace its antecedents in the history of ideas. The key learning point deriving from this discussion was that HRM as a phenomenon has a number of faces but that two in particular are notable. One of these is where HRM connotes a style of approach whose touchstones are the careful nurturing of, and investment in, the human stock. This usage was seen to relate to the human relations movement and it was tagged the 'soft' version of the phenomenon. The second usage was shown to emphasize the calculative, business-like treatment of labour with the accent being upon it as a 'resource' like any other to be deployed and disposed of in an economically rational way and with impatience towards institutional arrangements or procedures which interfere in that process. This aspect was dubbed the 'hard' version. Both versions share the presumption that decisions about the human resource are deserving of strategic attention because both start from the premise that the way in which this resource is managed will be critical to the success of the business plan. They also shared the understanding that HRM involves a distinctive departure from the standard practices of the post-war period in mainstream British organizations.

The nature of the phenomenon was therefore explored and elaborated. This was accomplished through a classificatory device which enumerated 27 points of difference between the new model and conventional practice. Important aspects of the distinctions thus drawn were shown to be that the approach was less procedure-based and that it gave a more explicit role to line managers.

Building on this classification, a range of theoretical issues was raised and a number of hypotheses drawn. In particular, the kinds of conditions which are likely to encourage, or conversely discourage, the development of this type of approach were postulated. The contingent nature of its application was used to make a particularly crucial point which has generally not been given the attention it deserves: namely, that when discussing actual cases it is necessary to distinguish between HRM as a 'style of approach' adopted or preferred by management, and HRM as a realized 'pattern of relations'. The point has far-reaching implications. It means, for example, that case analyses will have to examine: (1) managers' preferred approaches; (2) managers' actual practices; (3) the pattern of relations which results. In consequence of these distinctions, one final hypothesis might be drawn: that there are likely to be limits to the extent to which managerial action at the organizational level can, under normal circumstances, bring about a marked transformation of the patterns referred to under point (3).

So much for the conceptual analysis. The remainder of the book is devoted to a review and analysis of research findings. This task is begun in the next chapter with a case-by-case overview.

3

Mainstream Companies in Transition

In this chapter we tackle the theme of the management of change in a rather different way by moving on from abstraction to concrete instances. The purpose of the chapter is to introduce the 15 case companies in a pen-portrait manner and to provide an overview of the kind of changes to employment management which were found to be occurring. Further insight into the *detail* of what was occurring, an interpretation of the meaning of these developments and their implications, is provided in the subsequent six chapters.

By presenting here a thumb-nail, summary account of developments in these organizations, an understanding can be gained of the type of changes being introduced into these mainstream companies, the degree of commonality across sectors in the initiatives taken, and the extent and impact of such changes. In sum, we can begin to attend to the vital task of locating patterns of change in context.

For comparative purposes the cases are sequenced in a way which broadly allocates them to sectors. The full listing is shown in figure 3.1. We begin with the four motor companies and then, by way of contrast, move on to the three public sector organizations. This is followed by a third grouping of electrical, electronic and mechanical engineering companies one of which – Rolls-Royce – was, for part of the duration of the study, in the public sector before being privatized. The fourth and final grouping comprises manufacturing and service companies which, in the main, use process technology.

Figure 3.1   The case companies

```
The motor industry
   Austin Rover
   Ford
   Peugeot-Talbot
   Jaguar

Public sector organizations
   NHS
   British Rail
   Bradford Metropolitan Council

Electrical and mechanical engineering
   Eaton
   Lucas
   Massey Ferguson
   Rolls-Royce
   Plessey

Process industry
   Whitbread
   ICI
   Smith & Nephew
```

A feel for the thrust of the change programmes in these organizations is attainable first of all by consulting the schematic chart shown in figure 3.2. This lists the name of the case, the general theme of the change undertaken and the main component elements.

As this figure serves to emphasize, the welter of initiatives appeared to assume various shapes. Yet it needs to be understood that sometimes the change programmes were the same even though they carried different titles. To impose some order on this complexity, a common framework of analysis is adopted when briefly reviewing each case. This encompasses: commitment, selection, communication, participation, training and development, the approach taken to trade unions, and finally, a miscellaneous category to capture any other critical initiatives.

Figure 3.2 A schematic outline of change in the case organizations

Organization	General theme	Elements of change
Austin Rover	'Working With Pride' programme	Briefing system Zoning Zone circles Harmonization Family programme Attitude surveys New selection techniques
Ford	'Bargaining for Change'	Line management to forefront Employee involvement Investment in employee visits Flexibility
Peugeot-Talbot	Line management ascendancy	Communication QCs introduced Devolved management Training Increased ratio of first-line management
Jaguar	Human resource function to the fore	Extensive training Extensive communications Total quality Quality circles New supervisory role HR and IR dualism
NHS	From administration to general management	Appointment of 'managers' Performance indicators Resource management Performance-linked pay Interfunctional quality teams Customer-service initiatives
British Rail	From 'operational management' to 'business management'	Sectorization Customer-care programmes Devolved management Bargaining reform
Bradford Metropolitan Council	A social strategy	Promotion of an innovative culture Enhanced equal opportunity programme Training initiatives Organizational restructuring

Eaton	HRM philosophy implanted in traditional engineering context	Quality circles Line management to fore An elaborated HR philosophy
Lucas	Total quality	Systems approach Task forces Participation Training
Massey Ferguson	HRM/IR dualism	Workforce reductions Direct communications Involvement Mini-business concept Piecework retained
Rolls-Royce	Minor modifications to traditional pattern	Some direct communication Problems with team briefing Shop manager role 'Training for Change' programme
Plessey	Between two approaches	Reluctant maintenance of machinery Desire to build management leadership
Whitbread	Definite HR thrust	Strategic HR at company level Withdrawal of P and IR from sites Devolved management accountability Management leadership training
ICI (Chemicals and Polymers)	New receptivity to change	Devolved management Vision and culture change 'Quality improvement' programme
Smith & Nephew	Pragmatic, evolutionary shift from paternalism	Professionalizing of personnel Range of initiatives to invigorate line managers

THE MOTOR COMPANIES

Austin Rover

The evidence collected at the time of the research in this company (1986–7) was highly suggestive of a definite attempt to change the approach to labour management. Following the bitter medicine which Michael Edwardes had administered in the early 1980s to bring British Leyland, in his words, 'back from the brink', company management began, in the middle of that decade, to construct a new employment strategy which would more appropriately befit a quality rather than a quantity problem. The circumstances that they faced were inauspicious. Even today, the Procedure Agreement which regulates the negotiation machinery and such matters as shop steward-management relations is based on the so-called Blue Book which imposed the terms and conditions upon an unaccepting union negotiating body. Moreover, there had been a dispiriting period of plant closure and the workforce had been drastically reduced. For those who remained, discipline had been tightened. A management infrastructure from corporate level through plant management and downwards through superintendent to supervisory level had been introduced, which placed unequivocal emphasis upon a tough no-nonsense approach to achieving productivity.

It was in this climate that Andy Barr, the Manufacturing Director, was eventually persuaded, by a series of visits to the United States and a chance encounter with a management consultant, to attempt a wholesale change programme. The resulting package was given the title 'Working With Pride'.

The key elements revolve around the idea of raising quality by gaining employee commitment. It was envisaged that this commitment could best be sought through a cluster of measures which hinged on direct communication with employees in a way which does not rely upon the erstwhile practice of transmitting information via union representatives.

An early step in pursuit of the target of commitment was the re-organization of all manufacturing employees into 'zones' which were, and still are, intended to facilitate identification with a unit and to instil a sense of belonging. Each zone has a zone supervisor responsible for giving briefings on a regular basis to employees. At Cowley, over 100 of the 430 supervisors had been on training courses designed specifically for this purpose. It is intended that the zone supervisor will increasingly be the clear sole boss of that area – gradually encompassing all ancilliary and service functions under one general 'manufacturing' head. At Longbridge, for example, this idea has been pursued in some zones with all engineering and maintenance supervisors coming nominally under the production supervisor. Given a mis-match in numbers (there is far from a one-to-one equivalence in that a process engineering supervisor for example, would typically service an array of production zones) the experiment has involved designated periods when all relevant staff are on the zone. Photographs and names of all zone-related staff have also been posted in the relevant meeting areas.

The instances of success were recorded with satisfaction by many of the managers interviewed: over a thousand operatives trained in statistical process control (SPC) at Cowley with the expectation, therefore, of the self-management of quality in place of specialized quality inspection, and a high level of involvement with the work – especially on the prestige 800 series. On this project managers also report the cases of workers who have themselves taken responsibility for the painting and general re-furbishment of their own work area – a seemingly concrete signal of pride in work. Similarly, the 50 hourly-paid volunteers who gave up a free day to visit dealerships to help promote the new car are also cited with satisfaction.

On a wider cross-company front, support for the policy thrust of winning commitment has been pursued through the use of a 'family programme' which encourages new recruits to bring their spouses and children to visit the works in addition to open days and related social events.

The emphasis on direct communication is also revealed through the use of two other devices. One of these is known as the 'Road Show'. Initially, these were used simply to launch all new models internally to the employees, then it evolved into a series of gatherings of 400 to 500 where cross-sectional mixes of staff could meet for an hour every few months to hear a presentation and to engage in a question and answer session. The other is the graphic symbolism of the number of closed-circuit television installations scattered throughout the factories. These transmit news about company performance and other company-related messages.

The revamped policy has also meant, as the HRM model would suggest, a resort to more thorough and sophisticated selection techniques. In addition to biodata screening[1], new employees have also faced psychometric tests. Managers at Austin Rover were not the only car company managers to make the point, only half tongue-in-cheek, that the 'ideal' recruit was a male, mid-twenties with children, a mortgage and the 'right' attitudes.

Concerning the point in the model about 'participation', there were at Austin Rover definite signs of a tilt in this direction. The company had introduced 'zone circles' for this purpose. The number of these which had actually been successfully introduced by the date of this research were few, but they were accorded extraordinary significance by plant managers (notably less so by IR managers). The resistance to quality circles from the TGWU in particular, meant that their introduction was a long and painful process. But managers were intent on persisting despite union opposition – indeed the competition for the commitment of the operators on this measure became of symbolic as well as of practical importance.

The trade unions have so far not been involved in the Working With Pride initiative. According to one interpretation they have simply adopted a neutral passive stance, but according to others, some stewards are in effect seeking actively to counter it on the grounds that it is designed, long term, to undermine their position. At the present time, managers seem intent to press steadily on.

So, how can the Austin Rover case be summarized? Basically, the accent as it is perceived on the ground, is still on cost-cutting and meeting efficiency measures. Quite a deal of thought had gone into devising the Working With Pride programme and this is taken relatively seriously because it is seen to be supported by top manufacturing management. But even despite these advantages running in its favour, this change programme has yet to cut deep; the organization from a people management viewpoint can not yet be said to have been transformed.

Ford Motor Company

While many of the themes concerning quality, commitment and communication find echo also in the Ford case, the path towards the management of change here has been markedly different. In contrast to Austin Rover, for example, the line managers at different levels have been given a greater chance to influence the conduct of employee relations. Hence, at the national negotiations in 1985, plant managers from the main sites were instrumental in shaping the nature of the deal so that the productivity allowances were tied to a set of pre-negotiated changes in working methods. Moreover, the detail of what had to be delivered in terms of flexibility and revised working practices in order to earn this allowance was worked out and negotiated locally. The resultant negotiated contracts were comprehensive and very detailed. The outcome of the 1985 two-year deal was, from the company viewpoint, very satisfactory. For example, 500 different job titles were reduced to just 50 and after 17 years Ford finally removed the job evaluation system from the hourly paid group and replaced it with an approach which gives line managers far more flexibility in their utilization of labour.

In the Ford case of course it is important to remember that the American parent company has, to a considerable degree, been a leader in the 'new industrial relations'. The changes in Ford of America have been described by Kochan et al., (1986) and by Katz (1985). A key aspect was the EI programme. Not only did such measures put Ford in the leading ranks of the old smoke-stack companies but, according to John Stewart, Director of Human Resource Development for Ford of Europe since 1986, Ford was, in 1985, about 'middle of the pack' among even the top-line US companies 'such as IBM, DuPont, GE and Sears. Moreover, when measured in terms of the *progress made* by the company in areas such as creating programmes of change 'it far surpassed the others' (interview, Ford Central Office, Brentwood).

Participation was a key part of the set of managerial initiatives at Ford. The formal Employee Involvement package was inherited from the United States. It makes provision for two-way communications but it has been rejected by the manual unions although accepted by the staff unions. Ironically, however, in some plants it appears that on an informal basis at least, the practices of employee involvement have been more fully advanced among the manuals than the staff.

Commitment has also been pursued in this arguably most 'constitutionalist' of companies using a further American-sourced change package entitled 'Mission Values and Guiding Principles' (MVGP). The general statement on which this is based is reproduced in figure 3.3.

MVGP is supported by a bulky implementation manual. This contains centrally devised training and implementation programmes designed to cascade the MVGP message throughout the global Ford empire. The aim is to 'build understanding and commitment among Ford employees' (corporate vice-president's statement in the preface to the manual).

On the communications front, a key example of new departures was the so-called 'Trojan Horse' theme. Detailed business presentations have been made right across the company, contrasting performance measures in Ford with those of its major competitors – in particular with the perceived Nissan Trojan Horse in Sunderland. The shape of the message was outlined before the negotiations for the two-year deal signed in 1985 and it is seen by IR management as a very useful 'support' for the success of these negotiations. The initiative has continued on other planes after the conclusion of that deal. Essentially, it is Ford's version of the constellation of target-setting, performance assessment and communication devices that can be found in many British work organizations.

The continuing role of trade unions and industrial relations in this case is reasonably clear. At Ford the HRM-type activities operate very much in parallel with the IR machinery which continues to function. As might be expected from a management as sophisticated as that at Ford, there is little naivety about overnight transformation to a new order. What is notable, however, is that once again line managers – especially at senior level – are as willing, if not more willing, as personnel and IR managers to contemplate an installation of HRM approaches.

The current approach of Ford of Britain is dualistic: a continued systematic, careful, detailed and professional approach to collective bargaining. But this is now being accompanied by a new determination to put resources into initiatives which, until recently, would have been hardly contemplated beyond the level of occasional rhetoric. The mission, values and guiding principles form one part of this; the communication programme which stresses the competitive is another. Further details on both are given in sub-sequent chapters.

Figure 3.3 'Mission, Values and Guiding Principles', Ford Motor Company

MISSION

Ford Motor Company is a worldwide leader in automotive and automotive-related products and services as well as in newer industries such as aerospace, communications, and financial services. Our mission is to improve continually our products and services to meet our customers' needs, allowing us to prosper as a business and to provide a reasonable return for our stockholders, the owners of our business.

VALUES

How we accomplish our mission is as important as the mission itself. Fundamental to success for the Company are these basic values:

People – Our people are the source of our strength. They provide our corporate intelligence and determine our reputation and vitality. Involvement and teamwork are our core human values.

Products – Our products are the end result of our efforts, and they should be the best in serving customers worldwide. As our products are viewed, so are we viewed.

Profits – Profits are the ultimate measure of how efficiently we provide customers with the best products for their needs. Profits are required to survive and grow.

GUIDING PRINCIPLES

Quality comes first – To achieve customer satisfaction, the quality of our products and services must be our number one priority.

Customers are the focus of everything we do – Our work must be done with our customers in mind, providing better products and services than our competition.

Continuous improvement is essential to our success – We must strive for excellence in everything we do: in our products, in their safety and value – and in our services, our human relations, our competitiveness, and our profitability.

Employee involvement is our way of life – We are a team. We must treat each other with trust and respect.

Dealers and suppliers are our partners – The Company must maintain mutually beneficial relationships with dealers, suppliers, and our other business associates.

Integrity is never compromised – The conduct of our Company worldwide must be pursued in a manner that is socially responsible and commands respect for its integrity and for its positive contributions to society. Our doors are open to men and women alike without discrimination and without regard to ethnic origin or personal beliefs.

Peugeot-Talbot

Peugeot-Talbot enjoyed a remarkable recovery in the mid-to-late 1980s. This erstwhile failed British subsidiary of Chrysler was sold to Peugeot for just $1 along with a considerable inherited debt burden in 1979. The early part of the decade was a period of retrenchment. The Linwood plant in Scotland was closed and car assembly was confined to the Ryton plant near Coventry.

Since that time, a product-led recovery programme has resulted in an increase in employment again and has also seen the introduction of two-shift working. The big change in relations with the workforce is attributed to two main factors: a serious attempt to enhance direct communications with the workforce and the assumption, by line management, of responsibility for people management.

For employee communications a whole array of devices is used ranging from Industrial Society-style team briefing to professionally produced reports, newspapers and videos. The briefing is of the cascade type. The initial impetus stems from the top of the company and an outline brief is prepared reflecting the corporate-level information. This is fed down on a regular basis through the reporting structure. It is recognized in this company that the final stage is the crucial one, that is, the ordinary line supervisor giving an oral report to his team. For this event the assembly line is halted once a month for half an hour. The initial reaction from the shopfloor was sceptical. Likewise, the shop stewards mounted a campaign of resistance to the concept of a direct communication system which short-circuited them. However, management persisted and this device is now regarded, at least by nearly all managers, as a vital element in the attempt to place employee relations on a new footing.

The re-establishment of line managers' authority is also regarded as particularly crucial. The Director of Manufacturing, Colin Walters, insists that the 'production manager is King' and this was a phrase often echoed by others at Ryton including area managers and supervisors. Walters claims that personnel policy itself, not just the way in which it will be implemented, is now not the preserve of central personnel and industrial relations specialists, but is in the hands of manufacturing and the company

executive committee. The perceived role of personnel and industrial relations nowadays is, therefore, that of leading the annual
negotiations with the trade unions and of helping to 'coordinate'
practice across the company. It is argued that in the past, centrally led personnel and IR policies never really took hold 'deep-
down'.

A linked feature of the line ascendancy is the investment in
leadership training for line managers. This has involved outdoor
training and development and the general view from those who
have been on the course is that they returned 'inspired'. They
nonetheless tend to admit that a gap remains between management and the shopfloor.

Jaguar

Of the cases discussed so far, Jaguar is probably the one most
publicly recognized as having transformed its employment management approach. As we will observe, however, this conventional view exaggerates the degree of difference between the
various cases.

Jaguar was part of the BL empire for a period in the 1970s and
by the turn of the decade it was plagued by poor productivity,
indifferent quality and a falling market share. John Egan was
brought in during 1980 to turn the company around or, if this
could not be done, then to close it down. The story of revival has
been told many times. But what needs to be noted here is that
though that recovery can be attributed as much to the reinstalla-
tion of basic engineering principles as to the much-publicized
human resource initiatives. The extent of these initiatives should
nonetheless not be under estimated.

Jaguar certainly had devised an interconnected programme of
measures. A human resource management post was created in
1985 and a campaign was launched to win 'hearts and minds' (as
it was unabashedly called). This comprised all the main elements
we discussed in the previous chapter: an emphasis on direct communications; more careful selection; task level participation; investment in training and development. To promote identification
with the company, 'family days' were introduced. The new selection initiatives included psychometric testing for hourly paid

recruits. The trust in HR by most top managers as the way to proceed was very much in evidence:

> we see HR as the front arm, the leading arm of personnel. To get the best out of people you have to get them wanting to come to work and wanting to win. IR to us is a supporting activity only. That's the difference between us and say, Ford or Austin Rover. They would like to move from IR but don't know how. We are the other way around, we are a HR company with an IR function acting in support of that. We may not yet be Nissan but we are nevertheless distinctive in the way we approach HR.
>
> (director, Jaguar)

Yet even this special case revealed problems for HRM. Communication and participation were sought through team briefings, attitude surveys and a quality circle (QC) programme. But these have not been installed unproblematically, even at Jaguar. There was considerable resistance to both the survey and to the circles. For example, 56 circles were introduced between 1982–6 and the figure plateaued at this level. A major push from management increased the total number to 82 by 1987. But despite this at Browns Lane, the main site, no hourly paid involvement in quality circles has been achieved. All 35 circles at this location were on the staff side. This reflects the resistance by senior stewards. The 82 circles across the company meet once a month for an hour but there is some pressure to have this increased to once a fortnight. Noteworthy also is top management's persistence. Despite nearly a decade of experience with QCs and the attendant resistance, there was, in 1987, a renewed target of 200 circles across the three sites.

The theme of 'line managers to the fore' has also been pursued by Jaguar. Management 'leadership' is seen as vital. As one senior manager said, 'Categorically it is our key people issue in 1987 to 1988.' As part of this, extra recruitment of foremen was under way in order to take the ratio from the then 1:35 to 1:22. All new foremen were sent on a full-time, off-the-job training programme for six months. And a shorter version was designed for the existing stock of supervisors: 'The emphasis will be to change them from being progress chasers into fully fledged managers accountable for budgets and even for training and developing their own employees' (Manufacturing Manager, Jaguar).

The National Health Service

This is an instructive case because the National Health Service (NHS) seems to be peculiarly subject to serial reform and reorganization. So what was distinctive about the changes occurring at the time of the research and how far did they reflect the HR model?

The underlying drive was the implementation of 'general management' as recommended by the 1983 Griffiths Report. As the decade progressed the key themes which slanted its interpretation became those of accountability, target setting, performance indicators and new forms of managing budgets. Hence, apart from the (very pronounced) echoing of the line management theme, there was little at this official level to suggest a playing-out of the HR theme.

At another level, however, there were at least some indicators. For example, the whole battery of 'culture change' concepts and techniques were rife in this organization. The NHSTA as the national training agency was a leader in this field, but more interestingly, unit general managers were found to be not only familiar with these tools, they were actively experimenting with them. Team building, interpersonal skills, an emphasis on communication, team involvement in mission-statement construction and a constant resort to the notion of quality service were found in nearly all the units visited. Cross-specialist quality circles and problem-solving groups were being launched apace and the National Society for Quality Circles in Britain accordingly had many health authorities in membership.

So how does all this balance out? There was a perceived 'difference' in the nature of the change programmes in the late 1980s and NHS staff from various functions attested to this. But the case is instructive because in the final analysis as we shall see, the structural and budget-led 'reforms' were seen to carry most weight.

British Rail

The management of change in BR is a clear example of a business-driven approach with an extra layer of complication deriving from governmental pressures and constraints. The backcloth has been the objective to shift BR onto a self-funding competitive footing in as many areas of its operations as possible. The dilemma of course, has been that while seeking to meet governmental expectations in cost reduction this has led to increased conflict with the rail unions.

The first step was taken to divide up the railway into distinct parts or 'sectors', that is Intercity, Provincial, Parcels, Freight and the Network South-East. This allowed separate performance targets to be set and outcomes to be measured. Also, through this device, each component part of the organization was intended to be able to get closer to its particular customer base.

The reorientation was not helped by the fact that it occurred against a backcloth of budget reductions. There were various exercises to reduce administrative costs especially by reducing the white-collar head count at regional level.

A key thrust and one that was central to the theme of people management in organizational change was the attempt to shift the culture of the railway from a procedure-dominated, bureaucratic base onto a commercial, flexible, innovative and enterprising one. Pilot studies on 'organizational culture' in the Western Region were not sanctioned for extension elsewhere but a major Customer First Programme was mounted. And, following the period of the research, BR like many other of the organizations in this study invested heavily in a Total Quality Programme.

Concerning trade unions and industrial relations, BR were at the time taking steps to disengage from centralized bargaining. Various substitute forms were under consideration but following a major industrial action in 1989 the plans were withdrawn.

So the package of management initiatives in BR – sectorization, customer care programmes, devolved management and bargaining reform – while leading to an undoubtedly far-reaching set of initiatives, would not seem to add up to a package of change which could be called human resource management. While BR has been experimenting for some time with a number of the elements of HRM, including for example, new selection techniques and a revitalized performance appraisal system, even on these measures, the progress so far has been extremely patchy. What was happening in BR, was the introduction of a veritable welter of managerial initiatives – most of which failed to stick.

Bradford Metropolitan Council

Britain's local authorities represent another example of the nature and pace of change being propelled by central government. An array of legislative measures have recast the contours of local government – it impacts upon their methods of raising revenue, the scope of their functions and seeks to reorient them fundamentally in a customer-led way. Simultaneously, local government has been urged by the Audit Commission to revamp its *modus operandi* in its management of resources, most crucially its human resources. In effect, the Audit Commission has declared traditional administration to be defunct: 'the old consensus has gone' it states, 'and it is unlikely to be restored for some time' (Audit Commission 1988: 2).

The case chosen for inclusion in this study was the City of Bradford, a council acknowledged to have been at the forefront in pursuing these changes and one of the largest of the metropolitan councils in England and Wales. At the centre of Bradford's drive to make a step change in its employment management practices was its corporate plan which the council labelled its 'social strategy'. This was a policy document which sought to reorientate the total range of council initiatives in what was claimed to be a customer-led way. The personnel policies were, in turn, reassessed in order to engineer their compatibility with this.

It comprised a package of measures such as the localizing of services, training of staff in 'putting people first' and an acceptance of trade unions as partners in service delivery. Management was to be more 'vigorous' and a no-compulsory redundancy policy was adopted to assuage fears about the consequences of this. The case was particularly interesting because this organization was indeed committed to treating the unions as 'partners' in these changes. The design of the 'package' was consciously shaped by private sector 'best practice'. A series of workshops were held to which leading-edge practitioners and management consultants were invited to help diffuse their experiences. The personnel specialists in Bradford followed this lead by explicitly setting about changing their approach. They adopted one which they themselves described as the 'HRM way'. They devised a personnel strategy described as an 'HR strategy' built around more employee commitment and involvement, a reshaped organizational form to allow a speedy response to customers, more flexibility in reward packages, to allow for example, higher payment in areas of skill shortage, and a new push on the training front. Ironically, perhaps, it was the arrival of a Conservative-dominated group in 1988 which overturned much of this programme.

The Bradford case is especially interesting in two regards:

- it illustrates the point that in certain parts of the public sector there have been definite instances where attempts have been made explicitly to adopt a Human Resource Management model
- it instances a union-linked approach to HRM design in the British context.

ELECTRICAL AND MECHANICAL ENGINEERING

Eaton

Eaton Ltd has its major UK locations in Manchester, Aycliffe and Basingstoke and is part of the American Eaton Corporation. Eaton employs 41,000 people in 140 plants world-wide. Its development was based on truck and auto components including gearboxes and axles for heavy vehicles. It has, however, recently diversified into the electronics field.

The case is interesting here because it furnishes an excellent example of an American company which is at the forefront of HRM thinking, being confronted with British plant locations which are traditional, fully unionized and until recently, above-averagely conflictual.

The starting point for the new management initiatives is 'The Eaton Philosophy: Excellence Through People'. This philosophy, elaborated in a full-length book by a former manager of Eaton Corporation (Scobel, 1981) is constituted around a number of 'principles'. These, it is stressed, are not absolutes but are 'target conditions to be pursued at every Eaton facility'. In essence, they instruct managers to:

- focus on the positive behaviour of employees

- encourage employee involvement

- communicate in a candid, face-to-face way.

Other principles emphasize:

- training

- the maintenance of effective performance appraisal

- the selection of managers and supervisors who demonstrate an appropriate blend of human relations and technological competence.

What was the reality? In the British mechanical engineering plants this 'philosophy' was greeted with considerable scepticism – from the shopfloor and plant managers alike. Nevertheless, attempts were made to implement at least some of it. For example:

- quality circles were launched and a great deal of management commitment was put into them

- selection procedures were revised and 'cost centre' supervisors became responsible for helping to choose and then to develop the people who would work in their area

- senior managers attempted a more open approach to communications

- investment was stepped up in training and development.

Moreover, this is one of the (select) cases where some attempt was made to involve the unions in the change programme. At the Aycliffe site a no-strike agreement was reached locally with the AEU.

But another aspect of the reality is the degree of inter-plant competition for work. This was starkly illustrated following the loss of the Manchester plant by fire. Protracted negotiations ensued on new working conditions before the parent company agreed to reinvest in the site. This experience of vulnerability was undoubtedly a key factor in subsequent workforce attitudes to cooperation in change and is a classic example of the importance of context in the interpretation of HR practice.

In sum, if one asks how one of the more elaborated of the American HRM philosophies fares when transplanted to a traditional British engineering factory, the answer would have to be that, at this stage, the roots have yet to take hold and in consequence the flower is some way from showing. British managerial attitudes seemed to present as much of an obstacle as that of the shopfloor. As a result, the amount of planning and resourcing committed to installing HRM in the Eaton British plants has, to date, been limited. Perhaps in consequence, rather than despite this, there remains a degree of optimism among a minority of the managers that they are at a very early stage of something big and that things will eventually be very different.

Lucas

Lucas developed mainly as an automotive component supplier to UK-based motor manufacturers. As the British motor industry declined, Lucas ran into trouble. The group reorganized itself into three major divisions – automotive, aerospace and industrial. In planning for turnaround, corporate eyes have been firmly set on the international competition.

The organizational change programme devised to meet this competitive challenge included:

- devolution of decision-making and accountability to 135 constituent businesses

- decentralization of collective bargaining

- technological change

- a complete 'systems' analysis of its operating units which attends to their organizational structures, their cultures and their operating methods such as just-in-time (JIT) manufacture.

A key thrust has been the reappraisal of manufacturing systems and business systems. This has been underpinned and energized by a massive educational and training programme. The company was spending £40 million per annum on this, some 3 per cent of its sales. Following an attempt in the early 1980s to find a technological fix through off-the-shelf, consultancy-provided solutions, a key appointment was made at manufacturing director level. Dr John Parnaby, who was appointed to the post, had a phalanx of change agents at his command in the shape of a corporate group known as Lucas Factory Systems with some 200 professional staff available for 'internal consultancy'.

Each business unit was expected to develop a competitive achievement plan (CAP) which can demonstrate how the business will at least match the level of performance of their best inter-national competitor. The corporate strategy rested on a 'task force' approach with manufacturing and business systems methods injected straight into the component business units. Task force members are put through an intensive, one-week training programme. At the same time the most senior managers are treated to a two-week awareness programme about the total quality organization concept. The essential nature of this approach towards organization analysis and change derives from manufacturing systems engineering – not from personnel or human resource management theory. But the elements echo the HRM model: commitment to a focus on customer needs; continuous improvement; participation; and the view that every part of the operation of the business is 'a process which contributes to quality' and the restructuring of the organization away from functional bureaucracies and towards material and information flows.

Hence, at Lucas, many of the elements of a HRM approach are present but the leading edge derives from a manufacturing systems philosophy.

Massey Ferguson

Massey Ferguson is part of the Canadian based Varity Corporation a diversified industrial holding company. The Massey Ferguson Company itself has its main locations in Britain, France and Italy. The discussion which follows is confined to the Coventry tractor site which, in addition to undertaking assembly, also has a machine shop.

The company has a classic IR pedigree firmly located in Coventry engineering culture including, for example, a strong

attachment to the piece-rate payment system. It is highly unionized and, in 1987 still maintained a well-organized shop stewards
system with some one hundred and twenty-two shop stewards
and three full-time convenors. Changes to working practices were
hard fought and industrial action was relatively frequent. There
has been site bargaining since 1984.

It was into this environment that a human resources function
was grafted on in the early 1980s complete with an American HR
director. The MD was converted to the change in direction and
tended to issue memos and circulate photocopies of new-wave
ways of thinking in order to begin to effect a reorientation. For
example, extracts from the writings of Tom Peters and Lee Iacocca
were circulated. QCs, briefing groups and other employee involvement devices were introduced. These were often boycotted
however. Even the vice president's own direct briefing to the
workforce was similarly treated as the stewards claimed he was
'abusing the forum'.

The HR and IR functions continued, meanwhile, to operate
dualistically – that is it was rather more a question of coexistence
rather than 'in tandem'. There was speculation at one time that
IR would be taken over by HR but, as IR was already subordinate
to manufacturing the latter were reluctant to lose control over
this function. In the event, the American HR director returned to
the United States, the HR function was run down and by the late
1980s it had in effect been subject to a reverse takeover by IR.

The programme of change which failed, comprised an elaborate 'EI matrix' which recorded progress along the range of
'involvement dimensions' by function and by location. The
patchiness of the application was made evident by this. A couple
of years into the programme I found a very non-uniform situation. In most departments the EI matrix was no longer being
attended to.

An 'open style of management' was declared and salary ranges,
for example, were advertised on all jobs. Training programmes
were introduced which were designed to make employees more
'market orientated'. Briefing groups were launched and factory
tours for clerical workers were arranged.

But in 1987 the market situation for tractors had deteriorated.
Around one thousand redundancies were announced and the HR
function was scaled down. The number of shop stewards was also

drastically reduced and two out of the three full time convenors were placed back in manufacturing jobs. From the vantage point of the end of the decade, the managerial view was that the initiatives in the early to mid-eighties were premature and, in addition, they were launched without adequate preparation. The company is now setting about building on some of these ideas.

While the initial period may now be judged as 'a failed experiment' the underlying thrust is again becoming seen as the broad path to follow 'when the time is right'.

Rolls-Royce

The Rolls-Royce group has some 42,000 employees world-wide of whom 39,000 work in the UK. The main manufacturing plants are in Derby and Bristol with another 10 factories scattered around the UK. The company, which was privatized in 1987, produces engines for civil and military aircraft and also for industrial and marine use.

The research focused on one division – Industrial & Marine which is headquartered in Ansty, near Coventry. This business centred on repair and overhaul, marketing and product support. Most manufacturing is contracted-out either to other Rolls-Royce sites or to external suppliers. The Ansty headquarters therefore contains a significant number of technical experts.

New HR initiatives were found to be few in number. Great faith was placed however in the value of direct communication. The lead came from the managing director who believed it to be 'a major factor in maintaining morale, developing team spirit and motivating'. He affirmed: 'I have consciously planned my time to ensure that I can communicate and be visible to the workforce. I will stick to my general plans no matter what pressures arise to deflect me.'

Devices designed to deliver these objectives included:

- regular monthly briefings to all senior managers

- divisional director presentations to the workforce every four months

- a senior management conference held to address strategic issues every six months

- weekly meetings on an individual basis between a senior manager of each function and those managers immediately reporting to that person.

Nominally there is also a system of supervisory-based team briefings. But in practice the briefings were not working because they were blocked by steward opposition. However, management hoped to introduce the system gradually. One opportunity was seen in an incremental change to the site director's regular programme of talks to small groups in every shop in the plant (known at Ansty as the 'soapbox' meetings). The plan appeared to be to develop on from this by first substituting the work's manager for the site director, the production line managers for the work's manager and then, occasionally at first when the production line managers are 'unavailable', the soap box would be taken by supervisors themselves.

On a wider front, there are plans to extend appraisal beyond managerial grades into the monthly paid technical staff. Flexibility is also an issue though it is seen as double edged in that the company, under its present arrangements, has to pay for capability and it does not want to pay for something it might not use.

The company is also seeking an 'attitude change' so that new methods can be introduced more readily. It has installed 'task forces' to attack particular problem areas and it is hoped that this approach to active problem solving and quality improvement will eventually have a wider ripple effect. There was also evidence of the managerial restructuring we have noted in many other cases. Here superintendents had been removed and 'shop managers' became the new foci of attention. The old-style superintendents were regarded as not sufficiently technically proficient. The new shop manager's role has been staffed by using graduate entry and by drawing from the technical support staff.

The training dimension was also being given some attention. A 'Training for Change' programme had been launched mainly using line managers as trainers. The plan was to take every manager through this programme.

The trade union and industrial relations scene was fairly traditional. The shop floor workers were organized by the AEU and junior management was itself 95 per cent unionized – mainly by TASS. There were site-level negotiations with nine separate bargaining groups (though for some this was largely regarded as 'central bargaining in disguise').

In sum, of the 15 cases this one was among the group least affected by HR initiatives.

Plessey Naval Systems

Plessey Naval Systems is part of the Plessey Company plc which is an international company with major interests in telecommunications, radar, sonar, command and control and other related systems. Its activities embrace both hardware and software development and provision. During the period of the research the company repulsed a takeover bid from GEC.

The complex and intermeshing range of product groups and services resulted in a series of reconfigurations in company structure. The business division with which we are here concerned, Plessey Naval Systems, grew out of the erstwhile Plessey Marine which was in turn a constituent business of Plessey Electronic Systems Ltd (PESL) a major management company within Plessey. The structural arrangements are relevant in that they impinge on the question of who, in such organizations, can and will formulate and deliver new HR strategies. At the time of this research the individual businesses were broadly self-sufficient and the management-led initiatives within Naval Systems were therefore largely home-grown.

Plessey Naval Systems had 17 sites but was mainly located at Newport (Gwent), Templecome (Somerset) and Addleston (Surrey). It was divided into three product groups addressing the sonar, submarine communications and the naval command systems markets. Each site had its own personnel management arrangements. The sites were unionized but membership fell considerably short of 100 per cent membership. The hourly paid were organized by the EETPU and clericals and staff by the then ASTMS. Many people on site encapsulated the nature of the activity with the phrase: 'we are in the business of terminating wires'. Essentially, the Newport site, for example, was in the business of final assembly and test of naval electronic equipment.

Plessey Naval System management was highly proactive in the sphere of people management. The inherited industrial relations procedures were tolerated rather than nurtured and the main effort was directed towards direct communication with the workforce, an attempt to build employee commitment to the company and considerable activity was also underway in the area of management development.

Managers at Newport talked about transforming 'the culture'. The key to this was seen as a dual move to get the average employee on board through a sophisticated and integrated communications package while also building sound 'technical leadership'. These technical leaders/managers were to be identified through assessment centre techniques.

Most site managers agreed there had been considerable change in the approach to people management. The underlying theme was the notion of line managers being responsible for their 'own people' with personnel simply providing support when needed. But, as a senior site manager observed, the site was currently 'stuck between two strategies'. He was referring to, on the one hand, the aspiration to move towards a high-trust environment with open communications and teams which would largely devise their own ways of operating, and on the other, the persistence of the more centralized procedure-based personnel system.

The processes involved in managing the tension between these two approaches is a theme pursued in later chapters.

PROCESS INDUSTRY

Whitbread

The Whitbread company with a workforce of 35,000 and a turnover of £817 million in 1986/87 was decidedly one of the big brewers. Its financial performance is consistently sound and profitable. Indeed, despite the stagnation and even slow decline of the beer market and the public house industry in general, this company has continued to turn in profit increases of nearly 20 per cent per annum.

Like other big brewers it has been in the business of diversification in recent years. Its retail division, encompassing Beefeater Steak Houses, Thresher off-licences and Pizza Hut, has been the main engine of profit growth. This division now accounts for nearly 40 per cent of total group profits.

Here we are concerned with the brewery division. Key landmarks have been the rationalization of its production sites and a concentration into a few super breweries such as those at Samlesbury near Preston and at Magor in South Wales. These are large, purpose-built, green field site operations. The process of concentration was accelerated by the premature closure of the in-profit Luton brewery in the face of an industrial dispute in 1983.

Despite the conservative tag from city analysts, from an IR standpoint the company has been a leader rather than a follower certainly as far as the brewing industry is concerned and indeed even beyond. The senior management team have a definite view of the nature of their HR package (and it is significant that they do see it as a 'package'). It includes:

- devolution of managerial responsibility and accountability

- a drastically reduced personnel function

- a shift of responsibility for managing labour to the line

- an enhanced policy-advice and planning function for the remaining personnel team

- decentralized bargaining

- an approach to employee relations which seeks to shift from stratagem and confrontation to harmonious relations

- team working and flexibility.

There are now no personnel managers attached to the various sites but there is a human resource director at the head of the brewing division, beneath which there are four HR managers. One of the functions of HR at the divisional headquarters level is to produce the policy paper for the annual pay round. This is submitted to the board of Whitbread breweries, the parameters agreed and the maxima set. When approved in principle the package is disseminated and line managers are given responsibility for negotiating the packaging in their breweries. This is seen as symbolic of the wider culture change whereby line managers are held responsible for managing without a set of instructions to follow.

Such a policy requires underpinning by training. The company is described as one which has spent 'a fortune' on management training and development. Every manager had been on a one or two week training course in 'leadership'. First line manager training has centred on training in teamwork, and defining aims and objectives. Part of the change has been to move towards an open management style. The company was using attitude surveys on a regular two-year cycle. Significantly, given the limited HR developments described in the immediately preceding cases, Whitbread brewing is unionized but the union presence is clearly far less evident – particularly at site level.

Whitbread plc has produced a booklet and video proselytizing the 'Whitbread Way'. These media seek to express the principles concerning human resource management. It is noteworthy however, that in a covering letter, the Chairman, Sam Whitbread, traces these to the long tradition 'cherished since the company was established nearly 250 years ago.'

ICI

As one of the world's largest chemical companies with an extensive range of products, ICI needs little in the way of a general introduction. What is worth noting, however, is the extent to which, and the speed with which, the giant changed its posture when confronted with its trading losses in the early 1980s. In pursuit of its turnaround, the company rationalized and restructured itself. The company had become complacent and insular during its years of success but in the 1980s it began to look outwards with alacrity. Not the least important part of that change was in the sphere of labour management. In seeking to document its nature this research focused primarily on one constituent business: ICI Films, part of the then petrochemicals and plastics division. Following initial research at Wilton, interviews were conducted at the Dumfries site where 'Melinex' a thermoplastic polyester film is produced along with other high-grade film products.

Purcell and Sisson (1983) had classified ICI as falling within their 'consultors' sub-category of 'sophisticated modern' IR types. In this category while trade unions are recognized and collective bargaining is well developed, the intent is to minimize the extent of codified rules and conflictual relations. The preferred path is cooperation achieved through mature consultative procedures.

With some amendment that characterization remained broadly correct in 1987. Process workers were still 100 per cent unionized and company level bargaining was still the crucial foundation for employee relations. Local bargaining was supplementary to this and covered areas such as manning levels and shift patterns. There were, however, some important new initiatives which augured some shift from the traditional 'formula'.

The main thrust of the strategy of the senior team at Dumfries was highly suggestive of this rather different character. Their action plans centred on communicating a new 'vision' for the business, engineering a culture change, and implementing a 'quality improvement through defect prevention' strategy. Higher levels of commitment were being sought and steps had been taken to improve selection, enhance communication and encourage job and team level participation. The American guru, Philip Crosby, had been flown across to help devise the quality programme. The Dumfries view was that this initiative 'makes IR pale into insignificance' – though that was perhaps more of an aspiration than an achievement.

A summary view on this case might be that there were indeed signs of an attempt to shift the strategy. The prevailing consultation/negotiation arrangement had not been attacked head-on but managerial priorities clearly lay in other directions. Tracing the drivers for this was quite difficult. Central personnel at Millbank were seen as simply custodians of the national agreements. Divisional personnel were a source of advice and occasional initiatives. But the constituent businesses at site level were also encouraged to stamp their own character. The case is an interesting one because it illustrates the degree of shift from previously existing styles while the nature of the 'new approach' is only partially consonant with the HR model.

Smith & Nephew

Smith & Nephew has been a consistently profitable health care and consumer products group of companies. To a considerable extent it grew through acquisition. Its UK divisions are wholly owned limited companies each with their own formal boards. In recent years the group has invested heavily overseas, particularly in the United States, and these activities now account for more than half the company's turnover, revenues and employment.

The constituent companies, in the UK at least, are unionized – in most cases to a level of around 90 per cent density. Negotiation occurs at divisional level. Accordingly, at group level there is no personnel director but there is a group level 'advisory committee' staffed by the MDs of the various divisions. This high-level policy formulation group is supported by an industrial relations adviser. Each of the divisions has its own personnel function. It is at divisional level where policies are finally put into shape.

Smith & Nephew's employment management approach is highly pragmatic. It is a fiercely independent and, to a degree, parochial group of companies. It withdrew from the CBI and it views with suspicion 'foreign' ideas. As one corporate chief tellingly pronounced: 'our managers would not find Peters and Waterman helpful.' The personnel function itself has been rather weak in the past. But in the last couple of years an attempt has been made to upgrade it in each of the divisions and new appointments have been made of specialists from outside the company. The cautious, hesitant, character of the change process of Smith & Nephew is revealed in the following analysis made by one of the corporate level managers:

> It is difficult to put one's finger firmly on any new management initiatives because, in Smith & Nephew, things tend to happen by evolution. Nonetheless, in retrospect, a pattern can be discerned; we have gone through a period when the trade union influence had to be 'readjusted'. Now we have reached a stage where our managers have to manage better, be more positive, more effect-ive, do more than they did in the past, have to define what it is they wish to do, ensure their employees are pulling in the same direction. You could call this a new industrial relations or even a new phase of management. It means you've got to inform your employees better, train them better, allocate tasks better, identify the priorities better. They have to be more thinking.

The company has 'selected out' managers who have not responded to this new phase.

Another key factor is the increasing identification of procurement, sales and marketing as the priority strategic issues and not manufacturing and things related thereto. In addition, new product launches and a re-examination of company style and culture with the aid of a firm of consultants were the emerging themes.

Despite the pragmatic culture, the pace of change was clearly accelerating. The company had been regarded as dominated by 'old fashioned textile thinking with a mill owner mentality'. The shift from that was on a problem-by-problem basis underpinned by a more professional personnel approach.

Overall, the Smith & Nephew case is rather distinctive among the group of organizations reported here. Despite the old-fashioned feel about the place it had been markedly successful when measured in terms of profit growth. At first sight it would seem to be the least likely setting in which to find new human resource approaches and yet, in broad terms, it could be located in the middle band. It is only just coming to terms with starting to put its 'mill owner' approach onto a more professional footing. But, with its current thrust towards highlighting the proactive role of line managers at every level, it finds itself very much in tune with contemporary fashion.

CONCLUSIONS

This catalogue of 15 mainstream cases reveals, not surprisingly, a complex picture. But certain points can be discerned amid that complexity.

The first is that there is clear evidence of extensive and sustained activity directed at employment management matters. Moreover, management during this period had clearly seized the initiative and were experimenting with a host of approaches. They were conscious that the initiatives were different and there was a definite sense of new ground being broken.

But was there any underlying logic to this welter of activity? There was some degree of commonality in the initiatives, which extended even across the sectors. The touchstones were a retreat from proceduralism, an emphasis upon adaptability, direct communication with employees, 'managerial leadership', and the moulding of a more tractable employee stock.

Judging simply from the 'pen pictures' thus far, it can be deduced that the nature of these initiatives and the philosophies underlying them tend to give some qualified support to the HRM hypothesis. But a superficial view might be misleading. The depth and extensiveness of these initiatives were opened up as areas of doubt. For example, as the Jaguar case revealed, even the oft-cited examplars may turn out on close examination to reveal problems of considerable messiness and struggle. The undoubted HR initiatives here, as at Massey Ferguson and elsewhere, were found to be *running in parallel with the traditional approaches*. The concept of an integrated approach which figures so prominently in the abstract modelling turns out to be a rather distant aspiration. A possibility deriving from the cases would seem to be that the HR model as outlined in the previous chapter may be insufficiently subtle to afford the necessary insight into current change programmes. There is some *prima facie* empirical evidence to support the abstract propositions but there were also sufficient qualifications to merit a deeper level of analysis in the ensuing chapters.

There is also another important conclusion which can be drawn at this point: despite the commonalities there were also considerable variations. In the terms of figure 2.1 the initiatives ranged from 'weak' to 'strong' in their intensity and from 'hard' to 'soft' in their character. A range of explanatory factors could be hypothesized: industry sector, technology, the public-private distinction, the nature of product and labour market conditions – and perhaps most especially, the intensity of international competition. It would be premature to pursue each of these here. They are attended to in the final chapter. But from the overviews given in this chapter some of the interesting varying slants which were revealed between the sectors deserve immediate comment.

The motor companies and the other manufacturers tended to be the ones giving particular emphasis to team briefing, quality circles and functional flexibility. Yet there were important exceptions – two of the manufacturers (Rolls-Royce and Smith & Nephew) were found to be least influenced by this approach. The process companies were using technologies which placed little premium on the latter two initiatives. At Whitbread and ICI Films, the emphasis was upon consistent, trouble-free working. In all three public-sector organizations (BR, the NHS and the local authority) there had clearly been some infatuation with the tenets of the 'customer-facing' school of thought. Whitleyism was out of favour and could even be described as under attack – not only by central government but also by local authorities and health service managers. The long-standing procedural approach in British Rail was similarly under an onslaught. In each case the alternatives being explored had a familiar resonance.

Given the general commonalities, the obvious next question was whether these initiatives were being evenly pursued in each case or whether the picture was being muddied by a superficial application of fashionable techniques in some of these organizations while others might be applying them more genuinely. To answer this key question we need to take the analysis to a deeper level and that is the purpose of the next chapter.

Note

1 'Biodata' refers to biographical data. This a personal history inventory generated through the use of an extended application form. A personal life history is constructed so as to build up a profile of each candidate which can be compared against one or more 'preferred' profiles.

4

Managing Human Resources in Practice: A Thematic Analysis

The aim of this chapter is to examine developments in employment management by slicing through the research data on a thematic basis. This will allow direct comparison of the initiatives being taken by the different organizations whose broad progress was sketched in the previous chapter. At the very least, it would seem that there is an evident commonality of language and ideas permeating employing organizations in diverse sectors. Managers in health care, motor vehicle assembly, railways, brewing and local government are busy with talk of 'visioning', of clarifying organizational 'mission', of promoting 'managerial leadership' and pursuing 'excellence' – through, among other devices, effective communication, the linking of reward with performance, more systematic selection and through a more 'committed' and 'adaptable' workforce. Only a few years ago most of these managers would not have been using this language and probably would not even have heard of some of these terms. But is it only the language which has changed or is there evidence to suggest that something more fundamental is happening in the way that employees are managed?

The way evidence is reviewed in this chapter may be thought of as analogous to a high-altitude reconnaissance mission across a complex terrain. Notable landmarks are picked out for subsequent, more detailed, attention in the ensuing chapters. The first fly-past yields figure 4.1. This gives a broad brush summary of results across all 15 main case organizations. It juxtaposes the cases as listed across the top of the figure against the 27 dimensions listed down the first column. The 27 dimensions are those first introduced in the conceptual framework chapter (chapter 2: see especially figure 2.2, p. 35).

The 27 dimensions are condensed by homing-in on the HRM variant – that is the final column of figure 2.2. The scoring methodology is inevitably rather simplistic; it is indicative rather than definitive. A tick is allocated to a cell when the particular HRM-type characteristic was found to be broadly in evidence or where there were signs that significant energy was being expended to bring this state of affairs into being – that is it was a significant agenda item for certain key managerial players. A cross is allocated when none of the above conditions applied to any marked degree and a question mark is shown where either the item was on the agenda, though not a pressing issue, or where certain parts of the organization – such as a particular division or business unit – had registered the dimension as a key agenda item.

Even a cursory view of the figure reveals that these mainstream organizations were apparently engaged in some extensive experimentation. The patterns on the figure can be regarded as a pictorial representation of the welter of initiatives being taken by managements at this time. Of course, what the figure cannot do is reveal any of the subtle aspects associated with these moves. These aspects will require exploration across a number of chapters. In this present chapter the task is begun by examining, in turn, each of the main component spheres of human resource management. This is done in three sections: the first examines initiatives associated with the resourcing and utilizing of labour; the second section focuses on changes in leadership and motivation; the third and final section attends to training and developmental practices.

RESOURCING AND UTILIZATION

Under this heading we will review developments in the practices of:

- human resource planning
- deployment and utilization
- recruitment and selection

Figure 4.1 Full summary of results

Dimension	1	2	3	4	5	6	7	8	9	10	11	12	13	14	15
								The 15 case organizations							
Aim to go 'beyond contract'	✓	?	✓	✓	✓	✓	✓	✓	✓	✓	?	✓	?	?	✓
Impatience with rules	✓	✓	✓	✓	?	✓	✓	✓	✓	?	?	✓	?	?	✓
Prime guide to action: 'business need'	✓	✓	✓	?	✓	✓	✓	✓	✓	?	✓	✓	✓	✓	✓
Values/mission	✓	?	✓	✓	✓	✓	✓	✓	✓	✓	✓	?	?	?	✓
Nurturing orientation	?	✗	?	?	?	?	?	?	?	?	?	?	?	?	?
Unitarist	?	?	✗	✗	✗	?	?	✗	?	✗	✗	✓	✗	✗	✓
Conflict de-emphasized rather than institutionalized	✓	?	✓	?	?	✓	?	✗	?	?	?	✓	✗	?	✓
Customer-orientation to fore	✓	✓	✓	✗	?	✓	✓	✓	✓	?	?	✓	✓	✓	✓
Integrated initiatives	✓	✗	✓	✗	?	?	?	?	?	?	?	✗	✗	✗	✓
Corporate plan central	✓	?	✓	✗	?	?	?	?	?	✗	?	✗	?	?	✓
Speedy decision-making	✓	✗	?	✗	?	?	?	?	✓	✗	✗	?	✗	✗	✓
Transformational leadership	✓	✗	?	?	?	?	?	✓	✓	✓	?	?	?	?	?
General/business/line managers to fore	✓	✓	✓	✓	✓	✓	✓	✓	✓	✓	✓	✓	✓	✓	✓

Direct communication	?	✓	✓	✓	✓	✓	✓	✓	✓	✓	✓	✓	✓	✓	✓	✓	✓
Standardization/parity not emphasized	✓	?	✓	✓	✓	✓	✓	✓	?	✗	?	✗	✗	✗	✗	
Facilitative management	✓	✓	✓	✓	✓	✓	?	?	?	?	?	?	✗	?	✓	
Selection integrated	✓	✓	✓	✓	✓	✓	✓	✓	✓	✓	✓	✓	?	✗	✓	
Performance-related pay	✓	?	✓	✗	✗	?	?	?	?	?	?	✗	✗	?	?	
Harmonization	✓	?	✗	✗	✗	✗	✗	✗	✗	✗	?	✓	✗	✗	✓	
Towards individual contracts	?	✓	✗	✗	✗	?	?	?	✓	?	?	✓	?	✓	✓	
Marginalization of stewards	✓	?	?	✗	?	✓	✓	✓	✓	✓	✓	?	?	?	✓	
Fewer job categories	?	?	?	✓	✓	?	✓	?	✗	✓	?	✓	✗	✗	✓	
Increased flow of communication	✓	✓	✓	✓	✓	✓	✓	✓	✓	✓	✓	✓	✓	✓	✓	
Teamworking	?	?	✓	✓	✓	✓	✓	✓	✓	?	✓	✓	✓	?	✓	
Conflict reduction through culture change	✓	?	✓	✓	✓	✓	✓	✓	✓	?	?	?	?	?	✓	
Learning companies/heavy emphasis on training	✓	?	✗	?	?	?	?	?	✓	?	✓	✓	✓	?	?	
Wide ranging cultural, structural and personnel strategies	✓	✓	?	✓	✓	✓	✓	✓	✓	✓	✓	✓	?	?	✓	

Key: ✓ = yes (existed or were significant moves towards)
x = no
? = in parts

Human resource planning

It may have been a response to the demographic message and to the already tight labour markets in certain parts of the country in the late 1980s, but whatever the reason, there were signs that more attention was being paid to human resource planning.

Notoriously, the HR planning process has been the arena for prescription with a dearth of hard evidence that practice was in any way being affected. Even today, despite recent uncertainties about the state of labour supply, there is no reliable source of information about the extent to which companies do take a strategic approach to the acquisition, retention, utilization and improvement of their human resources. Surveys by NEDO (1988, 1989) and others, suggested that significant numbers of employers had an inadequate understanding of the demographic profiles of the workforce in the 1990s and it seems that even among those employers who did appreciate these changes, few had formulated plans for responding to the situation. One could begin to suggest that outside the traditional lifetime employment organizations, such as the large clearing banks or the civil service, many, if not most, employers continue with an essentially *ad hoc* and pragmatic approach to their human resourcing problems.

To a large extent, the findings from the 15 large case studies reported here would tend to support this suspicion. Even the basic raw data about the employed population in these organizations frequently did not exist in a usable form for planning purposes. For example, in the National Health Service, the way in which central statistics were collected meant that the Regional and District Health Authorities did not have a composite picture of the number of different types of nurses available. In effect, psychiatric nurses were being counted in with nurses who had specialized in paediatrics, and theatre-nurse statistics were computed alongside general ward nurses. Similarly, in the private sector engineering companies, human resource planning was also found to be frequently rudimentary. Even senior management succession planning, for instance, was in the main left to informal and *ad hoc* mechanisms devised by particular individuals. And even among the more sophisticated cases, where central personnel had drawn up a standardized mechanism complete with formal succession plans and elaborate profiles of the managerial stock, it was often admitted that the resultant piles of forms were hardly used because the information was quickly outdated.

Such instances might be considered particularly surprising given the number of commercial software packages on the market which purport to offer computerized human resource planning. Over half of the cases in our sample had in fact subscribed to one of these services but, typically, they were in the early stages of adapting them for planning purposes as opposed to the long-standing practice of using them for simple personnel records. One of the main difficulties was that while these systems purportedly allowed for inclusion of training records, experience and capabilities on the databases, the information stored was usually considered too schematic to be really useful for planning purposes. Typically, it was said that a trawl through such files might be undertaken in order to construct a 'long list' of possibles when moves were being planned, but, that the fine judgements required individual sifting. Even the suppliers of these planning systems were found not to be using them in their own organizations. Part of the reluctance to pin too much hope at this time on computerized human resource planning stems from the backlash to a premature attempt to produce 'mechanistic' planning systems in the 1970s. These were considered to be abstract and intricate mathematical exercises which served to produce technical models of supply and demand but which seemed to have little practical use. Put simply, the forecasts were frequently inaccurate and the implications for action were not clear.

But it would be wrong to conclude from this that no strategic thinking about resourcing was occurring in these organizations at the time of the study. One of the clearest examples was in fact found among the wider 'panel' of cases. Golden Wonder employs 3000 people on six sites. After the Hanson Trust takeover of the company from the Imperial Group, the company trod water for a while before being sold to Dalgety. The industrial relations approach of Golden Wonder has traditionally rested on company-level bargaining for most of the process operators. The pattern of relations in the various functions was described within the company as non-participative and even 'authoritarian'. But, on the human resource planning front, the company has taken a coordinated series of initiatives. The workload in crisp manufacture fluctuates depending upon seasonal peaks and special sales promotions. A temporary workers' agreement caters for employees engaged for periods up to 26 weeks. In any one factory the number of temporaries can range from zero to as many as 500. An average, however, would be some 200 temporaries for a few peak months.

There is 24-hour, three-shift working. In 1985 a proposal was put to the unions suggesting three categories of employees. Category One was to be the permanent workforce; Category Two would be permanent part-timers – that is those working two to three days per week but with an 'agreed flexibility' to work the extra two or three days in the week (for which no overtime would be paid until 39 hours was reached). A third Category was to be composed of the temporary staff. A ballot of the workforce led, however, to rejection of this scheme.

With the help of a team of management consultants the company then turned to what was known as an 'annual hours' package which involved the averaging out of total hours worked over a 12-month period so that what was worked in any particular week was no longer regarded as the critical factor. It entailed a planned reduction in work hours for the first category and an increase for the other two categories. The planning of the annual hours and the mixed composition of the labour force to reach the total required was accompanied by an 'integrated approach'. A policy document was produced which linked the issues of harmonization of conditions, training, progression, rewards and the flexible use of the different categories of labour. The company also seriously considered 'no-strike agreements' and to this end, managers visited various Japanese sites in Britain in order to glean ideas. The TGWU was seen as an obstacle to aspirations of this sort, however.

The company has a personnel director sitting on the board and human resource planning issues of the kind indicated, feature regularly in board discussions. There was a strike which affected most parts of the company in 1985 but since that date the integrated package has been rolled-out in a very determined way.

In formal terms the 15 case companies might easily claim to undertake human resource planning if prompted to reply to a survey question. But in practice, its usage was found to be very limited. Hence, this first tenet of the HRM model was found wanting.

Deployment and utilization

A conscious attempt to construct an integrated approach to human resource planning and utilization is also strongly in evidence at another food-processing company: Birds Eye Walls. Birds Eye is the frozen food subsidiary of the Anglo-Dutch Unilever company. The planning here centres on an attempt to alter radically the assumptions about the nature of labour requirements. The central thrust hinges on a plan to introduce 'teamworking'. This entails fully interchangeable process teams so that each individual can not only do other people's process-related jobs but, in addition, the teams are also responsible for their own routine maintenance. On a day-to-day basis each team decides who will do which task, including information inputting on shopfloor keyboards.

The team-focused human resource planning is part of a wider initiative across the Birds Eye Walls company known as 'Workstyle'. This package was carefully planned and negotiated in a series of working groups with employee representatives from each area. Agreement was reached with these groups, which included shop steward representatives, on measures which amounted to near total flexibility. This lengthy consultative negotiation process was undertaken on a site-by-site basis: failure to reach agreement at the Kirkby location was one of the reasons for the closure of that facility. The level of flexibility and associated training across specialized tasks was apparently more than met overall. One manager suggested that they had actually got more than was needed:

> We got it wrong: we have found we don't actually need that level of interchangeability. For a team of 10 to be efficient you may need only 7 to be able to do *x* and, say, 6 to be able to do *y*. We initially went for the whole lot. This, we later found was not necessary.

While the process operators teams were found to be fully operable, the engineers and electricians had drawn back. The aim was to combine fitters and electricians in 'mechanical-electrical/electronic teams'. Their fears were countered by managers who said, 'Don't worry about past job boundaries. Focus on the new sophisticated equipment we are introducing; that's what we want you to be concerned about'.

But the integrated planning process extends beyond team-working and flexibility. A number of erstwhile full-time employees have been switched onto part-time working. The Grimsby plant, for example, gained a majority of employees voting for this move as a means of 'saving the factory'. The resultant part-time resourced, four-shift pattern is highly economical with curtailed overtime, no shift payments and reduced holiday entitlement.

There is no doubting the way in which human resource planning has contributed a crucial element in the business plan. 'Workstyle' is billed within the company as an HRM initiative designed to underpin the rationalization programme, part of which is the concentration of production of frozen foods into a few technologically-sophisticated sites. As part of this the distribution side has been sold off to National Freight.

The factory closures and the simultaneous investment in new technology in the remaining sites were seen to open up an ideal opportunity to introduce a 'people-management change pro-gramme'. The plan was an attempt to 'harness initiative' – the stated aim was to raise expectations and to tap into that decision-making capability which ordinary workers display in their work lives outside working hours.

The 'Workstyle' initiative was described as 'holistic': it was frequently drawn in diagram form comprising the three interre-lated pillars of: 'responsibility/flexibility/quality'. The attainment of these three constituent features was seen to depend upon the teamworking concept. The package was presented as a means to make work more interesting and to foster greater responsibility. For example, Workstyle is described by the company thus:

> Workstyle which was introduced at Gloucester and Lowestoft is a concept which gives employee workgroups the responsibility for organising their own work, by their own methods, leaving man-agement free to manage. Workgroup members are encouraged to understand every aspect of the production process from start to finish and to take responsibility for meeting quality, cost and tonnage targets.
>
> (Birds Eye Walls Annual Report and Accounts, 1986)

As part of this concept, supervision was removed and the teams became self-supervising. In practice, however, the shift managers, to a large extent, still behaved as if they were doing the supervisory job. The managers were supposed to be raising their sights so as to tackle wider issues such as identifying training needs, setting priorities, auditing team performance, health and safety, planning and advising the production managers. Each shift manager (assistant manager) was typically responsible for two teams of 10 persons. They were held to account, in the final analysis, for the actions of these groups. As senior managers saw it: 'We have to have a single person we can go to to carry the responsibility'. In consequence, some assistant managers responded by being 'too interventionary' – that is behaving as if they were still supervisors. Others 'back-off too far and control has slipped'.

Taken together, the two cases of Golden Wonder and Birds Eye indicate that there are examples of consciously planned and, indeed, strategic action with regard to the resourcing and utilization of the workforce. The mechanistic manpower-planning models have been superseded and there is clearly evidence of a type of planning which attends not only to regulating numbers but is proactive in respect of part-time work and annual hours contracts, and proactive in the realm of radically different forms of labour utilization. This latter is illustrated particularly with the teamworking initiatives at Birds Eye which was dissolving traditional job boundaries and even helping to remove the whole supervisory tier.

Nonetheless, the two cases along with the other examples cited, also point to the difficulties which these sorts of initiatives encounter. Removing supervision leads some managers to try to fill that role themselves; it leads others virtually to abandon work teams to their own devices. The Workstyle agreements at Birds Eye have yet to embrace the critical constituency of maintenance workers. And at Golden Wonder, the new working patterns remain subject to future negotiation with the trade unions and cannot therefore be regarded as installed in perpetuity.

A key aspect of labour utilization in the 1980s was of course the question of the flexible deployment of the available labour resource. The concept of 'flexibility' loomed large in debate. Indeed, it figured so prominently that it sometimes appeared that this intermediate objective represented what many managerial change programmes have been largely about. Against the backcloth of controversy on this theme, what contribution can be made by the findings from these detailed case studies?

The first point to note was that, overall, the efforts spent by management to secure flexibility across a whole number of fronts was found to be considerable. Initiatives designed to achieve more flexibility in labour utilization were particularly notable in the manufacturing companies. For example, Plessey Naval Systems signed a formal 'Flexibility Agreement' with the EETPU. This stated that:

(i) existing hourly paid demarcation practices be replaced by total flexibility
(ii) the definition of 'total flexibility' is that employees will carry out every task within their capability
(iii) to achieve flexible manning it will be necessary for employees to learn new skills and develop existing skills
(iv) deployment will be based on business needs
(v) a revised flexibility grading structure will be introduced.

Four grades were introduced based on experience and capability. Ironically, as the bulk of the work was becoming more standardized and de-skilled the implied necessity for skill enhancement proved to be somewhat illusory. The expansion largely occurred in the lowest grade and even some apprenticed-trained skilled workers able, for example, to work from drawings, found themselves spending more of their days on routine assembly.

With the introduction of microelectronics into the Coventry telecommunications site of GEC, (another of our 'panel' companies), a similar situation was found to be developing. The implication that can be drawn from this is that strategic choice with regard to flexible utilization of labour will be influenced by technology. The drive for functional flexibility was, in general, especially important in manufacturing, but its importance varied considerably between situations where de-skilled operatives rendered it superfluous to those semi-skilled areas where the lack of interchange between tasks was seen as a major obstacle to be overcome. This latter situation prevailed most noticeably in the motor companies. At Ford, Jaguar, Peugeot and Austin Rover, there were definite attempts to facilitate inter-craft working and to expand the jobs of semi-skilled operatives to take in maintenance, inspection, cleaning and some responsibility for ensuring a smooth supply of material to the work stations.

In British Rail, a key initiative has been the 'traincrew concept' which has breached the long-standing divide between drivers and guards. The 1988 Traincrew Agreement reached between BR, the NUR and ASLEF provided for a new grade structure which is described as 'fully versatile':

> The occupant of the post whether designated Train (wo)man (Driver) or Train (wo)man (Guard) will perform the duties of the other grade provided training in that role has been received.
>
> (1988 Traincrew Agreement, Clause 5)

Measures of this kind are of course not entirely new: productivity bargaining in the 1960s as exemplified in Flanders' account of the Fawley Blue Book (1964) illustrates the point. But what is different is the extensiveness of the changes and the way in which they are underpinned by related developments. Thus, for example, a common observation in the 1960s and 1970s was that the buy-out of 'restrictive practices' was often phoney: in part because the agreements were frequently a thinly disguised side-stepping of the statutory incomes policies and in part because modified 'restrictions' emerged in their place. Under the current climate the accompanying real and extensive reductions in headcounts (as much as 30–40 per cent has been common in the larger manufacturing concerns) have meant that the pressure on those remaining to change their job scope has been of an entirely different order than before. This is not to say that 'flexibility' is necessarily sought as an end in itself or that it is always and everywhere desired by management. Patently this is not so. There are numerous instances where total flexibility is not seen as an appropriate goal. Management may expressly want a limited number of experienced workers to remain dedicated to a particular task – swapping and changing around would be regarded as wasteful and even dangerous. Similarly, the costs of achieving flexibility – whether incurred through training or through extra payment for skill attainment – may also deter.

Ford Motor Company provides an excellent example of the various levels of complexity. In 1989 the announcement was made that Dagenham, on the assembly side, was to lose the 'contract' for the larger, prestige models and would be reduced to the assembly of the small car, the Fiesta. This widely publicized event was simply one further step in a longer-standing series of cross-cutting calculations which involves, on a European-wide canvas, relative productivity, changes to working practices, quality, and inter-plant competition.

In retrospect, the 1985 agreement for Ford of Britain was a turning point and it serves to illustrate the way in which the company intended to head in the future. This agreement contained a crucial element which made part of the deal contingent upon productivity gains. The novel aspect was that although Ford retained company-level national bargaining, the productivity allowances package was devolved to plant level for detailed attention. These discussions and the resulting agreements were both extensive. The broad principles are incorporated in the national agreement. This states: 'productivity allowances are payable to employees who cooperate with local management in ensuring maximum capacity utilization and the efficient use of manpower.' The 'changed work practices' are itemized based on the three 'principles of versatility and flexibility; the acquisition and use of new skills; the elimination of inefficient lines of demarcation'.

The agreement set out the requirements for production operators and for craft employees. Regarding the former, it is stated that in order to qualify for the productivity allowances, operators must, as required:

   (i) seek, identify and repair defects (this includes the inspection and rectification of incoming work);
  (ii) be involved in techniques, such as statistical process control, to record and use results from control process measures;
 (iii) line feeding operators must procure and feed material to the work-place using the designated material handling equipment as required;
  (iv) make adjustments to, clean and lubricate equipment – this includes making corrections to settings, replacing worn parts and assisting, 'within their capability', craft employees who are carrying out maintenance duties.

As for craft employees, electrical and mechanical craftsmen 'must be flexible and versatile across the full range of their respective skills, and undertake any electrical or mechanical tasks outside their own trade subject to capabilities that are necessary to complete an assignment.' Both crafts have agreed to make the necessary preparations for work on equipment, including the use of lifting equipment and driving. They 'must also carry out line patrol, taking corrective actions as they identify the need and be mobile across a plant or operation' (The 1985 Agreement: 86).

While crossover between electrical and mechanical skills is not seen as attainable (for technical reasons) other than at the margins, the mechanical craftsmen 'must acquire and apply the full range of mechanical skills from all the mechanical trades' including advanced pneumatics and hydraulics. Payment is subject to meeting the standards set out in a formal training programme. The conditions specify that whether in body and assembly or powertrain, mechanical craftsmen are expected to be 'fully interchangeable' not only within their own traditional work areas 'but also central shop or toolroom and shopfloor maintenance'.

These conditions as set out in the national agreement are seen as the broad parameters: the detailed applications are the subject of local arrangement between plant management and 'in consultation with employees and their representatives'. As part of the deal the job evaluation system was abandoned and so too the grievance procedure for job grading.

So much for the formal agreement. But what has actually happened in the plants? The general estimate from various line managers at Dagenham and Halewood in 1987 was that they had, in fact, achieved 80 per cent of the conditions. Moreover, the remaining 20 per cent was usually seen as impeded by the want of investment in, for example, appropriate decentralized toolrooms (or 'cribs') rather than as a consequence of labour restriction. Allowance has to be made for a degree of bullishness in these crude estimates but even the stewards tended to endorse the general view that significant departures had been made from traditional practices, as a result of the agreements. A measure of reversion to past practice may, however, be expected. Already, for example, it was evident that where new dispersed 'cribs' for the mechanicals had been constructed in the machining and assembly areas, there was some struggle over the attempts by the craftsmen to develop these into closed havens instead of the envisaged open-plan workshops. Thus, attempts by the maintenance workers to have the cribs made fully enclosed with doors, ceilings and the like, were met with compromise agreements that resulted in the uppermost wall panels being sloped inwards so as to form semi-enclosed units. This small site of contention might be seen as likely to presage a more prolonged struggle over the amount of 'line patrolling' which can be expected.

Nevertheless, it would be a mistake to underestimate the degree of change. Underpinning the NJNC agreement on flexibility have been local plant agreements prompted by an entirely different calculation – namely, new work practices as a precondition for attracting investment in the face of inter-plant competition. This has been a feature of the engine plants in particular. Bridgend and Dagenham have had to compete for programmes for which continental plants, such as Cologne have been strong contenders. It has to be remembered that Ford is organized on a European basis for its manufacturing operations. The sourcing of any component, be it engine, gearbox, body or whatever, is thus potentially always a matter for inter-plant competition. The winning, in July 1985, of the in-line four-cylinder double-overhead camshaft engine for the Granada and Sierra models by Dagenham when it was initially regarded as destined for Cologne is a key case in point. To attract the £160m investment necessary to undertake this, Dagenham had to submit a detailed case built around changed working practices and cooperative labour relations. A series of off-site meetings between senior stewards and the plant management resulted in an extensive brochure documenting the agreed 'quantum change'. This involved locating skilled workers on production lines, oiling by operatives, mobility of labour within indirect functions and outsourcing of certain operations including some plant engineering.

In pursuit of these sorts of 'radical and far reaching' changes it is recognized that works committees are often placed in a difficult position *vis-à-vis* national officials and committees representing other locations. Accordingly, rather than insist on strict formal agreement, a 'tacit acceptance' was often deemed sufficient by plant managers. Conveners and senior stewards from the various plants tended to argue that while they face criticism from their colleagues for agreeing to major working practices' concessions, their critics were themselves 'hypocritically involved in similar agreements'.

There is also a considerable amount of exploration of 'scenarios'. In one plant during a joint meeting between senior management and senior stewards, the talk turned to future aspirations concerning the staffing of the machining area. The aim was clearly stated of having a 'team' of a dozen: four or five of whom would be oriented towards maintenance. Moreover, the production jobs were described as 'not old-fashioned production jobs' but ones entailing fault-tracing, monitoring, tool changing, adjusting and the like. It was estimated that such a team could itself take care of 75 per cent of the breakdowns which currently require the call-out of a maintenance engineer.

A twin-level push existed at Ford then. Locally, plants had to demonstrate cooperation and productivity (which is likely to involve, *inter alia*, flexible working) while at national level, the NJNC negotiated national agreement (the Blue Book) continued as an authoritative document which was amended from time to time. Also at national level, a Productivity Study Group had been meeting and this had buttressed the changes to working practices discussed above with a set of proposals relating to reform of the wage structure, which it identified as an inhibitor of flexible operation. As a result of this work, 500 job titles have been reduced to just 50. And, after 17 years of operation, the job evaluation process has been discarded in a move designed to allow line managers to be more directly responsible for the flexible use of the labour resource under their charge.

The overall view at Ford among the line managers charged with operating the system was a general satisfaction that at last the company had taken steps to improve productivity which had made a real and sustained impact. Indeed, the judgement seems to be that the company got far more out of the 1985 agreement than it had expected. The 1987 negotiations which led to a national strike were viewed, in contrast, as merely seeking the icing on the cake.

Peugeot-Talbot at Ryton in Coventry is another car manufacturer which has dramatically increased productivity. In the Peugeot case there is less room for doubt that the gains have resulted from cost cutting and new working practices rather than from investment in new advanced technology. Ryton remains a technologically traditional car plant given the present volume throughput (80,000 units per year). Nonetheless, productivity increased 100 per cent between 1980–8.

Here too, the changes to working practices have, in the main, resulted from a bargaining-for-change approach. In 1987 a new multi-craft grade (A+) with a 5 per cent differential was proposed.

Until that time the manual grade classification had been 'A' to 'E' with grade 'A' being the highest. It contained, for example, toolmakers, electricians and pattern makers. Negotiations at Peugeot include the national officers of the main unions (TGWU, ASTMS, AEU, EETPU). Agreement and introduction were not finally achieved until 1990. To qualify for the new grade, the craftworker has to have passed a specified training programme and be doing work of the specified kind. Until the late 1980s, maintenance typically involved a number of different specialists – for example, an electrician to isolate a defective machine, a millwright to remove the guard and undertake initial dismantling, and a toolmaker to repair the motor.

It is notable that Peugeot was not seeking full multi-trade working for all its craftworkers. It simply did not see the need for this, nor (and most important) did it want to pay for it. The limited amount of multi-craft working which the company sought was designed to involve what was described as the 'brighter of the toolmakers' receiving electrical and electronic training. After initial resistance, the stewards representing electricians have now shown a willingness to cooperate in this measure of multi-skilling.

The actual requirement for these multi-skilled 'A+ grade' craftsmen was viewed as likely to vary across plants. Initial estimates were that 20 per cent of craftworkers would qualify for this grade at Ryton where only a few hightech machines were currently in place, but a much higher proportion at Stoke where the factory management seemed to want nearly all their skilled people to be fully flexible. (Up to 90 per cent was initially envisaged by plant managers.) Central personnel was seeking to reconcile these wide disparities.

Even before this 1987 move, some considerable flexibility was in evidence – especially in the machine areas where operators were doing their own inspection, material collection, oiling and cleaning. These practices were coyly described as having simply 'evolved'.

In the main assembly areas the job-specifications remained more or less as they were. Few initiatives had been taken here where the prime requirement was routine and dependable accomplishment of fragmented tasks. The claimed outcome of attention to detail on the productivity chase is a regular schedule achievement rate of over 90 per cent. Indeed 100 per cent was said to be attained quite often. Between 1983 and 1988 there was a productivity increase which saw Ryton come from 30 per cent behind the French plants to an equal position during a period when the French plants themselves have increased their own rate of productivity. Ryton moved, as a result, to double-shift working.

The body-in-white at Peugeot-Talbot illustrates the point about how reduced manning implies a combining of jobs and an expansion of responsibility. At the end of the body-in-white-line there used to be 12 metal finishers, 3 inspectors and 2 additional rectifiers. One area manager commented:

> The rectifiers saw it as part of their role to try to slip jobs past the inspectors. Now we have just 7 men who do viewing and rectifying. Each is responsible for a particular car; they sign-off for it and they have a vested interest in it.

Notably, the manager continued by saying 'a problem is that they can be too good, that is be insufficiently commercially aware. In body-in-white there is always an element of subjective judgement.'

According to Colin Walters, the Director of Manufacturing at Peugeot-Talbot, the achieved level of flexibility at the Stoke machining plant was 'simply terrific'. He claimed, for example, that fork-lift truck drivers and inspectors also work on the machines. On the craft maintenance front, he said, mechanical fitters will also do some electrical work. He also suggests that the multiskilling idea of creating a super-skilled, super-flexible A+ grade actually originated in manufacturing.

In sum, with regard to the issue of the flexible utilization of labour, one of our continuing themes was again borne out – namely that even though most of the case companies were taking some initiatives in this direction these endeavours often did not translate into a markedly changed employment pattern. This again illustrating the point that 'strategies' and 'patterns of relations' should not be conflated.

Recruitment and selection

Apart from developments in human resource planning and developments in forms of labour utilization there have also been changes in resourcing practices with respect to recruitment and selection. As skill shortages began to bite – especially in London and the South East – employers began to treat recruitment and retention as a priority issue. To a considerable extent the wider pattern of flexible hours, of part-time working and the like, has been a response to supply-side factors rather than simply a shift in employment strategy from the demand side. Many of the case organizations, in their Southern locations in particular, were thus experimenting with non-standard hours and recruitment of older workers and were offering special terms to encourage women to return from child-rearing.

Among measures designed to attract and retain staff these organizations have also begun consciously to design and emphasize their training and development provision. In the graduate recruitment war in particular, the relative attractiveness of rival career-development programmes has begun to figure as perhaps the most crucial weapon in the armoury. If only for this reason, certain elements of the human resource management package have increasingly come to the fore. In order to compete for labour, companies had to demonstrate some provision for training and for career-development opportunities. Additionally, they supplemented these measures with others which were equally designed to signal that they nurture their human resource in some special way or could at least give it added value on the external labour market.

Other innovative ways to retain valued staff have, according to the media, mushroomed in recent times. With competition for able people increasing and the supply of young people decreasing, employers were reported as becoming more imaginative in devising new schemes to maintain some hold over capable employees. Career break schemes (which allow women to take periods of leave of up to five years to have children) and job sharing were just two examples of the kind of initiatives which attracted attention. Innovations of this kind were accordingly looked for in the 15 case companies. A few examples were uncovered but it has to be said that they were on a very limited scale and their impact was insignificant.

Developments in the realm of selection did, however, lend some support to those who propound the human resource management thesis. A key feature here has been the increase in testing designed explicitly to assess behavioural and attitudinal characteristics. The extent, however, to which these more sophisticated and systematic approaches can be, and are, deployed depends on the sector circumstances and on the kind of wider employment-management policies being pursued. In manufacturing, for example, psychometric testing of the kind marketed by management consultants such as Saville and Holdsworth, was found to have increased significantly. The motor companies, Jaguar and Peugeot-Talbot, were both using these tests in selecting foremen and even hourly paid workers. At Jaguar, psychometric tests were designed around dimensions such as 'independence of thought', 'team working' and 'cooperativeness'. The test batteries comprise over 100 multiple-choice questions and scores out of 10 were drawn up for each. The company encountered some resistance from the unions, however, to the proposal to draw upon current employees as a means of developing the appropriate 'profile'. The idea was to profile the 'better employees' as distinct from those regarded as merely 'ordinary and below average'.

Peugeot-Talbot uses assessment centres for selecting new supervisors and for the sales and marketing workforce. Its use of Saville and Holdsworth and their Occupational Personality Questionnaire (OPQ) test has, however, been more cautious than in the case of Jaguar. While personality and attitude testing was used extensively for management and some staff grades, testing for operatives was mainly confined to reasoning ability and mechanical aptitude. Nonetheless, Peugeot-Talbot and other case companies were watching developments at Jaguar with great interest. Devices such as 'biodata', which uses an extended application form to glean a mass of detail about a candidate's 'biographical history' for matching with an 'idealized profile', were beginning to figure in the selection literature at this time. These too were tested out. In the main they were not found to be making much headway. The case companies were pursuing a rather different tack – one which is designed to facilitate greater systematization and reliability in the perennially most-favoured selection method: the interview.

The key development here was the increased use of consultant-provided packages which offer a method, and the training support, to improve the selection process without abandoning the interview – indeed these programmes retain the interview at centre stage. The packages essentially involve training over a two-to-three-day period for line managers. They promise the tools to render the process less subjective. Extensive and highly structured documentation and role-play training promise to refocus the selector's attention away from the facility with which the interviewee expresses an abstract opinion and onto actual past behaviours and supposed 'typical-behaviour' responses to a variety of stimuli.

Whichever particular technique was being used by these companies, the underlying point is that more companies seem to be following the lead publicly made so evident by Nissan (IRRR 1986: 379; Wickens 1987) and other Japanese companies (White and Trevor, 1983). While workforces are certainly much reduced there would now appear to be more care taken in the selection of that reduced employee stock. Behavioural and attitudinal characteristics are playing an increasing part in this. An inference that might be drawn from this increasing resort to systematic selection techniques is that there is some expectation that a workforce could gradually be constructed which would be more receptive to the broad span of HR philosophy than is the case with existing manpower stocks.

The picture, overall, in the case companies concerning selection was that a number of them had launched initiatives which promised more systematic selection and a number had also set about trying to test for 'appropriate' attitudinal behavioural characteristics in their future workforces. Even among the remaining case companies, that is the ones without the psychometric tests and the like, there was evidence that they were addressing the selection issue with a new seriousness. As a corporate-level manager from the ultra-pragmatic Smith & Nephew company put it: 'I don't know about special techniques but we have without doubt given far more attention to the selection process in recent years – and here I also include the work we have done in weeding out the underperformers'.

LEADERSHIP AND MOTIVATION

Under this heading are grouped activities in the realms of:

- communication
- goal-setting, appraisal and pay
- participation and involvement.

The concept of 'leadership' or, 'managerial leadership' enjoyed a revival in the 1980s. The case companies, even those in traditional sectors, were showing a great deal of interest in it. Much of the stimulus could be traced to the influential work of Tom Peters (1985; 1987). The human resource levers associated with this were communication; goal setting, appraisal, and reward; and devices designed to elicit 'involvement'.

Communication

While communication might, on the face of it, appear to be at the 'soft' end of the continuum of initiatives it could prove to be one of the most significant. Where the expectation is built-up that each line manager will be engaged in direct communication with the workforce on a regular basis, this in itself may stimulate a need to formulate messages of substance. The activity also impels a revision of expectations about the managerial role.

What evidence is there of change in this regard? It would appear that many companies have made a step-change approach to this subject. Figure 4.2 illustrates the interconnected methods used at Peugeot-Talbot. This company prides itself on its employee communications. As the figure reveals, it has certainly installed a whole gamut of devices. The briefing meetings have now been running regularly for five years. To assist them the supervisors who are at the 'front line' of the briefing system, are provided with professionally produced briefing sheets and they have also been given training in holding team briefing sessions. 'Employee reports' and the annual financial report have been markedly upgraded and the result has been a regular series of prizes in intercompany competitions. The Ryton plant also has its own video studio and this is used to produce videos on a range of company-related topics. Figure 4.3 depicts a similar communications strategy employed by Jaguar Cars.

The device which these companies undoubtedly saw as pivotal was the face-to-face form usually known as 'team briefing' or 'briefing groups'. This involves the first-line manager in regular and systematic meetings with his or her subordinates. In terms of the absolute number of companies which had introduced devices of this kind, the results were impressive. Direct communication to employees using line briefing was taking place in 14 out of

Figure 4.2 Employee Communications at Peugeot-Talbot Motor Company Ltd

METHOD	PURPOSE	RECIPIENTS	SPEED	FREQUENCY
COMPANY OPERATIONS NEWS BRIEFING MEETINGS	Managing Director calls monthly Operations Committee meetings Operations Committee consists of 25 functional Directors Briefing Document contains details of meeting subject matter e.g. sales figures; financial information; employee incentive bonus; product news Line Management receives briefing document, adds local working area news. Work is stopped whilst managers give verbal presentation of the briefing document to employees All employees are free to ask questions at briefing meetings and receive either immediate or subsequent replies	All employees	Within 48 hours of Operations Committee Meeting	Each month
URGENT INFORMATION COMMUNICATIONS – IMMEDIATE DOCUMENT	To get very urgent information to all employees before the media (Known as a 'Red Document')	Distributed to functional heads ▼ Line management + Supervisors ▼ Then given verbally to all other employees	Information reaches all employees within 2-3 hours of document preparation	As required
GENERAL INFORMATION COMMUNICATIONS – GENERAL DOCUMENT	Communications news which is less urgent than that carried by 'Red Document' – but, which will not wait for inclusion in the next 'Peugeot Talbot Times' (Known as 'Green Documents')	All employees either: • verbally from super-vision • posted on notice boards	Information reaches employees within 2-3 days of document preparation	As required
IN-HOUSE NEWSPAPER 'TIMES' COLOUR TABLOID	'Local' newspaper for employees giving a blend of employee, Motor industry, company news Promotes and reports on various employee sports and social events, employee communications, retirements, appointments etc	Copy for each employee • Circulated to Company Dealers Press Libraries Other Companies Retired Employees	Normally distributed to all employees within 1 or 2 days of publication	10 issues per year

COMPANY OVERVIEW MANAGING DIRECTORS REVIEW	• Often preceded by a video presentation of major topics of current interest e.g. new model launch + analysis of past performance + future business plan • Presented to small groups of senior management at meetings chaired by the Managing Director • Trade Union representatives at separate meetings also chaired by the Managing Director	Senior Management ▼ Senior Trade Union Representatives ▼ Staff Content reported in brief meetings	2–3 weeks	2 or 3 times per year
COMMUNICATION – TRAINING VIDEOS	The Company produces, entirely in-house, videos dealing with specific subjects e.g. Quality campaigns, facility and operating changes, Pension Scheme administration. These are shown to employees normally as an extension of Briefing Meetings where there is the opportunity for questioning.	Identified groups of employees	Within one week of filming	As required
IN-HOUSE RADIO RADIO RYTON	In-house radio station for Ryton Plant covering the track areas – tapes prepared for Ryton Plant also played at Canterbury Street factory Broadcasts • anything from music to sports results • provides instant means of communi- cation on non-contentious items	Ryton and Canterbury Street Shop Floor Workers	Immediate	Broadcasts daily
LOCAL OPERATIONS NEWS SUPERVISORS BRIEF	Provides snap-shot of what happened 'on plant' the previous week Production achieved in each area – quality – appointments Gives detailed information relating to all work areas	All Supervisors	Distributed to all Supervisors in 1 day	Weekly
DIRECT CONTACT	Where necessary the Company communicates directly with employees, by mail in potential or actual dispute situations	Appropriate Group of employees	Distributed by mailing to employees home address or hand-out	As required
AGREED MINUTES	Jointly agreed Minutes of negotiations on Pay and Conditions containing TU submission and Company offer	Management Trade Unions Notice Boards	Immediate	During negotiating period
NOTICE BOARDS	Used to display up-to-date details on such matters as pay negotiation – job vacancies – fire/safety regulations – sporting and social events	Notice Boards are sited throughout all Plants	Distribution to all Notice Boards 1-2 days	As required

Note: Periodic surveys by questionnaire are carried out to assess the effectiveness of communication systems.

Figure 4.3 Structure for employee communication and involvement at Jaguar

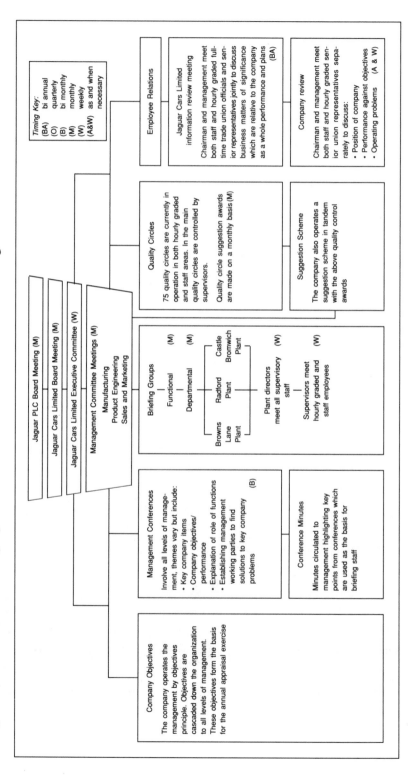

The following support services are provided to the employee communications and involvement framework:

- Video programmes

  To all employees (O)

  Themes vary from company performance against objectives. Key company items to new model information. All video showings are followed by a question and answer session involving a panel of senior Jaguar management

- Company newsletter

  To all employees (B)

- Monthly management bulletin

  To all levels of management including supervision (M)

- Individual plant supervisory briefs

  To management and supervision (W)

  Used as the basis for the plant directors weekly briefing meeting

- Notice boards

  Are sited in key areas across the three plants displaying the following information (W)

  Company information

  Production performance

  Quality performance

  Bonus achievement

  Union items

  General interest information

- Individual briefing sheets/letters

  To different levels of employee depending on nature of content (A & W)

  Circulation can be via: pay packets, letters sent to home addresses, manual circulation through supervision and/or display on notice boards

- Poster campaigns

  Displayed on notice boards (A & W)

  Recent campaigns have included: product quality and the hearts & minds/Jaguar sporting & social programmes

- Newscutting service

  To senior managers (M)

  Items of interest from the national and local press

Joint production committee

Manufacturing director and management meet senior hourly graded stewards to discuss:
- Manufacturing strategies
- Manufacturing performance
- Quality
- Operating problems   (M)

Plant production meetings

Plant directors and management meet senior hourly graded stewards to discuss:
- Production
- Quality
- Bonus achievement   (W)

Performance reports

Displayed on notice boards covering information in respect to:
- Production
- Quality
- Bonus   (W)

15 of the case companies. This finding accords with the survey of Britain's largest companies and public sector organizations undertaken in 1987 by the employee communications consultants, Vista. They found, in a survey of 222 organizations, that 86 per cent had installed a system of team briefing and 59 per cent claimed that it reached beyond the supervisory grades to all levels of staff. The Industrial Society could claim much credit for spreading the message. It had helped to introduce the system to some 400 to 500 organizations between 1984 and 1986 and many of the 15 case organizations had themselves consulted the Industrial Society for this purpose.[1]

Using the 15 company case research, it was soon revealed, however, that the real issue was not whether an organization 'had team briefing' but whether and how it was used in practice, and with what coverage across the organization. The case research suggested there were difficulties on each of these fronts. For example, it was rare to find a case where the system was being uniformly applied in practice. There were usually whole departments where briefings had not successfully taken root. The initiative in the unionized settings was also complicating collective relations. The shop stewards were in some instances rather better informed than the first line supervisors who were supposed to be giving the briefings. These supervisors said they felt exposed in transmitting a brief about topics where they might be challenged and be made to look foolish. This was particularly a complaint made by supervisors in British Rail for example. In about half a dozen of the cases the trade unions had sought to oppose the introduction of team briefings on the grounds that it was, they said, designed to bypass union channels. And of course it was. Though this was not usually its sole or main purpose.

Another development in the case companies was the practice of a certain number of key senior line managers of making direct presentations to whole departments of staff. Notable examples were at Ford Motor Company and Plessey. Works managers, plant managers and certain area managers seem to have found a confidence and competence to appeal direct to the workforce. In the instances cited, the shop stewards and conveners appeared to welcome, or at least gave grudging acknowledgement of the effectiveness of, these performances.

Goal setting, appraisal and pay

Staff appraisal had typically been around in some form in most of these companies for a long time. And with equal typicality the systems had fallen into relative if not, complete disuse. What was clearly evident in the 1986–7 period, however, was the renewed interest in revising and relaunching these schemes. For managerial employees, the new fascination with appraisal was in part linked to the vogue for defining managerial 'competences'. A number of the case companies were trying to construct their own organization-specific lists. These were normally used in assessment centres for selection into management and for developmental purposes. They were also frequently found, however, being used as check-lists in appraisal and report documentation.

An approach to appraisal which was also gaining favour was built around objective setting. The key development here was the increased insistence upon *measurable* targets. In this way this aspect of managerial appraisal was increasingly being linked to another – that is, performance-related pay. During the period under review, the traditional hesitancy about linking reward to appraisal was being shrugged aside. A further feature was the extension of the appraisal device from the confines of the managerial grades to supervisors, staff and, in a few cases, to hourly paid employees. Earlier survey work (Long, 1986) had suggested that it was part of a wider trend. The proportion of companies using appraisal for manual employees had increased from a mere 2 per cent in 1977 to 24 per cent in 1986. However, the evidence from the 15 case studies would suggest a need for caution in interpreting these figures. In instances where these mainstream companies were using appraisal for hourly paid employees it was on an 'experimental' basis and its coverage in the organizations was limited to only a very small percentage of the total workforce. For example, Smith & Nephew were talking about 'trials' in the past three to four years. The Birmingham factory had launched an elaborate scheme from a standing start. But 'it broke down. I don't think the MD was sufficiently clear about what he was trying to achieve' (senior S & N manager). Across the company, each division had its own particular system or non-system as the case may be. In certain divisions it was very evident that the nominal appraisal system was not taken at all seriously; a number of managers interviewed admitted they had effectively allowed it to lapse. At Plessey Naval Systems, performance appraisal for the manual grades was proposed in 1986. The scheme involved awarding discretionary 'uplifts' within the existing grade structure and these uplifts would have been consolidated into monthly salary. After three such supplements a regrading would be considered. During the research period, however, the plan was rejected by the EETPU.

Across the cases as a whole there was a definite interest in extending appraisal. It was seen as a logical tool commensurate with the moves towards harmonized terms and conditions with staff grades. Clear examples were found in parts of Whitbread. It fits also with the general aspiration to incorporate all sections of the workforce into an 'enterprise-commitment'. Individual appraisal, which could be used to set targets, monitor performance against targets, to counsel and to develop, was widely viewed as a vital tool of 'managerial leadership' which must eventually be made operable at all levels. The desire to reward individual performance also acts as a spur to further use of appraisal. Perhaps not surprisingly therefore it was also found that a key thrust in the changes to employment management so far as personnel specialists were concerned, was the drive to break at least partially away from collective pay arrangements and to introduce some variations based on individual performance.

Where individual merit payments have been installed in the mainstream companies this was often associated with the withdrawal of bargaining recognition from managerial groups. For example, the 1988 merit-based award in BR effectively put the managers union, TSSA, outside of the bargaining process for middle management grades. And in the NHS, the system of performance-related pay has steadily been rolled down from the most senior levels to embrace a wider and wider pool of staff. It is worth remembering that the encouragement of performance related pay and a departure from the annual pay round was part of the government's agenda of the day. Indeed, the merits of linking pay to profits as advanced by Professor Weitzman was echoed by the then Chancellor Lawson and floated in a Green Paper.

A further development in pay systems was associated with

changes to long-standing pay-bargaining structures. For example, the decentralization of pay bargaining at Lucas and the announcement by BR that it was going to withdraw from the 1956 Machinery were designed to align pay with particular market circumstances. Depending on the company, these circumstances may be geographical-based, occupational-based or, ultimately, can arise from the differential competitive performance of the separated units. This last point would apply rather more to the individual businesses in a company such as Lucas Industries, but the same concept underlay the proposed shift in bargaining arrangements in British Rail. As a BR manager argued when declaring withdrawal from national bargaining : 'the many existing levels of consultation and negotiation mean that individual and local issues are often not dealt with quickly enough in the competitive climate in which the railway operates'. In other words, the intention was to allow most matters to be dealt with by local managers. In the event, of course, these proposals became a key issue in the 1989 dispute with the unions and BR was forced to trim its aspirations in this regard – at least for the time being.

Involvement

The final subsection relating to the theme of 'leadership and motivation' concerns employee involvement. Again it was soon found that a large proportion of the case organizations was taking some steps seemingly designed to encourage a measure of direct participation and involvement. Perhaps of all the devices associated with HRM that of 'quality circles' has occasioned the most comment, the most inflated expectation – and the most cynicism.

The essence of the idea of quality circles is built on the twin facets of group dynamics and involvement in problem solving. The first element gives momentum: it allows diverse skills to be tapped, encourages a measure of simple fun, and it provides an audience for the demonstration of effective performance. The second element is pursued through a structured training programme in basic problem-solving techniques including, for example, brainstorming, problem identification, data collection, data analysis, cause-and-effect analysis and presentation skills. The two elements clearly potentially reinforce each other. In order to take advantage of the concept it is not necessary to abide strictly by the 'rules' of the pure QC format – though some consultants tend to argue that any *ad hoc* departures spell danger. Nonetheless, there are clearly many instances where 'problem-solving groups' and 'performance-excellence teams' are operating without the QC tag. Despite the (frequently deserved) charges of 'faddism' attaching to QCs, the underlying concept is undoubtedly prevalent in the case companies and it remains, for them, an attractive path.[2]

Nonetheless, many of the case companies had experienced considerable difficulty in launching and sustaining quality circles. The motor companies in particular were very keen to see them succeed and yet were also faced with some of the toughest opposition: much of it deriving from TGWU national policy. Austin Rover had made a determined effort. It had used external consultants, appointed a QC coordinator and facilitator and, had trained dozens of circle leaders. But, at the time of the study, after some 18 months of manoeuvering, only 20 circles had been successfully started. Moreover, none of these was in the main target areas: the two large assembly buildings at Longbridge. Jaguar has enjoyed more acclaim for its involvement of the workforce, but even here the record was not so very different from that at Austin Rover. Indeed, the cases were remarkably alike: there had been a similar degree of managerial effort and the same kind of patchwork response. Hence, in Jaguar also, the main car-assembly buildings had remained QC free. Peugeot-Talbot had pushed less hard. A quality control programme in the early 1980s was aborted but significantly, 'problem-solving groups', which amount to much of the same thing, have been installed with some success. 'Involvement' at Peugeot-Talbot is now described as mainly the responsibility of each individual area manager. One of these had led the way by introducing visual aids such as blackboards and easels, cartoons and drawings into his area. This met with some success including, for example, the volunteering by members of this area to spend some of their own time promoting cars at the annual UK Motor Show and at various dealerships.

Ford Motor Company, while keeping a close watching brief on these other cases, have not themselves so far attempted to introduce quality circles.

At Eaton Limited, the gearbox manufacturer, QCs had been running reasonably successfully for nearly four years. The circles were found to be meeting weekly for one hour in paid time and the company had a lengthy record of completed projects under its belt. But even here, in what must be considered one of the more successful exemplars of QCs in operation, it was evident that continued cooperation by the workforce and the stewards was contingent upon satisfactory industrial relations on a wider front. Thus, for example, during the annual wage negotiations, the operation of circles was suspended as the adversarial character of relations became more salient. This record of union opposition stands in contrast to the experience of Plessey Naval Systems at Newport. Here, quality circles had been introduced by the factory manager but they had been 'killed off' by middle managers who saw in them a threat to their own role. The ASTMS representatives claimed that the technicians especially had welcomed the opportunity to spread their wings and they further suggested that the union representatives were broadly in favour of QCs.

If one looks beyond QCs and problem-solving teams the state of play on 'employee involvement' is, if anything, even more uncertain. The enduring impression was that managers were increasingly of the view that it was a 'good idea' but specific initiatives were hard to uncover. Joint consultative arrangements, despite their continued appearance in survey results, were rarely given much credence by line managers. The predominant desire seemed to be for some vibrant form of task-based involvement. Even the overtly cautious Smith & Nephew company decided to give a corporate-level impetus to employee involvement of this kind. The central 'IR Advisory Group', comprising the MDs of all the divisions, championed the idea and tried to impel it and to monitor its progress, but, in the absence of clear guidelines the out-turn appeared insubstantial.

TRAINING AND DEVELOPMENT

It might be argued that the amount of training and development has to be the main litmus test of whether HRM has made headway in the British context. Sisson (1989) has argued that training and development are crucial, for it is not simply that the organization which fails to train will find itself dependent upon the external labour market and thus hardly in a position to regard its workforce as anything other than a cost. The organization that does train is more likely to engage in the other, complementary, aspects of HRM – if only to protect its investment. Moreover, the training company is also more likely to be able to draw symbolic value from its actions. It is sending a message that it values its employees and they are to be viewed as an important resource and this carries the potential to structure positive attitudes across a broader front.

If this really is the crucial test of the seriousness of mainstream British organizations to the full-blown HRM model, then it has to be said that few would pass it. Survey after survey has reiterated the point that on any comparative measure, the training record of British companies has been lamentable (NEDO, 1984; Handy, 1987; Constable and McCormick, 1987). While leading employers in West Germany, Japan and the USA spend up to 3 per cent of turnover per annum on training, the comparable statistic in Britain is only around 0.15 per cent. In the lead-up to the new Training Bill in 1988, however, the government began to suggest that the situation in Britain was not so dire as these kind of figures would imply.

There were also a number of independent assessments which hinted at a more optimistic outlook, at least at the organizational level in some special cases (Keep, 1989). In a patchy way this picture was reflected in the case companies. For instance, Jaguar cars had invested heavily in the system of 'open learning'. This was designed to encourage all employees to spend some time using company facilities to engage in self-development. But as this was widely regarded as a special case the important question is what were the other companies doing with respect to training and development? Does the macro-record of lamentable underprovision find echo here or are there new signs of change?

In fact, training and development practices were found to vary tremendously in the organizations studies. In many cases the dismal underprovision catalogued by the major surveys was clearly evident. Even the sporadic training that did take place was often dismissed as inadequate. For example, a Smith and Nephew manager spoke for many when he said:

Up to this year I've had no training whatsoever! The occasional in-company courses I've been on since then, such as presentation skills and chairmanship, have come too late.

And yet, sporadically, one encountered line managers in most of these companies who were receiving extensive training. Naturally, there was a degree of bias in the sample of managers whom one met. Those actively engaged in training and with promising career prospects tended to offer themselves forward for meetings, or, one was steered towards them because they were lively, informative and enthused. In these cases the range and impact of the training and development experiences often proved to be impressive.

Among the main case companies the revamped training practices at Lucas Industries probably represented one of the more dramatic and convincing instances of across-the-board upgrading of training provision. In fact, Lucas has had an above-average training record for many decades, but what is interesting about this case is the way in which the training had been revitalized during a very difficult period of restructuring and divestment in the 1980s.

Senior management contend that organizational transformation at Lucas had been driven by a rigorous 'systems engineering' approach. This, it will be recalled, has three elements:

- new technology

- alterations to the organizational system (most notably a devolution to strategic business units)

- new methods including, for example, Kanban and Just-In-Time.

The buttress to each of these three is 'a really major effort in training'. Indeed, at one meeting with corporate chiefs it was claimed that 'we are doing 50 times what Jaguar are doing'. The strategic place of training and development at Lucas stems from the intent to move radically from the standardization and divisionalization of the 1960s and 1970s 'which may have been appropriate at that time but certainly not so now', according to Dr John Parnaby, Group Director Manufacturing Technology. The new competitive conditions are seen as putting a premium on versatility. Under such circumstances 'our aim' said Parnaby, 'is not to substitute a new "method" but rather to help our managers and staff learn principles so that they can be innovative in their own setting. Local teams have to create their own solutions.' These teams in each of the 135 separate businesses can, if they wish, call on the assistance of a corporate 'task force'. At the end of the day, however, the SBUs are held responsible: Lucas operates on a 'loose-tight' principle using a combination of persuasion and pressure. Training has played a vital part in driving this strategy.

In the period 1985–8, Lucas has spent around £40m per annum on training which was equivalent to about 2.5–3 per cent of its total sales revenue. This expenditure was viewed as an 'investment' in that training and development was being called on to act as a major agent of change. The in-company consciousness of the key role of training was high. It was not seen as a poor-relation, peripheral activity, but as a potent source of change. The highlights of the contribution made by training in this company are:

- its link with the total strategy comprising marketing, product engineering, manufacturing systems engineering and business systems

- the highly evident top management commitment to it

- its role in developing and executing the competitive achievement plans (CAPs) which every business unit is required to have

- the installation of business and engineering systems into the SBUs

- and the underpinning of business task forces through training on an essentially project-requirement basis.

At the core of the Lucas turnaround strategy is the the transformation of Lucas manufacturing systems. As Parnaby observed:

competitiveness to world standards requires a fundamental re-design of our manufacturing systems and far-reaching changes in traditional working practices, habits and culture. Our most potent engines of change are the multidisciplinary task forces which operate mainly at business unit and factory level. Once the members of each task force have been given basic training in systems engineering, they then redesign their factory or business units on the basis of 'Just-In-Time' control systems. . . . they develop plans for marketing their products, improving quality, changing job structures, improving the performance of their suppliers and – not least – training all the people in the business unit.

This programme is so extensive that he estimated that by 1991 just about the whole of the workforce would undergo some form of training. (The fact that this was considered extraordinary even in a major training company such as this indicates the distance British organizations have to cover.) The delivery mechanisms included, in addition to the task force methodology, an active central training function which has reoriented itself from training delivery to training development; open learning centres; modular courses in manufacturing systems; and external masters courses.

The Lucas case provides an excellent example of a traditional, mainstream company which, in seeking to turn itself around from a loss-making situation, has sought a radical strategic response – part of which has clearly involved a drive to enhance the capabilities and commitment of its human resources through the use of training.

And yet the Lucas case is at the same time, instructive for another reason. Its training provision – especially its coherent, business-led analysis of the role of that provision – is distinctive for its singularity. Few companies – and this includes the rest of the cases involved in this project – could claim to match the emphasis upon human resource development which has been shown by Lucas. But despite this lead position, it has to be said that only a little digging around is required to reveal that the impact, when viewed from the stance of the intended recipients of such provision, is, even in this lead case, often minimal. The approach looks coherent, sophisticated and integrated when presented by senior exponents, but it is often experienced rather differently by shopfloor workers and indeed by many middle-level managers. Both groups relate how their own recent training experiences have been few and how the investment-in-people theme is countermanded by more visible messages of cost cutting and pressure.

To note these negative responses is by no means to mark out

Lucas for any particular criticism. The point extends well beyond such an exercise. What the case illustrates, is indeed, the extreme difficulty of formulating and implementing an HRM approach – in part or in whole – in the context of traditional businesses in Britain which not only inherit whole congeries of expectations and past practices but which, at the same time, have also been facing harsh competitive pressures. In this light, it may be seen that the difficulties encountered at Lucas – though their achievements should of course not as a consequence, be neglected – are reflective of a much wider set of problems which seem to be impeding the progress of human resource management in the UK.

SUMMARY

The chapter opened with a summary overview of the results from the 15 case studies. This revealed that, at least in broad terms, there *did* appear to be evidence of extensive managerial initiatives across the critical dimensions which had been identified in earlier chapters. It was recognized, however, that these results were only a pictorial representation of apparent change and that to be meaningful they required deeper exploration. This chapter commenced that task by examining developments in three main areas: resourcing and utilization; leadership and motivation; and training and development. The overall trend was incontrovertibly towards more individualized arrangements. Many of the particular devices had a rather patchy application but the pressure was found to be continuing in this direction. The basic tenets of HRM would seem to be enjoying some wide appeal among managers – if only in furnishing an aspiration and a sense of direction. The crucial importance of symbolism in helping to conjure the nature of that goal was very evident.

This chapter, which has examined different realms of initiative, reveals that there is by no means a uniform pattern of practice. Significant changes in such spheres as selection, training, flexible working and communication had clearly been driven some distance by case companies such as Jaguar, Lucas and Ford. But other cases such as Plessey and Smith & Nephew suggested a limited degree of change. And yet, what is also of some import is that in practically all of the 15 cases, the senior line managers were of a broadly common mind regarding the direction in which they wanted to travel and the kinds of changes they would like to see. The symbolic function of HRM in this regard was that it helped to provide some measure of logic to a host of often disparate initiatives. Hence, arguably, it was not the nature or content of employment management practices that was in particular contention but rather the process and feasibility of how to achieve the desired ends. It is to this issue of change processes that we now turn.

Notes

1 Where there is some legislative requirement, however, one might expect rather firmer monitoring. Section 1 of the 1982 Employment Act obliges companies with more than 250 employees to include in their annual reports a statement describing action taken to inform, consult and involve their employees. This provision came into effect in 1985. In June of that year the Employment Minister reported on a survey conducted by the Department of Employment on compliance with this section. The survey revealed 15 per cent did not report in accordance with the requirement. A further 40 per cent acknowledged the legal requirement but gave little or no detail of what they were doing. Of the remaining 45 per cent which did report, the largest proportion listed share schemes as their method of 'involvement', closely followed by company newspapers and line briefings (31 per cent of those surveyed). A broadly similar set of findings emerged from the ACAS/LBS (1986) survey of 300 company reports. This study emphasizes however, that the findings relate to what company report claim is being done, and these claims do not necessarily accord with what is actually happening.

2 Because of the difficulties of definition it is almost impossible to quantify the extent of operation of such groups. The National Society of Quality Circles (NSQC) which was launched in Britain in 1982 had 260 companies in full membership in early 1989: these included star names such as ICI, Barclays, Nat West, Tioxide and Rowntrees. It is estimated that there are some 5000 to 6000 circles functioning across the UK. The NSQC shrugs off scepticism about 'flavour of the month' by pointing to the 'marked increase in inquiries' throughout 1988 and early 1989. In January 1989 they were said to be running at 12–15 company enquiries per week (personal communication).

5

Managing the Process of Change

The focus of this chapter is upon the *how* rather than the *what* of change in labour management. An attempt is made to unravel the strands which can help explain the transition from one approach to another. In other words, the theme here is the process issue. This examination should therefore be of interest to analysts concerned with understanding how shifts in managerial tactics, strategies and behaviours are brought about. Likewise, it will be of interest to practitioners who are primarily interested in learning how managers in other organizations have engineered change.

From either position – and indeed from outside both – it may be observed that, in many ways, change processes can be of equal, if not of greater interest, than its content. How and why did one set of recipes for handling labour come to be replaced at this particular time with another set? There are other questions of similar interest.

- What is the mechanism of diffusion of practices within companies, across companies and between sectors?

- How do managers come to learn of 'new methods'? (It was very notable that when, during the interviews, managers were asked about their sources of information and ideas, many expressed surprise that they had never seriously considered this as an issue before.)

- What role were management consultants playing in diffusing ideas and practices?

- Was increased overseas travel a factor?

- To what extent were changes merely 'fads' and to what extent are they being institutionalized?

- To what extent have the initiatives been subject to careful planning?

- Are they part of a wider strategic change?

- If there is a corporate strategy/HRM strategy link, how is this achieved and by whom?

- What factors seem to promote and which inhibit the diffusion and institutionalization of new labour-management practices?

Experience with the case companies suggests that senior managers tend to ask three main questions of their own: how to 'intervene', where to 'intervene' and how to maintain change.

There are various theories within the discipline of organizational behaviour which have been advanced to help explain phenomenon of this kind. In this chapter, however, the analysis will be inductive – that is, the interpretation will start from the data. Nonetheless, there is obvious merit in having some understanding of the current state of knowledge as expressed in the extant literature in order to provide a platform for our own findings.

There is a burgeoning interest in the subject area now broadly known as 'The Management of Change'. MBA programmes typically have a module of this nature; books, articles and conference sessions increasingly seek to address the topic and practitioners increasingly seem to consider the theme as of significance.[1] The literature on the subject broadly falls into two distinct categories. On the one hand there are numerous prescriptive texts which proffer guidelines and check-lists on how to manage a change programme (Plant, 1987; Beckhard, 1987). On the other hand, there are the more academic studies which seek to describe how change has occurred in particular cases and, from these accounts, to construct generalized propositions about the actual process of change (Pettigrew, 1985).

The latter approach has enjoyed a considerable revival in recent years. This is related to the evident large-scale corporate 'turnarounds' in companies such as British Airways, ICI, Massey Ferguson and Chrysler and the dramatic reorganizations accompanied by attempted 'culture change' in organizations ranging from the NHS to British Telecom and BP. Antecedents of this genre are easily recognizable in certain classic works of 40 years ago such as Elliot Jacques' *Changing Culture of a Factory* (1952), Robert Guest's *Organisational Change* (1962) and Coch and French's 'Overcoming resistance to change' (1948). During the ensuing period, organizational development (OD) waxed and waned (Beckhard and Harris, 1977) until recent times when Kanter (1984), Peters (1988), Pettigrew (1985) and Morgan (1988) have once again thrust 'change' centre stage.

Yet while there are many common themes interwoven between these texts it is important also to note that the apparent unity of the 'subject' of 'the management of change' is somewhat chimerical. The 'OD' change-process techniques are often separated by some considerable distance from the way in which strategic change in organizations is, in reality, brought about. What is particularly notable about the literature on the management of change (both the prescriptive and the academic-analytical versions) is that it tends either to deal in universal generalizations without specific grounding in actual cases or, conversely, it is anchored in single-case studies. Ironically, both approaches result in the same kind of depiction of the supposed uniform features of change. But close analysis of the processes of change in the 15 cases studied here reveals quite clearly that these differed in significant ways. Study of the way in which changes were being made in these organizations was not greatly aided by the typified general lists which are characteristic of the 'guides to change'. Analysis of how changes were made across the 15 cases reveals indeed certain contrasting features. Some of the organizations, for example, steered a major new approach to labour management in a step-by-step manner; others launched total programmes. Some of the changes were progressed in a top-down, cascade way, others were bottom-up in character. In some cases the human resource or personnel/IR specialists were intimately involved; in others the process was clearly driven from elsewhere and these specialists were either marginal or even acted in opposition. The overall lesson about managing change was that there is no set formula.

And yet, while there were these evident diversities in approach, certain patterns were discernible. This is not surprising when it is remembered that to a considerable extent the wave of change which swept many along in the eighties occurred as part of a wide process of diffusion. Ideas were carried from one organization to another via conferences, consultants, the financial press, inter-company collaboration and so on. Hence, part of the language and lore of managers underwent a change. Certain commonalities began to emerge. Line managers, operational and staff managers from a range of functional specialisms became quite content to talk freely of their organizations needing further culture change. The necessity for line managers to 'own' solutions to organizational problems was widely discussed. Training and development programmes for managers in areas such as total quality gave further impetus to the spread of such ideas. For example, it is notable that the seminars run by Tom Peters and his BBC Enterprises' video package, *The Tom Peters Experience: The Customer Revolution* (1989) are marketed as tools to give the edge to quality managers, line managers and sales and marketing specialists, but the levers to be pulled to effect the recommended changes are primarily ones in the people-management arena.

In practice, there is no one standard formula. Managers were selective in the way they borrowed some ideas but rejected others. There was obviously a complex process of change at play. The accounts which suggest that HRM was somehow an almost automatic 'response' to heightened competition in product (and later in labour) markets are too simplistic. Quite clearly, one intervening variable was the micro-political struggle to defend and advance sectional interests between different managerial specialisms. These divisions within management run particularly deep in the British context and so it is not surprising to find that defensive routines and contestation between managerial groups has considerably coloured the process of change. But inter-professional or inter-functional competition has not been the only intervening variable. A further feature of the British scene is a continued ambiguity surrounding structural forms. Devolution and centralization are seemingly ongoing processes. The way in which the multi-divisional form and 'strategic business units' are managed, continues to raise doubts about where responsibility for certain activities rests. This is especially so in the arena of managing human resources and devising policies for this sphere of activity. A consequence of this is that given the lack of clarity about who can do what in HRM, there is considerable scope for diversity even within the same organization. Thus, one finds different practices and approaches and sometimes even cross-cutting processes which are allowed to flourish in the interstices of Britain's complex organizational forms.

The crucial consequence of these intervening variables is that the process of change is far more cautious, complex and variegated (in the British context at least) than the textbook treatments of 'the management of change' allow for. In order to bring these points into sharper focus it is necessary to pay regard to two key dimensions. These dimensions provide the basis of an analytical framework which can be used to help order and interpret the findings about change processes deriving from the 15 case companies.

A FRAMEWORK FOR UNDERSTANDING THE MANAGEMENT OF CHANGE

The two key dimensions are first, the extent to which managed change is unilaterally devised by management or is brought about by joint agreement, and second, the extent to which the path of change conforms to a total package or is characterized by a series of discrete initiatives. Both of these dimensions offer a continuum of possibilities. On the first, the change may range from being at one extreme unilaterally devised by top management to, at the other, jointly devised,[2] through a multitude of intermediate positions including consultation and negotiation. And on the second dimension the change may, in varying degrees, be incrementally constructed or launched as a total package.

By cross-cutting these two dimensions (see figure 5.1) a four-fold classification of 'types' of managed-change processes is revealed. The characteristic features for each type can be explored by using illustrations from the case studies. Before proceeding to the cases, it is necessary to explore a little more the nature of the two dimensions and the dilemmas they pose for practitioners. Taking the vertical dimension, the issue is whether the change process is characterized by a coherent, total plan with a mutually

Figure 5.1   Types of managed-change process

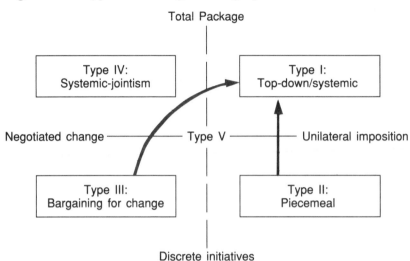

reinforcing package of measures or, whether it is characterized by a series of discrete and possibly even disjointed initiatives. It should be noted that the total-package approach leaves open the question as to whether such a programme is launched in one go or is phased-in. A common refrain across the companies was to extol the merits of 'eating the elephant a spoonful at a time'. As much as anything this was seen as necessary in order to allow middle managers themselves time to handle the changes in bite-sized portions. But it may also have stood as testimony to the fact that no fully formulated plan or package had been worked out. In the research itself, and in the accounts which follow, an open mind was maintained as to whether or not a strategic human resource existed. The aim was to seek out evidence which could support or refute such a position.

Whether launched as a package or in a series of discrete initiatives, there were also differences in the extent to which the changes were unilaterally imposed or jointly negotiated. This is the dimension raised by the horizontal axis in figure 5.1. In many respects the period under review witnessed a good deal of talk about 'imposition'. Much of this came from ordinary line managers who were often to be found in a bullish mood in the 1980s. A not unusual view was that the proposed changes should be put

Figure 5.2 Locational placings of selected case organizations on the managed-change map

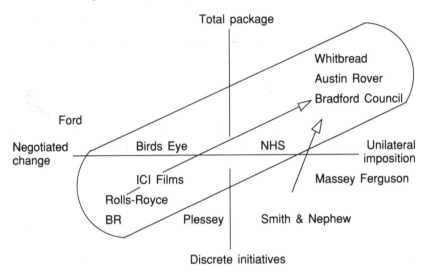

to the workforce and the unions (simultaneously, it was urged rather than giving 'special privilege' to the latter) and if, after a suitable (short) period, progress was not forthcoming, then the plan should 'simply' be imposed. This kind of scenario was certainly much more talked about than enacted but it would be a mistake to underplay the occasions on which it did occur.

As a general guide the case study organizations can be positioned on the conceptual map. The result is shown in figure 5.2.

Having explained the dimensions of the framework, 'types' of change process can now be explored using specific cases for illustration.

Type I: Top down systemic change

This pattern is located in the top right of the figure. It includes major restructuring programmes such as the shift to strategic business units and HRM packages which involve considerable interplay between their component parts. The strengths of such an approach stem from the fact that it is possible in this way to follow the rules of project planning. The vision can be drawn, the contrasts between the 'then' and the 'now' can be identified;

departmental and personal action plans can be constructed and their contents logically adjusted; timetables can be established and progress measured against milestones.

These features also contain the seeds of the weaknesses of the approach. The lack of participation in the programme design may lead to lack of commitment to it. Local managers talk of the 'not-invented here' syndrome and the consequent tendency to shun the ideas as foreign. Lower level managers, supervisors and employees may feel little sense of 'ownership' of the ideas. In these instances where the strategic plans claim to rest on principles of involvement and participation they are inherently contradictory if they are launched in this way.

Jaguar and Austin Rover   Obvious examples are Jaguar and Austin Rover. The 'Working With Pride' package at Austin Rover was designed and driven by top management without union involvement and it comprised a web of mutually reinforcing elements. The same can broadly be said of the interlocking package of measures at Jaguar. As one senior Jaguar manager expressed it, the trade unions 'were invited to come to the party but they declined to do so'. The points to be made here are that:

- there was a 'party' (something organized and planned) to go to
- the half-hearted attempt to involve the unions having failed, the company proceeded with its new human resource plan on its own terms.

But these were by no means the only examples of this type of approach to managing change. Two of the other cases from the 15, the local authority and the brewing company, also displayed similar features in the way in which they handled their change processes.

Bradford Metropolitan Council   Bradford Metropolitan Council sought to drive through a holistic managed-change programme under both the Labour and Conservative controlling groups.[3] The council's method of introducing these sorts of change has hinged, to a large extent, on a 'management development' programme. The lead-in to this had been a two-day seminar for managers and senior officers. Under the heading of 'Managing for Excellence' the seminar focused attention on four key interlocking concepts:

- customers
- people
- innovation
- leadership.

The messages which ran throughout all sessions were spelled out insistently – they included the need to 'get closer to our customers' and the desirability of 'developing a learning organization'. These messages were underpinned by further process-type symbolic rallying cries: the need to manage the transition 'from management as administration to management as leadership'; and the approach of 'top-down leadership combined with bottom-up involvement'.

These elements were derived from more than one source. The Audit Commission's agenda of 'The Competitive Council' was one trigger, another was the appointment of a new chief executive. In all three public sector cases, that is BR, NHS and the local authority, there were indications that one of the major triggers for programmed change was a politically dictated organizational upheaval.

The seminar programme itself included the explicit objective of learning from other organizations – most specifically from 'leading-edge' private sector cases. One of the cases which featured prominently was Tom Peters' review of 'Innovation in the 3M Corporation'. Under the Labour group, the strategic plan was launched carrying the title of 'The Social Strategy'. A web of interlocking initiatives was constructed embracing:

- equal opportunities
- employee involvement
- commitment
- changes to the selection procedure
- a quantum increase in training and development
- new forms of appraisal
- a revised reward package.

This set of measures was put together by the personnel director quite consciously as a 'human resource strategy' to mesh with the Council's corporate plan ('Social Strategy'). This organization-wide programme of change was supplemented by change activity arranged by the individual directorates. In these latter, significantly, it was the line and general managers who, having 'owned' the problem and the package at the initial stage then took the lead in diffusing the message. For example, in the key directorate of Enterprise and Environment, a follow-up management of change programme was offered, entitled 'Implementing the New Management Style'. In this, the departmental director, assisted by the chief executive of the authority, led a programme which included techniques of managing transitions such as 'evolving a focus of organization and leadership that succeeds amidst chaos and continuing uncertainty.' It also promised to reveal how to 'work on the development and implementation of the vision' of the department through 'empowerment, listening and learning'. The workshop, complete with brainstorming sessions, workbooks, videos and case studies was designed to help line managers 'work with managing change with immediate colleagues' using personal action plans and implementation strategies. Managers were told they would be taught to create 'flexible, fleet of foot' units, 'lead transitions' and to 'learn to love change, uncertainty, competition and challenge'.

If these phrases sound overinflated this is because they were. Few managers emerged with the secrets of how to accomplish these transformations. They did, however, derive a heightened sense of the possibilities of managing change and were generally more confident in their assessments of likely success. This kind of attitudinal restructuring helped lay the base for further change attempts.

Whitbread Breweries   Whitbread Breweries is another case which can be located in the Type I change-process category. There was a top-down plan of change with little in the way of negotiation. The change process nicely illustrates both the 'hard' and 'soft' aspects of HRM identified in chapter 2. As senior managers reported, there was definitely 'a conscious policy' to transform the pattern of industrial relations and to place them 'on an entirely new footing'. The context was a brewing company which, in the

1970s, was losing marketing share and was perceived to be fat and complacent. The Whitbread image was of thatched-cottage pubs frequented by retired gents who drank moderate amounts of gin and tonic. The company had, however, acquired licences for two leading lager brands and in 1968 it built one of the first 'jumbo breweries' in Europe, which it located at Luton. The human resource planning for this event was, in hindsight, seen as poor. The personnel function in those days was staffed by retired brewers who were transferred into personnel 'for a nice easy life'. At the new Luton brewery, for example, the manpower planning was poor and the staffing was soon seen to be excessive. Large numbers of workers were recruited from the nearby Vauxhall plant, from Electrolux and from other traditional engineering settings. Again, in retrospect, these were viewed as mistakes. Nonetheless, at the time, margins were high (45 per cent in some years) and the remit to the brewery managers and personnel was, in effect, that there were to be no disputes – at all costs. Meanwhile, the company was seen to be becoming increasingly uncompetitive in other areas – most notably for example, in distribution and in the management of tied houses.

A new senior appointment, shortly to become the human resource director, was made in 1978. This person came from a food retailing sector and his brief was 'to sort out Luton or close it down'. Within one year 'Luton Plan I' had been constructed. This resulted from a 'free thinking exercise' between the new HR chief, the general manager and two production managers. They started with the proposition: 'what plan would we write on a blank sheet of paper if we were starting on a green-field site?' (this, 10 years after Luton had been opened). In brief, drastic headcount cuts were made – from 900 to 600 and then to 300. Overtime was abolished, production workers were taken off day rates and put on salaries 'this would help them get mortgages more easily', supervisors were abolished and first-line managers were made responsible for handling disputes.

The plan was 'to move from confrontation and aggravation to cooperation and harmonized conditions'. Job flexibility was sought and the power of shop stewards became a target.

Despite these measures, industrial relations were not transformed at Luton. Following a major strike this flagship super brewery was closed. The symbolic significance of this move was felt throughout the company. The company continued with its change programme – and indeed stepped it up. Two new green-field superbreweries were built, one in the North and one in South Wales. The programme of closure of smaller, older breweries was accelerated. The broad parameters of 'the Luton Plan' were now installed country-wide. A resurgence of 'management leadership' was seen as critical. The first-line manager concept was embraced and harmonization of terms and conditions with production workers on a salary structure was pursued. Similarly, the personnel structure was changed as was the organizational structure. Regional companies and boards were dissolved. Personnel was removed from breweries: the new model was a strategic human resource function at the centre and only a clerical personnel administration facility at site level.

The source of this change process was seen as deriving from 'one or two visionaries' within the company – though it is interesting to note that these architects of change were not located at the corporate level. The plan was constructed and enacted in the Whitbread Breweries Sector: the other parts of the business 'have gone their own way'. How different was this method of change in eliciting a shift in working practices from old-fashioned productivity bargaining? First, said senior managers, there was no agenda of items: 'Blue Books lead to difficulties'. 'We didn't talk figures at all, we talked service and service requirements.' This aspect was particularly noticeable with regard to the delivery drivers – the draymen. A new joint company with National Freight Consortium was established. Drivers were put on a salaried basis, the salary level was pitched so that 55 per cent of the draymen would benefit from the change. They were given no job description and the tasks ranged from fork-lift driving to sorting out empty bottles, 'things they wouldn't have dreamt of doing in the past'. Five weeks holiday a year, stable salaries pitched at a higher level . . . 'we made it very difficult for the T & G to oppose it.' Managers painted a picture of a business downturn when overtime would not be guaranteed. There was, in total, a subtle combination of features. These ranged from a threat on the one hand to put all of the delivery work out to contract and, on the other, a very attractive carrot.

The implementation process in the breweries themselves was more problematical. Some managers found it difficult to operate under the new arrangements with few rules and few set practices, no set attendance hours and yet a day's work to be done. 'There was a reluctance by some of them to manage as opposed to merely administer and implement rules. We had to let quite a few go, though they received very attractive severance pay.' As for the remainder, 'we spent an absolute fortune on management development.' The new culture was inculcated in large part through a series of courses. The original 'Luton Plan' of an open, highly communicative, team-based, involved, participative non-proceduralized 'Whitbread Way' was thus eventually driven through across the breweries as a whole. It had failed at the Luton site but the subsequent shock closure and the combination of 'hard' and 'soft' elements helped to ensure that it could be installed elsewhere.

Type II: Piecemeal initiatives

This type is located in the bottom right of figure 5.1. Examples of these sorts of initiatives include instances where team briefing forms of communication were introduced following a visit from the Industrial Society. There were also instances where a few 'quality circles' were started, a suggestion scheme relaunched and performance appraisal introduced.

The drawbacks of this approach to change are well known to British managers. They talk frequently of 'flavour of the month' initiatives and they are well aware that credibility for future initiatives is being eroded. The piecemeal approach can also lead to inconsistencies between, for example, a revamped managerial 'leadership' and an 'employee participative' approach. Two of the 15 cases can be used here to illustrate aspects of this approach to change management. The cases are Massey Ferguson and Smith & Nephew respectively.

Massey Ferguson   At Massey Ferguson, the managing director had exposure to the works of Tom Peters and similar gurus during visits to North America. He developed the practice of photocopying sections of Peters' works and circulating them to all managers together with a covering memo. He also instituted a series of 'meetings with the chief'. These sessions were held both for union leaders and for selected samples of the workforce as a whole. Reports suggested that the climate of these meetings was tense, as the chief tended to dominate the events.

Meanwhile, a human resource director was appointed. The incumbent came from North America and he was very much attuned to OD-style thinking and modes of intervention. Yet, at the same time, the industrial relations function continued to operate quite separately and began to launch a series of initiatives of its own. The IR manager reported to the manufacturing director, whereas the human resources director did not. A whole series of disparate initiatives began to emerge from both teams and indeed from the managing director himself. At various times the emphasis was placed on:

- small group involvement
- open communications
- a re-examination of the incentive payment scheme which still continued to operate
- a reduction in the number of shop stewards
- flexibility
- subcontracting and so on.

At no point did each of these initiatives come together. There was no master plan. The initiatives were launched in waves and then subsided.

By the late 1980s following further cutbacks, redundancies, industrial action and reorganization, the human resources director returned to North America and the post was not refilled. The manufacturing director took early retirement and a new personnel team was appointed. They began the task of re-establishing a more cautious and in some respects a more traditional approach to labour management.

Smith & Nephew   In the case of Smith & Nephew, while a set of discrete initiatives also tended to characterize the approach, the way in which this was done was far less dramatic than at Massey Ferguson. The Smith & Nephew style was essentially pragmatic; its approach to managing change cautious. The corporate level (Smith & Nephew Associated Companies plc) oversaw the human resource practices of its constituent divisions and companies but did not seek to devise a corporate policy. There has been no centre-led change programme in this company. There is a corporate 'industrial relations adviser' who lightly monitors the developments within the divisions but he has no executive authority. Industrial relations are the responsibility of each of the separate divisions: Pharma-Med, Health Care, Consumer Products and Group Research.

The divisions were unionized and there had been no direct attempt to alter this state of affairs. However, within the framework of a remarkably stable pattern of industrial relations a series of discrete initiatives had been launched by management. In the main, these have not been seriously part of a negotiated change programme. Accordingly, the Smith & Nephew case can best be located in the bottom-right quadrant but fairly close to the vertical axis, as shown in figure 5.2.

The result has been a diversified pattern of personnel and industrial relations practice. This variety exists internationally as well as across the dozen or so British sites. The acquired American companies were described as having 'sophisticated personnel policies'. Two of the major locations are in South Carolina and Tennessee. They are non-union and the UK corporate managers expressed the view that 'sooner or later this experience is likely to have an effect elsewhere in our company but we don't really know'. The picture until recently has been very *ad hoc*. Negotiating with the unions was the responsibility of line managers and there was no central support for this. In the late 1970s, however, in response to a more robust industrial relations climate, an appointment was made at group level to furnish background IR advice. This role was discretely expanded by the next incumbent, but even today this central function remains slim and non-interventionary. The policy is still one of divisional autonomy, though an industrial relations advisory group (IRAG) has been established to 'share ideas' between the divisional managing directors. Across the different divisions, one finds a range of initiatives in the realms of selection methods, appraisal, training and rewards. But even within these divisions no one claimed that these amounted to anything more (for the moment) than a continuation of Smith & Nephew's pragmatism. There are hints though, that, as lessons from overseas acquisitions are absorbed, a gradual shift may occur. Hence this could be a further case to follow the directional arrows shown in figure 5.1.

Type III: Bargaining for change

This approach to achieving change is reminiscent of old-style productivity bargaining. Indeed, productivity bargaining may be considered as one subtype. A fairly standard mode was for concessions on working practices to be secured from different groups in exchange for compensatory payments.

The *ad hoc*, partial nature of this way of pursuing change is revealed in a number of regards. The targeted changes may not be linked in any coherent way with a broader human resource plan. The opening up of new possibilities on ways of working may not even be followed through by local managers. The hoped for flexibilities may, in consequence, fail to materialize. Even where they do, there is always the risk of new restrictions being gradually imposed. These features of productivity bargaining style approaches were not the only important aspects of this third type deserving of note. In one respect this type could be considered the most obvious path in Britain in the mid-1980s. The reasoning for this is not hard to trace. The representation structure and the bargaining machinery remained largely in place. But meanwhile, heightened competitive pressures were making radical responses more imperative. Added to this, there were the many publicized examples of apparently far-reaching changes in organizations across many different sectors. Under such circumstances long-standing habits would dictate that the way to proceed should be simply to draw up stiffer demands for concessions and take these to the unions with the residual threat of redundancies as a key bargaining counter.

In the United States this process of 'concession bargaining' became a common practice in the 1980s. Extensive ground was given by the unions in order to protect jobs. In Britain the device was not replicated in quite the same way. To a considerable extent this was because the nature of contracts in the two systems are of a very different kind. But in a more informal way, similar things were beginning to occur in Britain also. Added to the more traditional bargaining process were certain novel elements. It was not simply that managers stiffened their resolve in the face of union demands. Rather, the changes that began to occur resulted increasingly from managerial initiatives. Industrial relations specialists invited line managers to draw up serious 'shopping lists' of requirements. And personnel sometimes added their own themes – such as harmonization of terms and conditions – which they thought might lead to more significant long-term changes. But, in the main, the items on the shopping lists were lacking in strategic logic. They were characterized by traditional concerns:

• the availability of labour to meet peak demands (hence the move towards annualized hours agreements and new shift patterns)

• the scope to deploy labour where it was most needed at any one particular time (hence functional flexibility agreements).

What tended to be missing from this approach to securing change was any coherent vision of a radically different way of working.

The particular case chosen to illustrate this type of change process is ICI Films, but many of the other 15 cases would equally well have served, most notably, for example, British Rail, Plessey Naval Systems or Rolls-Royce. Indeed these other cases would probably more closely reflect the 'pure' characteristics of this type. But the ICI Films case is selected because it also makes clear that bargaining for change as an approach sits alongside other ways of seeking change in most of these cases. It re-emphasizes the point that the drift in Britain (at least in the late 1980s) was towards the top-right quadrant of figure 5.1.

ICI Films   The chemicals giant ICI is frequently discussed as though its human resource practices were of one kind. In fact, its divisions and indeed some of its sites are relatively independent. ICI Films in Dumfries is one such site. It manufactures 'Melinex' which is converted into photographic film and into propafilm for food packaging and computer tape. The site employs some 1200 people. Viewed from this location, ICI at the Millbank Headquarters was seen as having no central personnel policy – though there is central negotiation on wages, salaries and hours. Similarly, the general managers and works managers were seen as the architects of management style and organizational culture.

As one senior site official said, 'we don't have IR people who set out the path to follow, they merely proffer advice'. Central personnel are 'custodians' of the current agreements and they are also responsible for graduate recruitment and training. But, in determining how change will be managed, there is a view that the sites are largely responsible for their own destiny.

The process of change within this balance of power is fairly subtle. Site management noted that although they felt they had considerable autonomy 'if we were to openly declare that we were going to do something then there might well be attempts from various quarters to stop us.' When asked about his priorities, the works manager's response is instructive. It referred not to investment in plant or some minor change to working practices but to:

> receptivity to change: structural and cultural; the creation of a vision; the revitalization of the management team.

In practice, the method of change was an admix of negotiation on detail such as the move to the integration of the electrical and instrumentation trades on the Dumfries site, and a broader sweep of changes which have not been negotiated. These latter include for example, a massive drive on quality improvement through defect prevention. As the senior managers at Dumfries said, the quality initiative 'makes IR pale into insignificance'. The quality initiative was said to involve the adoption of entirely different approaches to the way work is done on site. Different standards of operation are required.

The thrust of change was talked about very much in terms of development, training and a consultant-led process of improved group working. Coverdale was used, so too was Peter Honey, the consultant. The latter had introduced behavioural analysis. And it was this approach to managing change which had captured the imagination of managers at ICI.

Another relatively discrete change initiative (and again one which had not been the subject of direct negotiation even though it was seen as vitally important) was the devolution of responsibility of section managers. These key staff are now more powerful. Plant engineers who used to report up the engineering chain have now been persuaded to report to their section manager. Engineers increasingly see themselves as attached to a product rather than a function. Other roles have been taken out of central support functions and allotted a clearer product management definition. Whole sections of staff and the weekly paid, ranging from turners and welders to accountants, customer service managers and distribution managers have been 'product aligned'.

A pivotal device in forcing through these changes at ICI Films has been a heavy emphasis on communication. This has been pursued in a multitude of ways but the mechanism which was constantly picked out as indicative of the new 'obsession of the general manager' was the quarterly meetings of senior site managers with representatives from every work group. Typically, some four or five representatives from each group would be present: a total of about seventy people in all. In addition, there was a practice of holding quarterly dinners to which the management team would invite, 'semi-randomly', selected individuals from each product group. Other devices for communication were also used; the timings and sizes of the meetings varied but the common theme was direct communication and an opportunity for a degree of two-way communication. But notably, these techniques were used alongside 'a more challenging and abrasive style'.

Overlaying these initiatives was the Crosby Quality Improvement programme sponsored by the erstwhile Polymers and Plastics Divisional Board. The Film Group chief executive was known to have volunteered his business to run this initiative (while Crosby was initially voluntary, it in due course became mandatory). The way this was done in ICI Films was to have line managers as trainers and facilitators operating under licence from Crosby. These managers included plant managers, maintenance engineers and a computer services manager. They were all 'relatively senior', in their 40s and 50s. They formed part of the wedge of change by running quality training programmes of 10 two-hour sessions for all 220 monthly staff.

A further relatively discrete initiative was the more careful attention paid to the supervisory role – including supervisor selection. The traditional method had occurred through temporary 'stand-in' prior to full succession. At the time of the study, ICI Films had introduced a framework of 'competency' in supervision derived from the McBer consultancy. This has been supplemented with greater attention also to the training and development of newly appointed supervisors. This includes a three-week, off-site residential course. Despite this, the relative lack of mutual reinforcement in this set of intitiatives was revealed in the continuing controversy over what was required of the supervisor. To what extent would the future model be of a highly technically competent or a people-management role? This had not been resolved but, meanwhile, the number of layers in the management hierarchy was being reduced and this was having a knock-on effect on the supervisors' task requirements. A manifestation of the indecision was the wide disparity in the span of control for supervisors in different parts of the site, For some the ratio was 40:1, for others it was 15:1. There was disagreement between managers as to which of these represented the desired target for the future.

Meanwhile, another change was the introduction of formal selection testing for ordinary operatives. During the three-year period 1985–8, all new operators recruited externally had been subject to a range of attitudinal, personality and intelligence tests. Management would have liked to have used this battery for internal staff also but union opposition had halted that side of the initiative.

One of the now familiar change techniques also figured strongly here. A new product, 'Melinex 5' producing high-grade film for X-ray plates and food packaging applications was set up in a separate (green-field) part of the site in 1985. The section now has 115 weekly staff and 16 monthly. These are organized into five shift teams of equal size. Each one is headed by a supervisor who reports to a plant manager. New working arrangements separate from those in operation in the rest of the site at that time were introduced. Flexible teams both within and between process and engineering were designed. People with trades backgrounds, especially those with controls and instrumentation experience, were recruited as operatives. One third of the operatives had worked previously in jobs such as radio and TV engineering, and some were ex-fitters. The process people were found to assist the trades but, conversely, the tradesmen only did a certain limited number of process-operator jobs. The special group of control technicians working on instrumentation and electronics was selected from the best of the technicians and given special training, some of it was provided by the suppliers of the equipment and some by the EETPU training college.

The supervisors' role in this red-circled area was redefined so that they became technical trouble-shooters and communicators. They have been freed from the administrative chore of staffing-up the shift. To forge and sustain shift-team identity all supervisors are rostered in the same shift pattern as the rest of their team. Equally, they take their rest periods together.

The Melinex manager's role was redesigned so that he looks not so much to the site manager as the four 'business managers' at Welwyn Garden City who head-up the four main product groups (photographic and packaging etc.). These business managers are the ones responsible for the bottom line; they make 'bids' to the Dumfries Melinex manager for the use of the facilities. As a result, the Melinex manager is encouraged to develop knowledge of the commercial aspects: the costs and the revenues for example.

Overall, the ICI Film's case at Dumfries illustrates a change process which is loosely coupled to, but not derivative from, a coherent central, or indeed business-level, plan. Separate initiatives are seen to derive from the various levels of the company including corporate, divisional, site and product-family level within the site. Many of these initiatives have been broadly compatible but they have had no common author. Similarly, while some of the changes have been negotiated with the unions – most especially those relating to flexible working – others have been pursued quite separately from the joint machinery. And significantly, it has been change which has been driven from outside the IR area which has proved to be the more far reaching. These initiatives have included the devolution of management, the restructuring into product groups and the emphasis placed on direct communication and culture change. Moreover, experience with the wider panel of companies (see chapter 1) suggests that where 'separate and distinct' facilities with their own special terms and conditions are introduced onto traditional sites, in due course there is normally a move to extend these special terms across the whole site. This 'trojan horse' approach to managing change is, noticeably, largely a feature of the Type III change process. It is an approach rarely employed in the other types. So much so that this device could almost be used as a determining factor in tracing and adjudging Type III cases.

Type IV: Systemic jointism

The fourth type of change process as shown in the top left of figure 5.1 refers to those situations where a total package is put together in a negotiative manner. This is undoubtedly the rarest of the types: at least in the British context. The reason, of course, is that in Britain, union–management relations are mainly confined to a circumscribed arena of pay and conditions. Indeed, the degree of joint regulation over non-pay issues seems to have declined during the period 1980–4 (Millward and Stevens, 1986: 251). The decline was most marked in private services and in manufacturing but the nationalized industries were found to be 'most immune from the trend' (ibid).

This state of affairs contrasts markedly with the way in which the transformation of industrial relations has been managed in the United States. In that country, as Kochan, Katz and McKersie (1986) demonstrate, the record of successful change has occurred where union leaders have been involved in corporate-level consultation on matters of strategic transition. The authors found that the most significant impacts of workplace innovations on the firm's competitive performance and employee attitudes occurred when innovations were:

> broadened beyond their original QWL charter ... to tackle issues that lie at the heart of competitive problems and the employment security of the workers. But to do this successfully the parties must confront directly the relationships between workplace participation and reform and issues that arise at the contract negotiation and strategic levels. (p. 175)

The same message also comes across strongly from Richard Walton in his analysis of the process of 'Innovating to Compete' (1987).

While there are no exact parallels in the British context there are a few examples of change processes which approximate to the fourth type. In this regard it is worth examining the manner in which Ford Motor Company engineered major changes in the mid-1980s.

Ford Motor Company   In the lead-up to the major comprehensive deal in 1985, Ford undertook an extensive preparatory exercise. It communicated a loud and clear message about 'the performance gap' between its British and overseas plants, and placed special emphasis on the gap between itself and the Japanese motor manufacturers.

In tandem with this 'softening-up', line managers became much more heavily involved than heretofore in the design of the negotiative package which was being put together nationally. The managerial agenda (including the requirement for a two-year deal) was then negotiated at the national joint council where an 'enabling' agreement was drawn up. The detailed negotiations on new working practices in exchange for a 4 per cent productivity allowance were then devolved to plant-by-plant negotiation teams. Through this exercise, comprehensive, American-style contracts were arrived at.

Meanwhile, Ford was also pressing ahead with the Employee Involvement (EI) process imported from its American parent. EI met opposition from British blue-collar unions but agreement on it was reached with the represented salaried staff. EI in Ford of Britain comprises an eight-stage process as shown in figure 5.3. What is notable about this process is the admix of management–union negotiation and participation arrangements for individual employees.

In the light of future events concerning the loss of the Sierra from Dagenham and the revision of the plan to invest fully in the Bridgend engine plant, the way in which the need for change was sold to Dagenham workers in 1985 is illuminating. The following is a verbatim transcript of the Dagenham engine plant manager's opening remarks to the special union–management committee convened to discuss the future of the plant and working practices within it.

> The position is, Dagenham engine plant has a chance of getting the I4 engine. Personally, I think, a good chance because of our recent track record. But I would put our chances a long way short of the 99 per cent quoted by *The Engineer*. Remember, a strong possibility is still the sourcing to a Japanese competitor . . . and we must still assume that Cologne is competing for the business.

These comments uttered as part of the negotiation for change approach are very much in line with similar methods used for example, by another case company (also, as a matter of interest, in an American-owned company): Eaton Corporation.

Figure 5.3 Ford's EI eight-point implementation plan

'EI means working in a different way than we have in the past. It is about including employees in the decision-making processes which affect their everyday life. It is not a panacea or a management tool but rather a joint process to create teamwork.'

There are eight steps to its implementation:

1 Local management-trade union agreement
  (essential for positive organizational change and the involvement of employees at every level)

2 Local Joint EI Steering Committee
  (a local joint group must form and meet regularly; early training in effective meeting processes is essential)

3 Briefing employees on EI
  (steering committee members in labour-management pairs to conduct these, with third-party consultants, in small groups to facilitate discussion)

4 Selection and appointment of an EI Coordinator
  (appointed by joint steering committee; internal to the site selected from interested applicants. The coordinators' role is to support and later to train problem-solving groups and to provide a link between them and the rest of the organization)

5 Information gathering and diagnosis
  (interviews with sample of workforce, managers and trade union representatives dealing with their perceptions of the site. Interviews conducted by third-party consultant, data fed to coordinating committee and then to workforce)

6 Training
  (first phase awareness workshops of two days' duration for mixed groups of middle management and union leadership exploring EI in depth; second phase: skill training workshops for problem-solving work groups)

7 Problem-solving group launches
  (at all levels of the organization)

8 Monitoring and support of groups
  (coordinator and consultants meet with problem-solving groups and continue training and coaching; leadership and facilitation; the process spreads)

Type V

One of the most characteristic ways in which change was being managed could best be located towards the very centre of the cruciform depicted in figure 5.1. Here, the 'programme' of change is neither a total package nor simply a series of discrete initiatives, but in a sense occupies a space midway along this axis. Likewise, this method of change is neither unilaterally imposed nor openly negotiated but again exists somewhere along this continuum. Strictly speaking therefore, this set of approaches is perhaps not a 'pure type'. Nonetheless, it aids the clarity of the presentation to locate them on the figure. Under this method the broad 'spirit' of the change is signalled and certain key structural moves executed, but the total picture is, intentionally, merely adumbrated. Extensive scope for the exercise of local initiative is preserved.

In this type of change process the nature, clarity and sustainment of the signals are crucial. These signals typically comprised both structural and cultural elements. In the cases studied, the quintessential structural messages of this kind were the shift from formalized, bureaucratic and centre-led administrative systems to more ambiguous, devolved forms. These new configurations were typified by the creation of strategic business units (and in the public service sector, their equivalent, the local service delivery units). These were underpinned by further structural shifts of symbolic import: the changeover to short-term contracts; the creation of personal rather than collective contracts; performance-related pay, and so on.

The methods associated with this form of change hinge on the following:

- the stark spelling out of what is not acceptable and some broad guidelines as to what is
- intense activity in 'management development'
- extensive use of consultants and 'facilitators'
- experimentation with OD-type exercises and techniques.

This type of change process can be illustrated by considering examples from the NHS and Birds Eye Walls.

NHS   In the NHS, the impetus to change set in train by the Griffiths Report leading to the replacement of administrators by 'general managers' has been a major change event, the ripples of which are still being felt. But the 'model' of what general management would look like at Regional District and unit levels was left vague. Intentionally so. Certain broad pointers were provided in a variety of ways: for example, via a series of messages from the NHS chief executive who took on a high-profile role; through the launch of a management bulletin clearly identified as emanating from the 'management executive'; and through influential guides to good practice such as the glossy 'Better Management Better Health' publication.

The NHSTA has been active in fleshing out the new culture and an important monograph by Tony Turrill (1986) published by the Institute of Health Service Managers, entitled *Change and Innovation: A Challenge for the NHS*, has enjoyed wide circulation and utilization within the service. Forewords by Len Peach and Sir John Harvey Jones set the tone of the manual which in many respects is a digestible version of Richard Beckhard's many works on OD. The perspective adopted accepts and indeed welcomes continual change. It celebrates 'leadership' rather than administration or direction. The associated techniques which it recommends, such as jointly agreeing core purpose, mapping the environment, sharing priorities, force-field analysis, commitment planning and allocating and accepting responsibility, were found in the case research to have all been spread widely in various health districts.

The political moves at national level have been given extensive coverage in the press. Less well covered have been the actual processes of change within districts and units. The analysis of how change has been managed can best be revealed at these levels. Hence, in what follows, insight is given into first, district-level change process, and second, approaches to managing change at the unit level.

In one of the health districts studied, organizational development as a way of driving change had been especially embraced by the district general manager and by his unit general managers (UGMs). A series of 'corporate management workshops' were being held. At these, techniques such as 'environmental scanning', 'domain demand mapping', 'visioning' and other workshop activities were pursued religiously.[4] One concrete outcome in 1987 was the production of a district mission statement. But these general managers went further than that, they reported that they felt positive about this process of managing change and they expressed a commitment to gaining a familiarity with the concepts and practice of organization development. The unit general managers also took these techniques back to their units and cascaded them through their own management teams. The way in which this was done can best be revealed by following through the subsequent behaviour of just one of these unit general managers.

Like many unit general managers encountered during the course of this study, this individual was very active, energetic and capable. Most notably for our puposes here, he was also, like many of the others, highly persuaded by the concepts and methodology of OD. He had encountered these at a number of venues – most recently at the Nuffield Centre for Health Services Studies at the University of Leeds and also at the White Hart management training centre. As pointed out earlier, this transmigration of the mystique of OD from a few specialist and marginal hands into the mainstream of general management is of considerable significance. It can imbue the line and general managers with an attitude to change and equip them with a methodology (however lacking in completeness that might be) which has been largely neglected by mainstream IR commentators. The significance arguably resides less in the power of the techniques themselves than in the sense of direction and most importantly, the conviction which its converts possess.

A crucial feature of this is the extent to which managers of this persuasion actually think about the change process in a highly self-conscious and (in some respects) sophisticated way. For example, this general manager was using the process of generating a mission statement by his newly formed management team as a team-building exercise, and as a way of securing consensus on fundamental objectives and agreement on a strategy to achieve these objectives. As a result of his attendance at process workshops at the Nuffield Centre he had already prepared his own statement of mission for his unit and had explicity set out his vision for the future. But these documents he kept hidden. He observed:

The process for the team to construct its vision and statement of mission is very time consuming. Why don't I tell them my vision? The reason is they need to develop confidence; they are frightened to express their views in case they are slapped down or in case they are seen as stepping outside their remit. Anyway, if I did the whole process would simply appear as if it were the old consultation system. In any case, it would be too partial.

This set of remarks reveals the sensitivity and subtlety of one, not untypical, unit manager in the NHS. It takes some measure of restraint to 'hold back' from demonstrating 'the answer' and the 'leadership' which, on the surface at least, would be shown by revealing the prepared solution. Instead, he encouraged the continuance of a whole series of workshops where OD-type techniques were used (with the help of a facilitator). The general manager was, moreover, also acutely conscious of related ambiguities and difficulties associated with this approach to change management in his organization. The team, he felt, would be experiencing difficulty in determining whether he was 'part of the process' as simply another member or whether he was adopting the roles of judge, appraiser or teacher. In addition, he commented upon the tension between the 'workshop behaviour' and everyday management style. There was the ambiguity of authority in the workshop setting. Was every team member of equal standing during these 'protected' periods? In addition, there was, he thought, some suspicion that the series of workshops and the presence of the facilitator must imply some criticism of the team. They cannot have been acting appropriately in the past if they were having to 'learn new ways'. This caused considerable anxiety.

But the UGM, while concerned by this anxiety was also quite capable of utilizing it as a way of unfreezing the status quo. The general management concept had to be introduced, understood and sustained. The new management arrangements in the unit were to be much more than simply new job titles, new people in posts and the reallocation of responsibilities. Nothing less than a new style of managerial leadership was being called for. He went further:

I am seeking to drive through, or rather bring about, a radical revision of the management culture. I want to establish new expectations of organizational behaviour in this hospital and higher levels of service delivery and performance outcome.

In pursuit of these, the UGM instituted the OD-style workshops while simultaneously undertaking supportive structural changes. The workshops were run in part, as a management development exercise. The techniques employed included the familiar ones identified above. Structurally, hierarchy was reduced, authority was devolved and a radical shift was effected from the traditional functional-specialism reporting hierarchies to a looser, task-based system. In a written statement released to the management team it was even boldly claimed that 'the hierarchical structure has been dismantled'. This was undoubtedly an exaggeration but the statement is nonetheless significant given that its author was the general manager!

The general management group in this unit was evidently highly committed to OD. Operational matters were, it seemed, rather crowded-out from the agenda of the executive meetings. The coordinating role of the senior team was, as a result, undoubtedly compromised but the general manager was aware of this. He was intent on forcing the issue. Executive meetings, as well as workshop meetings, attended centrally to the issues of 'management identity', 'team development' and the analysis of other organizations in order to diagnose what made them successful. The prime aim was to make a new management style and culture manifest. The hidden agenda was to remove 'negative feeling' about 'general management', that is that it was autocratic; that it represented a 'takeover', and that it was simply a device to make cuts.

In the workshops, representatives from the various specialisms were involved. The most problematical group was found to be that which comprised various 'support managers' – domestic services manager, head porter, medical records officer and works officer. Given the difficulties which this group had in the workshop, the general manager and assistant general managers held a series of informal meetings with them to help the tensions and problems to surface. The GM's reflections on these meetings are illuminating:

> these sessions identified a number of very strong concerns. They were still not clear about the purpose of the workshops or why

they as individuals were there. They had a continuing suspicion about not knowing what it was that was really wanted out of them at these workshops.

The observation by the general manager highlights the clash in perspective between a group which had been used to debating definite proposals and a GM who had fully accepted the transformative potential of OD and of keeping these things loose and ambiguous.

The nature of this fifth 'type' of change process is also further revealed by the way in which managers down the chain not only themselves received these ambiguous messages but also acted in a way which extended this approach to their own reporting managers. The importance attached to this form of change process in this health service unit can hardly be over emphasized. In addition to the management development workshops which were happening every two weeks, the general management group itself met monthly to oversee and coordinate the activity of the unit as a whole. This body 'will in the future', said the GM, 'be solely concerned with corporate management development activity. The intention is to give support to individuals coping with change and further, to enable them to be motivated and competent to lead other managers through continuing change.' The objective is to have similar OD activity occurring in every department. It was notable, however, that clinicians – that is the doctors – had not been involved. The general manager when asked about this re- plied 'I don't think they would join us on these workshops even if they were invited. Anyway, they would intimidate the rest.'

If one examines closely the outcomes of departmental and unit workshops which have been asked to discuss such issues as the 'new management role', 'visions', 'mission', 'new culture' and the like, what is remarkable first of all is how similar they are from unit to unit and district to district. But second, the consonance with NHSTA and other national-level aspirations and current views relating to the appropriate management style is also high. In some regards at least, therefore, the relatively subtle and apparently non-dirigiste change process in the NHS has enjoyed considerable success. Whether this survived the Kenneth Clarke onslaught which followed is another story yet to be told.

Again, however, one of the major observations arising from

this case is the tendency of the change process to drift in the direction of the arrows shown in figures 5.1 and 5.2. It would be fair to say that:

- there was an underlying logic to the initiatives being taken and indeed that these had the coherence and significance of a strategic thrust

- that without doubt the nature of that thrust was of a character which differed from traditional personnel concerns and yet carried massive significance for the labour-management approach.

Birds Eye Walls   The process of change at Birds Eye Walls also falls roughly midway along the negotiation/unilateral dimension and similarly so on the programme-discrete initiatives dimension. In introducing 'Workstyle' the company had a vision of the package of interlocking measures it wished to introduce and it was prepared to consult extensively upon these. What it did however was to set up working parties separate from the ongoing negotiation machinery to discuss the Workstyle concept and its implementation. Some trade union representatives sat on these working parties and were able, it was claimed, 'to take off their trade union hats' from time to time. These working parties produced written recommendations for the organizational planning of each of the frozen food plants. In effect they wrote the job descriptions for each team with flexibility built in. It is notable that the agendas for these meetings were emphatically focused on issues concerning 'quality of working life' and the 'creation of interesting jobs' rather than on debates about demarcations and the like. The working parties spent two to three days on each future team's area – examining their sphere of operations and laying down plans for multiskilling. They researched current operations, paying close regard to what tasks were being done, how they were done and how they might be done. These joint working parties were, in effect, engaged in work study and process redesign. They accepted the remit of searching for flexibility and also the principle that every team member would be capable of undertaking a range of the jobs done within his or her team.

The Birds Eye change process was thus also moving in broadly the same direction as the other cases referred to. Labour management on the sites had traditionally hinged around joint regulation and the changes to working practices were of the productivity bargaining kind. The way in which change was being managed using the Workstyle Programme was now further along the horizontal axis of figure 5.1 towards the right (i.e. with a reduced emphasis on union negotiation). Second, it was also further up the vertical axis, that is the changes sought could be (and were) clearly articulated by managers as constituting an intermeshing plan. The Birds Eye managers did have a vision of where they wanted to be and they had worked out a strategy (with project and process elements) of how to get there. At the time of the research the package was new and it was partial rather than comprehensive – hence the placing of this case in the centre area of the model. Nonetheless, the direction in which the methods of change were moving were unmistakable.

CHANGE AND DIFFUSION

Having reviewed the major 'types' of change process illustrated by the case research it will be found useful in this final section of the chapter to focus on certain key lessons which actually cut across the types. Two such generic themes are worthy of special comment. These are first, the way in which changes to prevailing 'recipes' for employment management are triggered and then diffused across an organization and from one organization to another; second, the way in which champions 'sell' change of this kind.

Triggers to change and its diffusion

The case material emphasized the importance of the diffusion of ideas about possibilities and practices. As noted in previous chapters, one of the most remarkable findings was the extent to which line managers had embraced the lexicon and outlook of 'culture change', 'commitment', 'units as mini-businesses' and the like. The way in which this had come to be was seemingly a result of a diffusion process which was operating along a number of fronts.

One such front was the extent to which these organizations had learnt from overseas. They did this first of all through visits to associated and competitor companies. The number of managers at all levels who had themselves experienced such trips was quite high: around 30 per cent of the 350 interviewed. Many of the companies had also sent supervisors and shopfloor employees on these journeys. But there was also another key way in which these organizations had learned from overseas: by direct acquisition of foreign companies or through joint ventures at home and overseas. Austin Rover for example, was cooperating with Honda. This, as I observed, literally amounted to Japanese quality specialists working directly on the lines at Longbridge as well as exercising more subtle influences through product and process design. Lucas, another case company, had massive involvement overseas and it was also absorbing Japanese production practices through licencing agreements and joint ventures.

To take just one example of a Lucas UK site. The business had been failing in the early 1980s. At the time of the research here in 1987, the general manager was visiting Japan three to four times a year and he described the 'attitude change' of himself and his senior team as a result of these visits as 'dramatic'. Of probably even greater importance was the learning from the licensed business activity which had involved extensive importation of Japanese systems. It would not be accurate to say that this was the main objective of the deal but there was a definite spin-off along a number of fronts: 'the quality ethic', manning levels, working practices, communications, supervisor selection and the like.

Before managed change could begin, certain key figures (i.e. people with the power to make things happen) had to become acutely aware of the need for a different approach. 'Acutely' means the awareness became a priority issue and not merely a vague notion that there might be scope for something new. This 'need sensing' was more readily elicited under extreme circumstances – that is when general dissatisfaction with performance was compounded by some trigger condition. The observation that it 'helps to start with a crisis' has been made by a number of observers of managed change. Escape from complacency was aided at ICI by the shock of the deficit in 1980–1; the trigger to start doing things very differently was prompted at Eaton in Manchester by the complete fire loss at the factory; at Jaguar, radical change commenced when John Egan was appointed with the remit to achieve turnaround or close; a similar trigger occurred at Whitbread Breweries starting at Luton.

The argument concerning the crisis point is that organizational practices or ways of doing are maintained by offsetting vested interests; stasis is the result of an uneasy power balance. These conditions are most easily disturbed and tipped when a crisis is sensed. Geoff Armstrong, at the time of the research a Director of Metal Box and Chair of the CBI Employment Committee, argued the point in a more robust way. He propounded the view that because of the tendency for old habits to re-establish themselves and for complacency to creep back in rather rapidly, there was merit in engendering an almost permanent sense of crisis. This could be engineered through the timely release of information, through periodic reorganization and through a constant flow of initiatives.

Such a proposition can be seen to veer to the 'hard' end of the HRM spectrum. Offsetting this thesis was the view held by managers on the 'soft' wing of HRM that it is not possible to win commitment from a workforce that lacks a sense of security. This position usually meant not that insecurity in 'crisis-sensing' should never be countenanced but rather that it should be of the short-sharp-shock variety, subsequent to which, trust should be re-established as quickly as possible.

A distinction has to be drawn between 'need sensing' when it occurs as a 'trigger' which sets off, say, a chief executive on the search for solutions, and 'need sensing' as a longer-term process involving the winning of acceptance of the requirement for change from a wide constituency across the organization. In the case of Austin Rover, key line managers had at least half 'bought-in' (as they themselves would term it) to the 'Working with Pride' change package because it was seen as championed by the manufacturing director, a figure of some considerable credibility in their eyes. Part of that credibility derived from the fact that he was previously regarded as a no-nonsense production man with his feet firmly on the ground. And part stemmed, more pragmatically, from the fact that he was seen to hold the manufacturing purse strings which could resource the training and other expenditures which would be necessary. There is clearly an important point here. The power and credibility which changes of an HRM nature will carry or fail to carry are critically dependent upon the access to resources which the champions of change have and/or are perceived to have.

Given these two factors, it is interesting to explore how this manufacturing chief had himself been 'converted'. The story was widely told that he had been called on by various management consultants in the early to mid-1980s but to little effect. However, following a particular visit to certain car plants in the United States, he returned to the UK in a more receptive frame of mind. Within a few days of his arrival a reapproach from consultants who had previously made no impact happened to coincide with this altered consciousness and the new approach began to take shape. The need for a change in course direction was thus accepted by the manufacturing director and his close associates. The 'selling' of the idea to the rest of the managers and to the workforce at large was a different matter. At the time of the research in Austin Rover, the acceptance of the idea from middle managers was highly conditional and tentative. Notably, the scepticism was particularly acute among certain plant-level industrial relations officers (more so indeed than among line managers at the same level). On the shopfloor, the change in direction was less consciously perceived. There were certain pockets – particularly where careful selection brought together small groups working on prestige projects – in which the ideas about quality and involvement had been adopted. But, for the workforce as a whole there was still a long way to go before the new package would be understood and accepted.

A closely related learning point was the apparent need for an alternative 'model' of how things could be. In the terminology of some of the case organizations, there had to be a 'vision' or at least a sense of new possibilities. This is where the HRM phenomenon had proved so crucial. Many of its critics have focused on aspects of its contradictions and incompleteness in the model but this has often resulted in seriously underestimating the ideological power which the set of ideas labelled 'HRM' has carried. Human resource management, as we argued in chapter 2 clearly has its ambiguities, but it would be a mistake to dismiss it on these grounds alone. If it did not exist some other term would undoubtedly be invented to signal the range of alternatives to previous (uneasily prevailing) conventional wisdom.

The real question therefore is how this generalized view of 'an alternative way' to manage labour is translated into a set of values which are internalized and a set of practices which are institutionalized.

This part of the process is by no means as straightforward as authors in the field of 'managed change' seem to suggest. Numerous organizations have now drawn up mission statements expressing worthy sentiments whose breach in everyday activity merely serves to accentuate their superficial and hollow character. But Ford Motor Company has tackled the issue with customary thoroughness – producing an elaborate manual and training package as a means towards the dissemination of its statement of mission, values and guiding principles. In addition, Ford managers, like Peugeot-Talbot managers, are issued with pocket-sized plastic covered cards carrying a printed summary for easy reference. Nevertheless, even in these exceptional cases, while specific instances of shopfloor behavioural change can be cited, the notion that a new coherent vision has been widely internalized is somewhat fanciful.

Commentators invariably refer to 'the need for top management commitment' by which is normally meant top general management commitment including that of the chief executive. The high profile role of Colin Marshall at British Airways – including making a personal appearance at nearly all of the numerous training sessions during the Putting People First programme is even today cited as crucial by BA's staff. The absence of a similar example at British Rail during its change and customer care programme was likewise as frequently noted and lamented by BR middle managers. Meanwhile, the lesson has been fully learned by chief executives in other of the case organizations – notably, as remarked above, in the case of Bradford Metropolitan Council where the chief executive officer is taking a very high-profile role in steering a new direction in organizational management, and the same was notable in the NHS under Len Peach.

And yet, the preceding 'guideline' has to sit alongside the one which points to the need to instil a sense of 'ownership' of the integral elements of the change programme at lower levels in the organization. Achieving this balance between the sense of being led from the top and yet also a sense of personal stake in the ideas would seem to require a subtle exercise in communication, team building and involvement. It suggests a departure from the 'blue print' approach to an iterative process whereby a learning-oriented organization is engendered. The attendant talk, however, of 'thriving on chaos' despite its take-up in the lexicon of a number of the case organizations appeared not to have achieved the same kind of intuitive appeal among the bulk of British managers.

What had struck a chord was the wide dissemination of diagnostic and process-oriented change techniques. Brainstorming, systematic data gathering, visioning, force-field analysis, self-analysis, organizational climate analysis and the like, each enjoyed a boom period in the mid- to-late-1980s. Large numbers of British managers were even found to be going along with, and seemingly relishing, devices such as peer and subordinate assessments as ways of generating data for subsequent developmental workshops. Of significance was that these training-methods-cum-organizational change processes were being made widespread by diffusion through managerial ranks rather than being proselytized by specialist purveyors of OD. As numerous managers reported when talking about their experience on such programmes, 'at least they have given us a common language' by which they also meant a common way of thinking about problems – in effect a new mind-set. One result of all of this was the easy familiarity with which engineers, industrial chemists and a host of other specialists talked of 'management styles', 'organizational culture' and a range of other behavioural concepts. Town hall departmental heads, area managers in car plants, pharmaceutical section heads and their equivalents in all types of organizations, were found to have not only a certain familiarity with these sorts of ideas, but more significantly, unlike the situation a decade or so ago, many of them had begun to embrace the language, lore and logic of this approach to understanding and interpreting organizational life. This had occurred to an extent which, in some cases, seemed naive. Excessive simplicity notwithstanding, this diffusion of behavioural models and methods is undoubtedly part of the explanation of how the change in direction is being managed. This, of course, could be its Achilles heel: while the evangelical spirit is a powerful force to counter inertia, its capacity to be self-sustaining over the longer term is more open to question. As one of the departmental heads at Massey Ferguson complained, 'We are told with trumpets playing and drums beating about the start-up of new initiatives but no one tells us when they have finished.'

Concerning the issue of diffusion of a set of new ideas once they have taken root, a number of lessons were derived. One of the case companies, Ford, provides an excellent example. It is important to remember when talking about diffusion that the manufacturing business of this company is organized on a pan-European basis by Ford Europe. (The separate 'national' companies are, in the main, sales and marketing enterprises). In consequence, the diffusion of ideas and practices is extensive. During this study Ford was undertaking a Europe-wide review of supervisors and the future role of supervision. The task force was staffed by line managers from a number of European countries. The explicit objective was to explore how the new 'managerial leadership' ideas being proselytized at the time in the literature might be translated into line management practice across these countries. Meanwhile, Ford of Britain had also just completed its own extensive research on the human resource and industrial relations practices of Japanese companies operating in Britain. The intention to learn from within and from without the organization can thus be clearly seen here.

Diffusion was also occurring through 'networking' within Britain. One of the wider panel companies in the study, Stanton, on the Nottinghamshire–Derbyshire border, referred to the interchange of information on a regular basis with an extensive range of companies in the region. This data included pay rates but was increasingly also taking in a wider range of employment practices. This kind of interchange was also occurring on a nationwide basis between the motor companies. Those managers charged with the task of planning future negotiation packages and employee relations strategies tended to meet each other at least twice a year.

A further channel along which new practices were spread was found to be provided by management consultants. There had been a massive growth in consultancy in the eighties. Some of this resulted from the slimming of large corporate personnel functions in the early part of the decade. One repercussion was that in the later part of that decade it was increasingly common for the in-house, overstretched, personnel chief to look outside for assistance. The extent of this practice has hardly been comprehended. Two of the organizations reported that they had found no less than 100 different consultants working with them in personnel-related areas. These were separate consultancy contracts ranging from large human resource consultancy firms to individual consultants. The measure of their impact in diffusing practices, assumptions and models across the British employment scene has yet to be made. But among these 15 case companies alone, the extent to which the same names of particular consultancy practices (such as McBer, PA, Saville and Holdsworth, Coopers and Lybrand, and indeed of individual consultant 'gurus') tended to be cited, was quite remarkable.

A further instance of diffusion evident in the cases was the process whereby key 'messages' were transmitted internally within these organizations. There had been a considerable increase in communication devices of all kinds: company videos, newspapers and magazines, briefing papers, special meetings with the chief executive and so on, some of the companies such as Peugeot at Ryton had even established their own video production studios on site. These and other channels of communication were used to transmit messages which reinforced the new approach to management. More powerful still perhaps were the symbolic impacts from managerial and supervisory restructuring with devolved responsibility, changes to the reward package, new evaluation methods and similar devices whereby 'expectations' were altered and 'attitudes restructured'.

Selling change

The significance of this process certainly exceeded the attention given to it in the literature on industrial relations and personnel management. What was found to be happening was, in essence, a far greater degree of preparation by management than heretofore. At its most basic, there was a shift from being reactive to being proactive. But the way in which change was handled went beyond just this. Not only was the content of the change more carefully prepared but the way in which it would be handled, the process, was also more carefully planned. This planning included, *inter alia*, paying regard to the timing of various announcements; their sequencing; who would make the announcements; to whom; and using what medium.

Crucially, line managers in the companies were found to be willing to spell out the need for and the reasons for change. The 'solutions' were introduced only after these messages had been fully transmitted and understood. This part of the management of change hinged on the capability and willingness of line and general managers to make proficient presentations to assemblages of employees. A good deal of attention has been paid to the difficulties which many supervisors have had in handling briefing groups. Such observations fairly reflect the reality encountered in the cases. But what has received far less comment, and yet deserves more, has been the practice of area managers, departmental managers, plant managers and the like to stand up in front of shopfloor and other employees in order to 'explain' the current situation in that department, section or company.

It was found in the case organizations that these presentation sessions usually included an analysis of the situation facing the company and section, problems being encountered and proposed remedies. At such events the 'data' was often professionally marshalled and the case delivered with confidence. The investment in 'presentation skills' had seemingly paid off in these instances. A central aspect of these events was that shop stewards and similar union representatives were invited along simply as employees: the case being elaborated was not couched as a negotiating outline but as an analytical review and set of proposed measures. 'Imposition' was not a term to be encountered at these events but implicitly it lay in the background. Typically the picture was: this is the problem, here are the solutions, this is what is going to happen. The question and answer sessions were cast as further opportunities to explain the details of the measures prepared by the management team.

Successful delivery of this 'selling' of change hinged on a series of mutually dependent aspects: careful preparation (the collecting and collation of relevant data, the analysis of such data, the construction of a plan); training of line managers to make competent and convincing presentations; and the clarity with which line managers were seen as 'responsible' for these measures. They had to be perceived as 'owning' the solutions rather than merely transmitting messages from a distant and alien personnel function.

Obviously, these conditions were not always met. Hence, there were clear examples where proposed changes came to grief: the data had not been well prepared, it was incorrect, outdated or incomplete; the analysis and plans drawn from the data were faulted; managers making the presentations were not sufficiently competent either through lack of training or lack of capability or lack of conviction. In such instances, the proposed changes had not sold well. But what was surprising was the number of instances where line managers were able to carry their workforces and the lack of opposition: even in settings with well-organized unionism such as Ford Motor Company or Whitbread breweries.

There has been a great deal of rhetoric concerning the notion of 'Managerial leadership' in recent years: often it has remained at the rhetorical level. However, the instances referred to above indicate that in certain cases the leadership theme had been taken seriously and had informed practice. Illustrating such a process is extremely difficult (interview responses, let alone survey responses, tend to be peculiarly unreliable in this sphere). Probably the best way to make the point is to draw on one such instance which I directly observed.

This event occurred one morning in 1987 on the Ford Dagenham Estate. One of the plant managers, working with his area managers, had devised a plan for reducing costs by reorganizing the work in a machining area. The problem was that if the plan was to work it required two important changes from the workforce – first their cooperation in moving from the production of one set of parts to the production of another set half-way through each week. Second, it required the introduction of a new twilight shift. No extra money was on offer nor were any other inducements held out. The 'case' had to be sold direct to the workforce (some 80 people) by the relevant area manager. This was to be attempted at a special meeting in the old canteen at the start of the morning shift.

At the appointed hour the men were assembled and seated in a rather cold and uncomfortable setting unconducive to extended debate. The shop stewards for the area and the plant convener and deputy convener were seated out at the front. The area manager arrived 'chauffeur-driven' in one of the plant's electric vehicles. Flanked by section heads he strode to the front and commenced his delivery. The style was relaxed, down-to-earth, occasionally jovial but very direct. In essence, 'the problem' was explained as uncompetitive costs in the production of two powertrain assemblies. The danger of at least one of these ceasing production altogether unless the 'uneconomic' low volume levels could be compensated for by more flexible switching each week between one job and another was explained. The 'solution' was then described – this involved the introduction of a 'swing shift' and the necessity for the shift, on certain days of the week to be ready to finish the scheduled run on 'Power Train I' and relocate themselves to a different area of the factory to commence work on 'Power Train II'. Questions were then invited and the area manager fielded these himself. One issue of concern was the extra time that would be needed reporting to work and in lost break time because of the distance between the two work locations. The area manager dealt with this one by promising to keep this under review during the first few weeks of the new work scheme.

After about 40 minutes the area manager and the rest of the management team departed and the convener and stewards were left to address the meeting. The tone was essentially a 'realistic' one of the economics of inter-plant competition and the perilous state of 'Power Train I' because of its age and its low volumes. While some minor problems were noted with the management plan, the overall message was that the reorganization was neces-sary. There was very little opposition from the floor. A vote was taken and the plan was accepted almost unanimously.

This was just one observed example where change was sold to the workforce by a middle-level line manager. At the meeting where he put the case directly to the 80 men, no other member of management had spoken: neither the section heads nor the plant employee relations manager. The event was a clear example of managing change through 'leadership' built on careful preparation – involving both project planning and process planning (even the detail of the uncomfortable draughty venue had been taken into account) combined with an assertive, confident delivery.

CONCLUSIONS

It was evident from an analysis of the cases that there were in fact different ways in which change was being managed. There was no single best way to 'managing change' or 'overcoming resistance to change'. The differences between the cases could, to a large extent be explicated by comparing them along two dimensions. These dimensions were: a total programme approach versus a discrete initiative approach on the one hand, and a negotiated versus an imposed approach on the other. Cross-cutting these dimensions allowed four main types of change to be clarified (plus one mixed type) and the case companies were located in relation to each other using the resulting map.

It was also noted that there was also a tendency for the process of managed change to move towards the first type. There were signs, in other words, that changes were being more carefully planned by managers; they were learning from each other; they were more willing to act outside the negotiating machinery and they increasingly saw the more significant thrusts as indeed coming through this other channel. Above all, the initiatives were being viewed more and more as *linked*. They were not merely opportunistic. To this extent there was a notion that the process was becoming more strategic. The human resource elements – new policies on selection, appraisal, reward, communications, deployment, utilization and development – were increasingly seen as integrated. And this integrated approach was more likely to have an exposure at senior levels – including the board.

These, it must be repeated, were only tendencies. But they are significant. Much of the debate in the 1980s was very partial and one-dimensional. Was macho management a reality? Were unions being bypassed? These were the archetypal questions. The point about the processes noted in this chapter is that something far more complex was occurring and potentially far more significant. Whether the tendencies will endure is a different matter. A change in government, further influence from Europe, a more sophisticated union strategy and other similar factors could well drive the approach to managing change in a very different direction. A prime candidate for reassessment must be the dualistic approach itself. If this were to happen the directional arrows shown in figure 5.1 could begin to veer towards the top-left quadrant.

In total, the cases demonstrated that the process of managing change was at least as interesting as its content. We have found in earlier chapters that erstwhile 'formulae' for managing employees were under challenge during this period. This chapter has helped to fill in some of the detail about how this was being handled. Changes to the 'accepted' or at least 'recognized' way of doing things were problematical for managers. Some sort of 'trigger' to commence a switch was necessary; then those individuals sensitive to the change had to 'champion' an acceptable alternative among their colleagues. As we saw, those with access to organizational resources tended to carry more weight in steering such a course. Even when a critical mass of managers was persuaded, the diffusing of the newly recognized 'best practice' was by no means assured. The ideological power of the 'idea' of human resource management was, for some, the critical factor in mobilizing resources. In those cases where HRM, *per se*, was not to the fore, the fact that other comparator organizations were evidently forging ahead in novel ways, seemed, in itself, to provide the necessary impetus. Hence, in both indirect as well as direct ways, the ideological significance of the HRM model to employment management change at the time of this research, should not be underestimated.

Notes

1 Many examples can be given of this growing interest. The National Economic Office in association with the Training Agency has sponsored research, run conferences and published on the topic. A major conference entitled *The Challenge of Change* was held under its auspices in London in September 1988 and this was opened by the Secretary of State for Employment. NEDO then published a lengthy report *Managing Change* in September 1989.
2 Conceptually the other end of this continuum would be unilateral planning by employees. However, as we are here concerned with an analysis of managerial initiatives this conceptual possibility falls outside the present purview.
3 A fuller account of the process of managed change in Bradford can be found in Storey and Fenwick (1989) and Storey and Fenwick (1990).
4 These are standard OD techniques. 'Domain demand mapping' refers to a simple exercise which identifies, on a diagram, the key constituents whose demands must be attended to in one form or another. Each constituency or 'domain' (such as customers, suppliers, professional interest groups) has listed against them the kind of demands that they are perceived to be making. 'Visioning' relates to a range of exercises whereby groups can share their scenarios for three, five and ten years ahead. Such exercises are likely to be used to reach some consensus about key objectives.

6

The Part Played by Personnel Specialists in the Management of Human Resources

The kind of developments discussed in previous chapters cannot be expected to leave personnel specialists untouched. Sufficient momentum has built up in many organizations to make it very difficult for personnel specialists to control either the speed or the direction of change. A number of key questions therefore arise:

- What part has personnel played in shaping developments to date?

- Is HRM a friend or foe to the personnel specialist; is it a threat or the most significant opportunity to have arisen for personnel in the last 20 years?

- Could it provide the much sought-after path to the centre of corporate influence, or, is it a development which threatens further to marginalize a function which has always been peculiarly prone to anxiety about its status, standing and contribution?

Reaction from within the specialism and from spokespersons closely associated with it has been divided upon these issues. Torrington and Hall (1987) adopt a rather negative tone but another prominent commentator and practitioner in the field,

Michael Armstrong, writing in the IPM magazine *Personnel Management*, adopts a decidedly more welcoming note. The fear of marginalization, he maintains,

> is groundless if personnel managers play their proper strategic and proactive role as business partners in the management of the enterprise and the people who work in it, but we ought to be concerned about the fact that there are chief executives who seem to be saying that their personnel function is failing to deliver what they need as a key contributor to their strategic thinking. (p. 31)

In a later contribution to the debate, Torrington (1989) appears to shift ground. He suggests that HRM is but the latest 'addition' which takes its place as part of a long line of innovations and new beginnings which, during its history, personnel management has successfully absorbed. Different 'self-images' have been dominant in personnel during different periods of evolution and giving rise to 'a current situation where successive waves of management approaches to getting value for money from employees now dominate personnel thinking, without the initial welfare concern being abdicated' (1989: 57). Torrington makes a spirited defence of the personnel tradition enriched by its successive phases and is scornful of suggestions which would lead to any dilution of the distinctive contribution of the specialism. HRM is 'but a further dimension to a multi-faceted role' which will 'probably embellish personnel expertise and authority'. But, personnel

> remains a distinctive management specialism whose practitioners derive their expertise from an understanding of one or more of the ways in which people, individually and collectively, engage with the need to be employed and the needs of organisations to employ them. . . . the recruitment, development and management of resourceful humans is a more complex, interesting and expert task than the management of human resources. This is needed at all levels in all organisations as a specialist activity, no matter how skilful line managers become with their 'competences', and no matter how exotic the offerings of consultants. (1989: 66)

The personnel manager is a 'general practitioner' occasionally called in by the line managers who ordinarily manage their own health but, from time to time, need advice on diagnosing puzzling symptons. That, for Torrington is the distinctive contribution of personnel. But, to what extent does this depiction reflect what is happening in practice? What part, in reality, have personnel managers in the mainstream case companies been playing apropos the new developments?

Information on this was gained not only in the traditional fashion – that is from personnel managers themselves – but, more unusually, from line and general managers. From the picture built up in this way what became evident was that, even in those companies which were moving ahead with major initiatives, personnel specialists were adopting different stances. Some were clearly still trying to act as the custodians of collective agreements and formal procedures; others had retreated to a position where they proffered advice and guidance, when asked, about matters such as labour legislation and labour market information. Such withdrawals from the front line signalled, in some cases, the adoption of a more strategic overview role for personnel; in other cases it was symptomatic of a general pulling in of horns. There were a few instances where personnel were apparently at the leading edge of change.

These differences will require fuller description and explanation. But before systematically mapping them a few illustrative quotations will help to set the scene on this diversity. The first two exemplify practitioners from the 'regulative camp':

> Our general managers always say they want to handle their own affairs and that they are anxious to manage their own local bargaining but they have little idea of what is really involved, of the resources required, of the capability needed, of the complexity . . . in my experience they soon come running back to us.
>
> (group personnel director)

This statement indicates a distinct lack of enthusiasm for an enhanced role for line managers. The next one more specifically expresses severe reservations about the kind of changes that human resource management change packages normally embody:

> I meet with the works committee at least twice a week, to sort out industrial relations issues. The [particular company] initiative is

all very well but it will never remove the need for this kind of work. To be perfectly frank, there is a lot of scepticism about it in the plant. This may not be what you have found at head-quarters. . . .(plant-level industrial relations officer, Austin Rover)

The lack of enthusiasm for the package of changes, albeit for different reasons, is here revealed among personnel practitioners across different levels. Corporate personnel chiefs and factory industrial relations officers can still be readily found who are fundamentally attached to the procedural, contract-negotiating approach to labour management. These practitioners regard negotiation and grievance handling as highly specialist functions which require a distinctive contribution from personnel. Such a stance conceivably leaves open the question as to whether these specialists might nonetheless accept that HRM-type initiatives might coexist with proceduralism. This is a possibility we will need to explore, but meanwhile the point to note is that a large number of the personnel specialists interviewed for this project were clearly of the view that other managers needed as much reining-in as employee representatives.

One group of personnel specialists had, however, clearly shifted from this position. The following examples make the nature of this shift sufficiently clear:

I used to have to spend nearly all of my time firefighting. Nego-tiations were endless. Now I have time for what I always thought personnel should really be about, that is manpower planning, selection, training and development. . . .
(personnel specialist, Rolls-Royce)

In the 1970s, relationships were managed as if the whole thing was about 'contract-negotiating'. That's not my view of what we are here for. We are here to deliver a service to patients – our clients. The role of personnel in this is to promote the conditions which will allow this to happen. Quality of service is the key and our immediate customers who set the appropriate service level are the unit general manager and the rest of his management team.
(unit personnel manager, National Health Service)

The stance taken by these two personnel specialists from very different sectors is clearly rather more in tune with the kind of developments in human resource management which we have been tracking. But they can hardly be said to be drivers or devisers of change. Other personnel practitioners did, however, claim such a distinction:

> Personnel, in this organisation, is fully integrated into the business team. We have helped shape the kind of company we now are. Our success as a company has resulted from a full recognition that our only assets are our people. The integrated approach that has been taken to managing this resource . . . through clearly communicating our objectives, through finding the right people, rewarding them appropriately, continually seeking to develop their potential and managing the culture change . . . these successes have derived, in no small part, from the effective contribution of personnel.   (personnel specialist, Jaguar)

So far in this chapter, all of the illustrative quotations have been taken solely from personnel management sources. To give a more rounded picture it will be necessary to examine the relationship of personnel with respect to HRM from the perspectives of managers outside that function. But for the time being the statements do serve at least to indicate a crucial point: namely, that personnel has reacted in varying ways to recent developments. In a very few cases personnel specialists have been in the vanguard, but in the majority of cases they were found to have taken refuge in a rather more reactive stance. In order to take the analysis further it is necessary to elaborate a rather fuller conceptual framework than the one-dimensional contrasts which have typically been used to understand the personnel role.

A CONCEPTUAL FRAMEWORK

Where previous commentators have pointed to the variations in personnel, the basis of their contrasts has normally rested on dichotomies such as 'maintainers' versus 'innovators', or 'strategists' versus 'firefighters'. For example, Terry Lunn, the Personnel Director of Joshua Tetley & Son, contrasts personnel specialists who essentially 'maintain' systems (bargaining arrangements, selection and the like) with 'innovators' who have 'broken down large centralized bargaining units into units that employees and managers alike can relate to', and who have revised pay systems, communications and the like in line with the flexible, individual-ized approach of recent years. The terminology echoes Legge (1978), though Lunn's 'innovators' seem closer to Legge's 'conformist innovators'.

The most frequently cited typology in the last few years has been that devised by Tyson and Fell (1986). Focusing on a continuum of 'low-discretion' to 'high discretion' they draw on the building industry metaphor to help identify clerk-of-works, contract manager and architect 'types'. Although Tyson and Fell are careful to point out that they are not claiming any of these is universally 'good' or 'bad', there is a strong implication that the 'architect' model is the more sophisticated approach. Similarly, there is an implicit argument that there has been an evolution in this direction. This same point applies to Lunn's argument noted above.

Using a different continuum, however, it could alternatively be argued that a not infrequent path over the past 10 years has led from an up-front contracts manager to whom line managers were expected to defer on labour-relations matters (the person who told them what they could and more frequently, it is said, could *not* do), to a state of affairs whereby personnel stepped back and adopted a 'customer-led' approach. He/she responded to requests for information, and for advice on options but forsook practically all claim to be an arbiter or decision maker.

More recently, given renewed confidence by the human-resource management concept, a further model was sometimes talked about by personnel managers in the study – that of 'full-team member'. In this posture the personnel manager seeks to avoid being 'the person who says no' and yet also eschews the passive, customer-led (i.e. simply reactive to line-managers' requests) role. The full-team member aspirant tries to escape from the dichotomy of playing the policeman or playing the servant. It was not entirely clear how this stance differed from the 'architect' model but the emphasis had seemingly subtly shifted from the 'liberal' tendencies embodied within the 'deviant innovator' type to a position more synchronous with 'business needs'.

While these models reflect some of the variation in contemporary personnel practice and therefore help to correct for the simplistic unilinear, representation of the historical development of personnel, they nonetheless fail to capture adequately the

Figure 6.1   Types of personnel management

patterns found in the case studies. This may be because the models so far discussed are limited by operating along the single dimension. The data from the cases suggested a need to overlay the interventionary/non-interventionary dimension with a second one: that is, the extent to which the type of intervention which does prevail is strategic or tactical. When these two different dimensions are cross-cut it gives a 'map' (see figure 6.1) which more adequately reflects the range of practices found in the 15 mainstream cases.

Four main types of personnel practitioner were identified. Each took a very different view of the new developments in people management and acted accordingly. 'Advisers' acted as 'internal consultants'. They were in tune with recent developments but left the running to line and general manager colleagues. 'Handmaidens' were also in reactive mode but their contributions lacked the consistency of the previous type; they were predominantly customer-led in the services they offered. To a certain extent they were in a client/contractor relationship with line managers but to an even larger degree they were more submissive in the role they played than even that phrase would suggest. The figurative term 'handmaiden' is used in order to signal this type of subservient, attendant, relationship. 'Regulators' were more interventionary. They formulated, promulgated and monitored observance of employment 'rules'. These rules ranged from personnel procedure manuals to joint agreements with trade unions. Practitioners of this kind were operating within the traditional IR paradigm. These were 'managers of discontent', seeking order through temporary, tactical, truces with organized labour.

The 'changemakers' had higher ambitions. They were seeking to put relations with employees on a new footing – one which was in line with the 'needs of the business'. Typically, this meant eschewing the regulative approach in favour of a management style which engendered employee 'commitment' and a willingness to 'do the extra mile'.

It is of course this fourth group, the 'changemakers' who were the ones most in tune with the new human resource management initiatives. But even among these people there was an important variation in the nature of their 'strategic' approach which should be noted. This will be made clearer when we examine some instances in more detail, but basically it hinges on the difference between those changemakers whose strategic interventions stem from a distinctive human resource perspective and those who now adopt an approach which is, in effect, indistinguishable from the rest of the business team. In these latter cases one witnesses the subsumption of personnel under the prevailing (usually management accounting) business logics of the senior team. It is in this contrast in the approach by personnel directors that the 'hard' and 'soft' aspects of human resource management, as discussed in chapter 2, once more become manifest. The 'hard' face brings to the fore the quantitative, calculative and business strategic aspects of managing and planning the headcount in as 'rational' a way as any other economic resource. The 'soft' face by way of contrast, emphasizes the unique qualities of the human resource and thus seeks to unlock its potential through the use of an altogether distinctive set of techniques. These include, for example, paying close regard to motivational aspects, to two-way communications with this human resource, to the developmental potential and to the whole issue of 'managerial leadership'.

What this adds up to is that even within the changemaker/ HRM 'type' of personnel management there is a disjunction which goes to the very heart of what HRM is all about. How these conceptual differences are made manifest in practice is best examined by attending to some actual cases. The section which follows illustrates the range of ways in which personnel managers in the 15 case companies enacted their roles during this period of change. It is as important to examine how personnel specialists behaved even when they are not taking the lead in HRM – a situation which obtained in over half the cases.

The advisers

A considerable number of the personnel managers interviewed stated that they had changed their approach from a 'rule maker' and 'custodian of the procedure' stance, to a less assertive, advisory, role. Essentially, their response to changing conditions had been largely to withdraw their personal physical presence from the everyday labour-management interface. They had switched their attention instead to conjuring the 'tone' of the new relationships as well as figuring out the details of the increasing number of management-led initiatives in areas such as new shift systems, new manning levels and working methods.

Thus, one of the Ford Motor Company plant personnel managers made the point starkly, stating, 'I am just a humble adviser.' He elaborated the point thus:

> I try to ensure that discussions are between line managers and their opposite numbers on the trade union side. Me and my people are not to be seen as go-betweens or, still less, as people who make the line managers roll-over. The line managers have to have the commitment to the solution. I like to see them getting on with it and I like to keep out of their hair.

Corroboration of this point comes from the plant manager of this same establishment. Referring to the handling of IR-type issues he emphasized:

> I don't accept the excuse from my area managers that 'GK [the personnel manager] told me not to do x or y or to do A and B . . .', I say to them, 'You're the manager! You have the responsibility. You make the decision.'

Nor is this phenomenon (the greater responsibility of the line), something which is only occurring at the level of plant relations. As is well known, Ford Motor Company in Britain has been negotiating nationally for many years. The professionalism brought to the task by such luminaries as Bob Ramsey and Paul Roots might have argued for a continued reliance on a top-down, IR-run machine. However, the significant departure in winning increased productivity came not in the 1987 negotiations but in 1985. At this time, plant managers played a far more influential and decisive role in devising the national negotiations strategy than they had done for a very long time. One of them described the situation in the following terms:

> The last company negotiations were a breakthrough because the plant managers themselves were directly and heavily involved ... we of course listened to personnel but in the end we took it upon ourselves to define the nature of the package. This marks a very significant departure fom the way we behaved with Paul Roots. He was a brilliant tactical negotiator but in the end we have to ask what he achieved for us. In contrast look what we got for ourselves in the last negotiations ... in the toolroom we moved from eighteen job categories to just one, we moved to dedicated line maintenance. The semi-skilled are now virtually totally flexible, so, in addition to their machining, they do oiling, check fixtures, arbors and guards, replace bulbs and so on.
>
> (plant manager and member of NJNC)

As with any 'account', the possible bias has to be considered here. The newly assertive line managers have a vested interest in claiming exceptional outcomes from their own involvement. John Hougham, the successor to Paul Roots as Personnel Director, Ford of Britain, does not quite see the situation in the same way. Nonetheless, the general character of the changing role for personnel being described, does begin to emerge. It certainly expresses the situation which many senior line managers would like to see happen.

This 'adviser' role type is clearly compatible with the devolved, business-manager pattern adopted by many organizations for their line and general managers. As Colin Walters of Peugeot put it, the 'manufacturing line manager is king.' If line managers are encouraged by chief executives to run their units as 'mini businesses' then at the plant level at least, personnel managers are cast in a service-advisory role.

In large multi-site companies, however, especially those with central bargaining – such as Ford and Austin Rover – the switch at plant level from custodian of agreements and trouble-shooter to adviser still leaves open the possibility of a different role for personnel at the corporate level. If one looks at the statements from plant managers in the Ford Motor Company, the implication is that they see central personnel as providing negotiating expertise, but the package being negotiated is, they claim, increasingly devised by the line and less by the personnel specialists.

The handmaidens

Moving clockwise around figure 6.1 brings us to the 'handmaiden' type of personnel role. Like the 'adviser' this type adopts a largely non-interventionary posture but the kind of contribution made is now more of a service-provider at the behest of the line. The handmaidens were enacting an imposed role rather than one which they had elected to adopt. This level of responsiveness to 'customer requirements' often resulted from a period of prolonged buffeting in the shape of reorganizations, shifts in priorities and culture, budget cuts and similar threats to traditional, and relatively stable, personnel and IR roles. It could also be witnessed in those cases where reorganizations had meant that 'personnel', in any managerial sense, had been withdrawn from site level.

A poignant illustration of the 'prolonged buffeting' variant can be gleaned from British Rail, an organization in which the formal procedure has long been paramount in labour relations and where the personnel department at Corporate and Regional Levels has also long been regarded by many operations managers as unduly powerful and rule bound. Following a lengthy period of critical questioning arising out of the business-sector reforms, the five regional personnel 'baronies' clearly began to show the strain. One of the regional personnel managers expressed the degree of retreat in the following remark:

> We had a meeting last week with the new subsector managers. We set out our stall and we said to them 'look, here's what we do, now, what do you want to sign-off for?'
>
> (regional personnel manager, British Rail)

One has to appreciate that in this organization the regional personnel managers, backed by their substantial departments, had erstwhile been extremely powerful. To be reduced to the ploy indicated in the quotation was a humiliating experience even though in due course the balance of power did not shift quite so dramatically as it once seemed as though it might.

The 'sub-sector' managers are the extended arms of the business-sector directors heading up Inter-City, Provincial, Parcels, and the other BR 'businesses' which had been superimposed onto the pre-existing BR production-management structure. They had become powerful figures, largely, as the quotation indicates, because they held the purse strings. In effect, any internal services (including personnel) if they were to survive had to be paid for and thus chosen by these business managers. This did not mean the introduction of an internal pricing mechanism in the normal sense. But it did mean that personnel's activities were in the process of being closely scrutinized by the sector managers and that there was an explicit understanding that any parts of that service the latter judged not to be of value to their business requirements they would simply refuse to fund. The 'contribution' of personnel was thus to be weighed by these business managers. As a response, some personnel specialists saw little option other than to serve by giving the business sector managers whatever they wanted or, more accurately, were willing to pay for.

The extent to which some business-sector managers began to exercise this potential is shown by looking at the relationship from the other end – that is by listening to the expectations of these 'clients'. One key representative of this select group expressed himself thus:

> I basically deal with the production managers and as far as I'm concerned the personnel managers serve them. However, what I do want is definitely more 'say' on the types of services offered by the RGMs [Regional general managers] and naturally much of this relates to what Personnel are doing. It means I want to look at job descriptions, I want to look at management development . . . yes I really want to know what it is that I am paying for.
> (business manager: Inter City)

With this rather stark and direct financial lever being held over personnel it is hardly surprising that some practitioners sought to defend their departments and their staffs by retreating to a position which, in effect, said 'what the customer will pay for the customer can have'. There was one tactic which was used by quite a few of their number, however, and that was to point-up as graphically as possible the series of out-turns which could be expected if various services were cut or 'deselected'. To this degree even the handmaidens could influence the agenda.

At a lower level, personnel specialists operating within this 'type' were found to be engaged in servicing the routine requirements of the line. The personnel presence in the Whitbread brewery locations was of this nature. Their activity involved fulfilling a clerical and welfare function. For example, those undertaking 'personnel servicing' were doing initial selection screening. They maintained record systems for absence, sickness and pay, handed-out forms on request and administered their processing. These junior personnel people were usually not answerable to head office or regional personnel managers but reported instead directly to line managers. Much of their activity such as that concerned with collating information on payroll, headcounts, sickness-absence and the like, was originated by the accountancy function. It should be noted that this was a new development for Whitbread. In earlier years there had been a significant industrial relations and personnel presence in each of the larger breweries and indeed within each of the former regions.

Welfare was another manifestation of the type. It involved visiting sick employees, counselling and generally 'simply being available for advice'. An example of this orientation was found in a number of the Smith & Nephew divisions. The benevolent-paternalist tradition was occasionally still evident. On one of my visits a personnel officer spent a considerable time, for instance, responding to a request for guidance from an employee who had been summoned by a court in connection with a driving offence.

The third facet of this quadrant can involve the IR cycle. Where a unionized workforce generates grievance for settlement through a recognized procedure, some of the organizations had retained the practice whereby a personnel specialist is 'called down' by either the superintendent or departmental manager to explain the prevailing rules and regulations. The issue at hand may be some dispute over holiday-leave entitlement, overtime or shift patterns. In resolving the local issue the firefighter may make minor modifications to the rules but on an *ad hoc*, 'this-time-only' basis. This mode of IR firefighting then, differs from the more interventionary kind which will be discussed in the next subsection. It often involves a 'special favour' arrangement which is recognized by both sides as an exception to the rule rather than a change to the rule. Examples were encountered in most of the engineering companies, including Rolls-Royce, Eaton and Massey Ferguson; and, from the panel cases, GEC.

Whichever of the three facets was emphasized, the handmaiden role, although sharing the non-interventionary end of the lateral continuum differed from the adviser type in that the service offered was of a more routine administrative, or at best tactical kind, rather than being in the nature of strategic advice.

It was found, however, that both types could exist even within the same plant. Thus, in one of the mechanical engineering sites there was an older 'traditionalist' IR manager who was widely seen by the stewards and the supervisors with whom he had to deal, as having been through 'the school of hard knocks'. In former years he had been a firefighter-cum-trouble-shooter who although perceived as a 'bit of a tough nut' had won the respect of both sets of constituents. Until the past five years or so, troublesome day-to-day decisions on such matters as whether to allow pay for a period of doubtful 'sickness absence' had been routinely referred to him. Under the new policy of 'line resurgency' such issues had now to be settled by the supervisor in the first instance and, if contested, by the departmental manager. Coexisting within this plant was a relatively new 'human resource manager', senior in status to this firefighter although junior in years. He had identified himself in a relatively cautious way with the new order and tried to introduce more 'forward-looking' policies and practices – quality circles, harmonization, new 'uniforms', better communications and the like – which had echoes of Nissan in Washington. Ironically, perhaps, this shadow of a changemaker role had not won support from either the supervisors or stewards. Indeed, both groups reported in interviews that they regarded him as 'too distant', 'too intellectual' and even 'a snob'.

The regulators

Personnel specialists of this type are decidedly interventionary in the conduct of people management but their interventions rarely involve engagement with the wider business strategy. In many regards they represent the classic IR manager – responsible for

devising, negotiating and defending the procedural and substantive rules which govern employment relations.

They are to be found at both company and establishment level.
Some of their rule-making activity may appear to have 'strategic'
character in that it occasionally involves such 'big' decisions
as union recognition and membership or non-membership of
employers' associations. But these sorts of decisions are rarely
recognized as of a corporate strategy nature by senior business
managers.

This is not to say that their rule-making interventions are of
low significance. They devise and sometimes negotiate rules which
bear upon the smooth operation of the enterprise. This may be
done during annual negotiations for such matters as pay rates,
hours and holidays or, more long term perhaps, they are also
engaged in drawing up rules and procedures bearing on recognition and negotiation structures. Perhaps on a shorter-time
horizon their engagement in 'bargaining-in-grievance settlement'
can result in significant revisions to rules, or even new rules being
created during contract periods.

In a company or plant where the personnel specialist plays a
regulatory role the line manager may feel displaced and upstaged
or, in time, may readily abdicate managerial responsibility in
labour matters to this specialist. A quotation from an IR manager at one of the Rover car assembly plants illustrates this point:

> It is only a few years ago that the production managers here would
> pass all their IR problems on to us. More than once I have come
> into this very room [a conference room] to find a plant manager
> facing a group of stewards whose lads had already walked off the
> job. As soon as I came through that door the so-called manager
> would stand up and say 'ah I'm glad you've arrived to sort this
> out' and then he'd head off out!

What is important to note from this example is that even in
this rather traditional case company the IR manager is speaking
in the past tense. The point of his remarks was to indicate the
extent to which the situation had changed.

Debate continues, however, among observers and academics
about how far things have changed in this regard. One side of this
debate suggests that the IR machinery is still in place and con-

tinues to operate in practice. The other side paints a picture of the IR regulator as a defunct species. Perhaps not surprisingly, given the climate, many personnel and IR managers themselves subscribe to the view that they personally, have not only shifted emphasis from negotiation to such modern activities as training and development, communications, selection, leadership and the like, but that they had really 'always believed' that these latter were the 'proper functions' of personnel and that the strong emphasis on negotiation in the 1960s and 1970s was something of an aberration.

Many academics, schooled in sophisticated debates on pluralistic and radical perspectives were perhaps too readily persuaded of the extent of the spread and the measure of adherence to pluralism. So convinced were some that, when encountering a chance exponent of unitarist philosophy, there was too ready a temptation to dismiss the spokesperson as 'unenlightened' or 'retrospective'. The deep-seated suspicion among practitioners of the notion that there really were multiple sources of legitimate authority in economic enterprises was almost certainly underestimated. Indeed, perhaps most telling on this point are the remarks made by a relatively young yet senior group personnel director from one of the 'panel' companies:

> I graduated from Aston University. Pluralism was most definitely the message. But I soon found it doesn't work in practice.

What is important about this statement is that it signals a considered rejection of the pluralist perspective by a personnel specialist – admittedly one who has speedily gained a seat at the board of directors. The practical outcomes of such a 'revised' position should not, however, be underestimated. Referring to one of the group's recent acquisitions he talked of his plans for reform. This involved: a pull-out from the NJIC, replacement of incumbent managers who 'lack confidence', and of an intent to 'impose' a new package by a certain date – piecework will go out and base plus bonus will be in. Rates will be restudied: 'We have been accused of "doing a Murdoch" but we hope to persuade the president of the union that there is no choice. We have wasted too much time with the stewards and the local officers.'

What is the connection between the regulatory role for personnel management and the human resource management movement? In large measure the brouhaha over HRM reflects the journey of departure from the post-war consensus in industrial relations which found its apotheosis in the Donovan package. Formalization, proceduralism and collectivism were the watchwords. Each of them has been challenged by HRM.

Whether one places emphasis on the 'hard' or 'soft' version of HRM, its impatient dissatisfaction with the proceduralist approach is all too clear. From the 'hard' side comes the criticism that the long, drawn-out appeals and referrals are simply inappropriate in a fiercely competitive and fast-changing climate. The efficient and effective utilization of the human resource, it is argued, requires tough decisions – for example, on downsizing, closures and divestment – decisions of a kind which almost by their very nature do not readily lend themselves to negotiated compromise. And from the 'soft' side with its emphasis on individual selection, direct communication by managers to 'their employees', investment in training and development, direct involvement of employees, tailoring individualized pay to individual performance and similar nostrums, the regulator's arguments about 'dual process' and about honouring agreements and observing custom and practice are anathema. But the crucial point insofar as these 15 mainstream companies are concerned (and by extension for many more organizations in the British context) is that, in some way or other, human resource management-type approaches have to coexist with proceduralism. How this is accomplished is the central theme of chapter 9.

The 'regulators' came under pressure from line and business managers who adopted a highly proactive and interventionary approach – even extending into the 'personnel domain'. Thus, returning to the BR case, but taking it up a step from regional level to central headquarters, the research uncovered a bullish mood among the British Rail managers at that time (1987). As one claimed, 'We muscled-in to bring about the train-crew concept . . . though we were content to let personnel sort out the details.' This claim is interesting in more than one respect. Not only does it say a lot about the attitude of the new business sector managers towards personnel, it is indicative also of a view, prevalent at that time, which held that operational managers too had been pusillanimous in their dealings with personnel during the previous period. In reality, all the major change initiatives of the 1980s had derived from a trawl of operational management views concerning possible alterations to working practices. The train-crew concept (which moved towards the dissolution of the strict separation between drivers and conductors by providing a career link) had itself been one of the ideas emanating from the operational managers. Indeed, one of the senior operational managers interviewed during this research claimed to be the person who formulated the idea and to have written a systematic paper on it showing how it could be implemented. Whatever the actual origins of the idea, the business sector manager quoted above is nonetheless clearly of the opinion that it was the new breed of 'business manager' which had driven ideas of this kind through to completion.

One reaction by regulators to this sort of pressure has been to warn rampant business managers who, for example, too readily espouse the unqualified merits of devolved bargaining that there may be a price to pay. Not least, they maintain this may arise because the capabilities of local managers actually to handle such affairs has yet to be demonstrated in practice. Arguments of this kind were voiced for example in Lucas, British Rail and ICI.

A further defensive move by the regulators has been to step up their bargaining-table demands so that they can approximate the changemaker role. This bargaining-for-change approach can be illustrated by the case of Ford of Britain. We noted in chapter 3 how the company in Britain had sought to build on its 'constitutional' approach by importing a degree of 'jointism' from the United States. Instead of bypassing the unions (as many other British companies embarking on a change programme have done) the company has tried to 'build relations' with union leaders at national level and to encourage negotiated change at local level.

The American notion of 'jointism' rests on the premise that constructive relations can be forged if extra efforts are made to engage the union in wider, less conventional, perhaps less contentious, areas. The formal employee involvement (EI) programme derived from America, largely met opposition from the manual unions in Britain though it gained some acceptance from the staff unions.

The bargaining-for-change approach was, however, stepped-up in earnest in a two-fold way. First, at national level, the key two-year productivity deal of 1985 marked something of a breakthrough for the company and managers still judge this bargaining-for-change deal to have won significant concessions.

A different kind of bargaining placed the future of particular plants in jeopardy unless the rates of productivity could be seen to render them competitive with foreign locations. As we have already seen, the traumatic closure of the Dagenham foundry at the heart of the Dagenham estate was profound and salutary. Subsequent talk of inter-plant competition for investment was taken very seriously.

In these ways, personnel at Ford has played a far more astute game-plan than many other personnel specialists in Britain. They have both managed to offer themselves as partners to the aspirations of key line managers and yet to have maintained a separate distinct professional role for themselves. They have not forced the pace nor have they held rigidly to traditional positions. Above all, they demonstrably helped deliver the goods. As a result, the regulative approach at Ford is far from over. There was the experimentation with the stalking horse of the proposed single-union electronics plant at Dundee. Although this would have marked a departure from the national multi-union agreements, central personnel went along with the plan on the grounds that it could be presented as part of an entirely separate division. Its eventual loss, however, did no particular damage to personnel.

The changemakers

This role type denotes the natural location of the human resource manager proper. These personnel specialists make a highly proactive, interventionary and strategic contribution. The orientation is away from bargaining, away from *ad hocery*, and away from 'humble advice'. It is, in fact, the antithesis of all of these. The dual forms of integration explained in chapter 2 (integration of the different aspects of resourcing, planning, appraising, rewarding and developing; and the further integration of all of this into the business plan) are the characteristic features of this type of personnel approach.

But to what extent does the changemaker role exist away from the prescriptions in the text books? Recent recruitment advertising by blue-chip companies suggest, and promise, that reality might match aspiration. Thus, one of the companies in an advertisement for a personnel manager painted just such a scenario:

> Personnel is part of the total management system and shares with line managers in running the business – contributing from vision to results, and operating in the forefront of change management. It acts in partnership with line management and provides expert advice on all aspects of manpower management. These include not only traditional personnel areas such as training and employee relations but also the most fundamental issues of company business policy and philosophy.

An impressive and exciting scenario; but is this kind of personnel practice really happening in Britain? Recent evidence from an IRRU Survey (Marginson et al., 1988) suggests that HR planning of this kind is very exceptional. And data from the cases researched during this project would broadly confirm that finding. Even where human resource strategy issues were found to figure in the written corporate plan their presence was very limited and the aspirations were typically cast in general terms.

In order to interpret the case research material on this point it is necessary to pay regard to the two variants of the change-maker type noted earlier in the chapter. The first pursues the 'hard' version of HRM and identifies fully with the board (and/ or top executive team) and its understanding of 'business needs'. The accounts of two of the personnel directors in the study (and endorsed by colleagues from other functions) suggested a close affinity to this version on their part. As one of these personnel directors reflected:

> We always have to remember that we are in business to make money. That is really what it's all about in the end. My portfolio on the board nominally takes in personnel and corporate affairs. But, to be perfectly honest, I don't regard myself as a personnel specialist anymore. . . .

When I asked him to describe the human resource strategy he was pursuing he replied:

> Our strategy is to seek maximum utilization of our human resources in just the same way as we seek to do so from our other resources. We are not here to devise sexy career opportunities. . . .

The kind of contribution made by this individual was a subject I took up with his senior colleagues. The MD summarized the general feeling:

> D T [the personnel and corporate affairs director] is very much a team-player. As for a 'distinctive personnel contribution', as you put it, I don't know. In fact, I'm not really sure what these personnel people actually do. But if we didn't have [D T] we would certainly miss him, well I would. . . . We've got a very good manpower planning system in place now, we used to have chronic overmanning – that's now a thing of the past. We have cut the number of locations by half and that was achieved without a single dispute; our people are now fully flexible. . . .

Both personnel directors operating in this mode seemed to be seeking to maintain their credibility by subsuming personnel within the dominant business culture. Similarly, within the panel companies, cases were found where the personnel director minimized the 'personnel' persona and emphasized instead the board director role. IPM membership was downplayed or even abandoned.

Conversely, those approximating rather more to the 'softer' variant tended to highlight the distinctive nature of their input to the team. They stressed the importance of tapping the creativity and commitment of 'resourceful humans'. Hence, they made a virtue of the unique nature of the HR director's contribution to the board. These aspects are illustrated by the following observations:

> The monthly board spends about three quarters of an hour out of its total of two and a half hour meetings on human resource issues. Currently our need is to shift the organization from being technically-oriented to being technically-business oriented. My contribution is to produce policy proposals which will help the company make that culture change.   (HR director)

One of the (technical) colleagues of this person confirmed this account:

> Chris has brought a breath of fresh air to the board. Our 'analysis' of people-management issues in the past was clouded by our obsession with relative remuneration packages and the like. We now have a much wider vista; talk of retention, development and career

planning has become more meaningful and more serious. Oddly our people-management policies now also seem to make far more business sense. The board feels more in control of the massive culture change which we are undoubtedly undergoing.

This kind of impact emanating from personnel was, however, unusual among the case companies. Much more frequent was the admission from personnel that the major initiatives on Total Quality, on Career Planning, on Top 300 Strategic Review Workshops, and so on, had 'regrettably' originated outside the specialism. A number of these sorts of initiatives, however, had subsequently been delegated to personnel for their routine administration. As one said:

> I have to admit that TQM and the Top Management Workshops represent two of the main thrusts in our management development strategy and, to be perfectly honest with you, they are now the major planks in our human resource strategy as a whole. You are correct in saying that neither of them was launched by us. We sort of inherited them. . . .
>
> (personnel director, manufacturing company)

Such cases reveal an interesting aspect of the contest between symbolic realms. Here, the personnel specialists had evidently stayed with the traditional mode of operating and had seen little need or little chance of switching to some new approach. However, changes which deeply impinged upon their realms of practice were, meanwhile, being forged by other key actors in the organization. These changes had so successfully taken hold that personnel had little option in the end but to accept the implementation and maintenance role in respect of them even though they had played no part in the origination of the practices which had now, by default, become part of their 'main thrusts'.

There is an additional angle to this. It may well prove, in the fullness of time, to be an ineffective way of managing change because with so little early involvement, personnel may harbour little real commitment to these central new planks in their portfolio of activity. Any faltering on the part of the innovating champions or some other alteration in the balance of power may result in these inherited programmes simply being allowed to run out of steam.

Where personnel had adopted a changemaker type stance the state of affairs was very different. For example, the Ford of Europe Employee Affairs function (a separate body from Ford of Britain Personnel) had developed an overall strategy designed to 'lead and support the personnel strategy in each National Company'. The focus of this Ford of Europe people strategy was on 'open communications, skills development and motivation'. The first of these, communications, was being driven through by extending the mission, values and guiding principles (MVGP) package, through 'state of the nation' presentations and upgrading senior management/union and works council communications. The skills development substrategy is built on a seven-point plan which includes attending to a complete skills analysis, targeting a standard 40 hours training per employee per annum and so on. The third component, motivation, has a six-point plan embracing the 'assessment of new reward systems and ownership programmes to enhance loyalty', extending the 'specialist Growth Path' to reward and retain key skills by opening up career ladders and, of particular note, 'increasing rewards and recognition for participative managers achieving objectives'. Other related measures are an increase in hourly and salaried employee involvement in launch planning and a reduction in the distinctions between hourly and salaried people.

This Ford of Europe, overarching HR strategy is also elaborated on a country-by-country basis with particular features emphasized for Britain, Spain, Germany and Belgium. Of particular note in the British context is the explicit intent to 'incorporate' lessons from its Ford's 'Japanese Companies Study' into the Ford of Britain Personnel Strategy.

The Ford case is suggestive of a high-level HR strategy in a mainstream company. The Ford of Europe Employee Affairs Directorate have adopted a changemaker stance. They have committed the strategy to a formal written policy document and have succeeded in winning a significant place for this in the company's overall business strategy. As the illustrations reveal, the bias of the contribution is towards the developmental, motivational and employee communication aspects of HR – that is the 'softer' variant of the changemaker personnel type.

What is perhaps most instructive, however, is that despite the sophistication, the painstaking preparation and planning, and even the pan-European vista, the impact of this kind of personnel-driven change package, at least in the British context (the case research did not extend to the European continent), was considerably less at plant level than some of the other initiatives we have discussed in other companies which were championed from outside personnel.

In reviewing both subtypes of the changemaker role, it can be seen that in practice it is very difficult for senior personnel specialists to get the balance right. The top-team players had tried to position themselves as repositories of specialist skills and yet as also equally comfortable when dealing with general business issues. They had tried to be 'professional' in the technical sense but certainly not in the occupational-interest-group sense. Their salient aspiration was to be accepted fully as team members and they were criticized if they appeared to be anything other – and yet their unique value to the board lay in their latent nonconformity.

When reflecting upon the whole range of 'types' it is notable that even when there was a recognition of a job to be done with regard to the people-side-of-enterprise it cannot be assumed now that personnel specialists will be seen as the appropriate people to do it. At a time when direct communication with the workforce is seen as a potentially powerful instrument of corporate persuasion, many companies turn to their Public Relations departments for the necessary expertise in devising the appropriate kinds of 'campaign'. Similarly, motivational campaigns of the 'hearts and minds' variety are frequently perceived as best referred to external consultants. The internal promoters for these, as we have seen in the previous chapter, tend often to be key line managers and not personnel. Moreover, where an internal specialist function is created to handle some of the developmental aspects of human resource management, these innovative units may well be outside the traditional personnel department. In sum, even in those cases where 'strategic changemaking' occurs within a mainstream organization, it cannot be assumed that personnel specialists will be able to claim it as their own.

CONCLUSION

It was noted at the beginning of this chapter that there are basically two aspects to the question of the nature of the link between personnel specialists and developments in human resource management concerning:

- the role played by these specialists in devising and driving the changes
- how personnel has responded in those cases where the changes have come from outside the specialism.

The 15 case organizations and the additional panel companies revealed examples of both.

The evidence suggested that 'personnel management' as a function has adopted no single stance with respect to HRM. In some cases the values, concepts and methods of human resource management clearly provided a fillip to personnel's flagging fortunes. A new credibility with line managers had been gained and even main board directors had begun to express an interest in its activities. But, in other cases, personnel had seen initiatives and programmes introduced and championed by senior managers from other functions and had played no active part in their conception or roll-out. Personnel's access to, and readiness to embrace, the new symbolic realm was seen to be clearly variable across the case companies.

In order to help 'map' these different actions and reactions a 2×2 matrix diagram was developed in the chapter as a way of summarising the research findings. Of the four 'types' of personnel specialist behaviour identified, one, the changemaker type, was seen to be particularly consonant with the human resource management model. Most of the major change programmes in this set of cases had originated outside personnel. It was notable that of the 15 mainstream case organizations, no more than two had personnel specialist teams which approximated to the changemaker type.

When compared with the debates within the personnel specialist domain this is a surprising finding. For within personnel the talk has been of 'devolving' functions to the line, and the 'paradox' of having to 'give HRM away' in order to maintain a presence. Judging from the information derived from the 15 mainstream cases this sort of discussion begins to look somewhat fanciful.

The findings overall thus indicate that personnel in the mainstream companies had not been the main drivers of the new paradigm. Another issue is how this (and the degree of variety which was found to obtain) might be explained. Insofar as the regulators still outnumbered the changemakers in most of the companies, part of the explanation might be sought in the traditional opportunism which Sisson (1989) had traced to the institutional and structural characteristics of the British scene as a whole and which derive from particular historical circumstances. But, given that despite this historical legacy variation was nonetheless evident a further level of explanation has to be entered.

In most of the mainstream companies personnel had found it 'safer' and more attractive to remain attached to the proceduralist symbolic realm. It was perceived as the pragmatic choice. Personnel had grown used to more occasional gung-ho adventurism on the part of some of their line and unit manager colleagues. In the past they had usually managed to see off these naive challenges. Furthermore, personnel had built up a vested interest in the traditional paradigm. By and large then, this state of affairs was the 'norm' for the mainstream companies. But as we have seen there were exceptions.

The main group of exceptions actually came from outside the mainstream cases. In the panel companies which were usually smaller and certainly more varied in terms of ownership and sector, the likelihood of encountering a personnel director who had adopted the changemaker type role was far higher. It appeared then that the attachment to the traditional paradigm in the mainstream companies had something to do with the characteristic features of these organizations. It was in these large, unionized and proceduralized organizations that for a variety of reasons personnel had remained more attached to the traditional mode. This was in part no doubt due to the difficulties of escaping from that paradigm because of the pressure from trade unions and significant others. But it was also because personnel had their own vested interest in that paradigm built around practised realms of expertise such as negotiating and built around power plays *vis-à-vis* other management functions.

While the majority of the personnel managers and directors in the study would not be easily locatable within the changemaker 'box', it would be fair to say that quite a number of them – at least a half – had aspirations to move in that direction. Further, in sporadic fashion, the same number could already point to some initiatives which had a similitude to this position, albeit lacking in consistency and strategic integration.

These results suggest that the terms 'opportunism' and 'pragmatism' which Sisson (1989) has used to characterize the practice of personnel management in Britain are ones which largely remain pertinent despite the considerable developments which have taken place in the way human resources are managed. This was perhaps to be expected given that, as Sisson observes, the roots of this stance taken by personnel in Britain are traceable to deep structures inherited from the past. But the weight of this historical legacy might similarly be expected to extend across the span of managerial specialisms in this country. And yet when viewed in the round, change as we have seen, has somehow occurred in the management of human resources. A review of the key part played in this by line and general managers is the purpose of the next two chapters.

7

The Part Played by Senior and Middle Line Managers in the Management of Human Resources

According to the model described in chapter 2, a key attribute of human resource management is the shift of responsibility from the personnel specialist to the line manager. Usually, at least when described in the personnel literature in Britain, the shift is depicted as the 'devolution' of certain personnel activities to the line. This implies a voluntary, strategic review by personnel specialists, out of which has come a reasoned reallocation of responsibilities. But there is also another account which explains the origins of the perceived shift and this one is rather less flattering to personnel practitioners. This alternative, more critical account suggests that under conditions of intensive product market competition, personnel simply failed to produce appropriate ways forward to meet organizational needs. This line of argument is illustrated in the preface to Beer et al.'s (1988) book on human resource management. They observe:

> Line managers trying to improve organisational effectiveness perceive conflicting perspectives, directions and values emanating from various specialists in the personnel function . . . General managers faced with an array of external and internal pressures, are beginning to demand that managing human resources be approached in an integrated, proactive, and strategic way, one relevant to their business and management problems. (1988: x)

As this implies, personnel specialists may not have given away part of their role but rather had it taken away.

Be that as it may, in most discussions, while the notion of a 'devolution' of human resource management from the specialist to the line manager is asserted, the matter is there left to rest. There has been a noticeable lack of examination of what this has meant in practice. It is time to shift attention from personnel specialists in this debate towards those managers who may well be playing a far more central role in labour management than current literature would seem to reflect or even acknowledge.[1] The purpose of this chapter is to remedy that neglect by drawing upon the case research.

But before presenting the data it will be worthwhile outlining those elements of the roles of senior and middle-level line managers which can be gleaned from the literature.

LITERATURE ON LINE MANAGERS

The literature is useful first of all in helping to clarify the meaning of 'line management'. Traditionally, the role has been defined in terms of the distinction between 'line' and 'staff'. The historical antecedents to this distinction are traceable most especially in the military organizations of nineteenth century Prussia but the distinction can even be found much further back in ancient Greece (Haimann, Scott and Connor, 1978: 190). Concern about the damage this duality might do to the 'principle of the unity of command' was the aspect which exercised the classical administration minds of Fayol and Gulick in the first half of this century. Despite periodic speculations that the line-staff concept might have outlived its usefulness (Logan, 1966) the distinction has proved to be remarkably robust. The aspect which attracted most attention hinged on the real or potential conflicts which this fissure in the management division of labour might engender (Belasco and Alutto, 1969; Stewart, 1963; Browne and Golembiewski, 1974).

'Line' functions have been defined as those 'which have direct responsibility for achieving the objectives of the company' in contradistinction to staff activities 'which primarily exist to provide advice and services (Stewart, 1963: 32–3). Accordingly, whether a particular role and function is 'line' or 'staff' will depend on the company's objectives. In a research laboratory where new products and processes are the prime aim, the researchers will represent the 'line' but in most other structures these people would more usually be regarded as in a staff-support role. Despite the potential complications the distinction is, for the most part, readily understood and is widely used by practitioners themselves.

One of the main problems in trying to interpret changes to the managerial role from a reading of the literature is that so much of that literature is based on future speculation. As Dopson and Stewart (1990) have shown, a large proportion of those studies (e.g. Peschanski, 1985; Kanter, 1986; and Drucker, 1988) which predict a decline in middle management in terms of numbers and a reduction in their status and opportunities due to information technology, have failed to base their accounts on empirical evidence. In contrast, those studies which drew upon actual research have tended rather to point to the enriching of middle management jobs (Millman and Hartwick, 1987; Buchanan and McCalman, 1988; Nonaka, 1988; Dopson and Stewart, 1990).

The 'gloomy view' of middle management 'blues' (Thackeray, 1988; Dickson, 1977; Hunt, 1986; Scase and Goffee, 1989; Goffee and Scase, 1986) is countered by Dopson and Stewart (1990) who conclude that their recent study 'does not support the dismal picture of middle management' (1990: 12).

While the general literature on 'middle management' as cited above tends to be insufficiently focused for our purposes here, publications in the specifically IR/personnel area relating to the role have, conversely, been too restricted. Thus, for example, one of the very few studies to report on 'the involvement of line and staff managers in industrial relations' (Marsh and Gillies, 1983) illustrates this point. The authors restrict themselves to reporting on the extent to which the managers they interviewed were engaged in 'talking' to union members and union representatives, were 'handling grievances', or were 'negotiating'. It was concluded that these managers 'seem in general willing to regard IR as part of their job and to accept this situation with no noticeable resentment' (p. 38).

The *Workplace Industrial Relations* survey (Millward and Stevens, 1986) also tackled the role in terms of 'involvement' in various types of 'personnel matters' as traditionally defined. On average, works managers reported that they spent a quarter of

their time on 'personnel matters'. The proportion varied sub-
stantially depending upon whether the factory was British or
foreign owned. The British plants had factory managers spending
more time on such issues, mainly, it was thought, because professional provision was less readily available than in foreign-owned
companies.

It is relevant to note that works managers, were preoccupied
with the same sorts of personnel issues as were personnel managers (according to rankings on a pre-ordained list). Thus, 97 per
cent of works managers compared with 96 per cent of personnel
managers reported that they dealt with disciplinary cases and the
proportions were 'not very dissimilar' in all of the other areas
listed (recruitment, training, IR procedures) although personnel
managers were more likely to be responsible for pay systems and
job evaluation. Nevertheless, the majority of works managers even
included these issues as part of their own job responsibilities. As
for manpower planning, 96 per cent of works managers reported
this formed part of their jobs compared with 83 per cent of personnel managers.

This is about all the *Workplace Industrial Relations* survey had
to say about works managers. As can be seen, it is confined to
'types of involvement' but even this limited data is indicative of
the considerable level of engagement these senior line managers/
general managers had in areas which are more commonly regarded
as the proper province of personnel specialists.

The survey also contains information about the relative influence of departmental managers and personnel managers on a
range of specified issues as judged by works managers. Five types
of issues were used as indicators. In fact the items chosen are not
by any means a representative list of decision areas which impact
on people's experience of work. They omit the issues of work
design, technology, communication, control and the setting of
goals: that is, key aspects in the management of human resources
and ones where it seems likely that line managers have considerably more influence than do personnel. But even on the more
traditional personnel and IR topics chosen by Millward and
Stevens such as appointments, discipline and negotiations, their
own evidence shows that departmental managers were judged to
have increased their influence far more than personnel (p. 44).

The suspicion that line and general managers were more heavily engaged in IR issues in the 1980s is also given support in the work of Edwards (1987). His study of 229 factory managers found these people to be 'quite heavily involved in decisions with a labour element' (1987: 114). Moreover, a marked reduction was recorded between the date of this one and that of an earlier Warwick Survey (Brown, 1981) in the proportion of respondents perceiving the IR specialist function to be 'much more important' (19 per cent compared with 56 per cent). The nature of factory managers' engagement in human resource management under the new conditions, found Edwards, is directed towards 'creating the broad conditions in which workers would see what management was doing and understand why' (1987: 134).

Edwards' book is one of very few to tackle the issue of middle management involvement in labour management, but as a survey-based analysis it inevitably leaves untouched the question of *how* these and other line managers actually engage in the management of people. This, however, is especially important because, as Edwards detects, there has been a trend (in large manufacturing establishments at least) towards what he terms 'enlightened managerialism' – that is an attempt to involve labour in rather particular ways in the meeting of business objectives. Examination of the precise nature of this practice requires close-up research. This is especially so when the shift in the labour-management approach is accompanied by, and indeed in no small measure brought about by, a change in the very nature of the middle-management role itself. Moreover, all of the previously referenced sources are silent on the part played by *senior* managers in human resource management.[2]

EVIDENCE FROM THE 15 CASES

The analysis which follows is structured so as to answer the following questions:

● In what precise way is the role of the middle and senior level line manager changing and in particular what does the concept of the 'expanded' role mean in practice?

● What implications are organizations drawing for the recruitment and selection of these managers?

- What kinds of management development and training are organizations providing to equip line managers to handle these changed expectations?
- What evidence is there of a change in attitudes and behaviour among line managers?

Overall, the case research revealed quite clearly that line managers were becoming far more important in determining how human resources would be used. This increased responsibility for people management has two key aspects. Line managers have come to the fore in this regard not only as the crucial delivery mechanism for new approaches in employee relations (responsible for example, for direct communication with employees) but, more assertively, as themselves the designers and drivers of the new ways. Both aspects carry implications for personnel as a specialism but the latter aspect, which suggests an invasion of the policy-making territory by 'non-specialists', is clearly the more threatening for personnel managers. A key contention of this chapter is that the nature of the changing role of line managers is intimately linked with the kind of changes which are taking place in labour management.

Developments at Austin Rover, Ford, Peugeot, Massey Ferguson and the other manufacturers in particular, showed that even without 'bidding' for a policy-making role in the human resource area, line managers were projected rather more centre stage in human resource management. In addition to the requirement to be more 'up front' in directly briefing employees, the whole raft of measures involving 'managerial leadership'; the shift towards more individualized forms of pay; of more appraisal; of devolved management accountability; and of deproceduralizing, all led to a more prominent role for middle managers.

But in addition, as noted above, there is also a second angle. This concerns the question of the part played by non-personnel specialists in formulating the revised patterns of people management. In a number of the case organizations, personnel managers were clearly not the prime movers in redrawing the architecture of labour relations. On the contrary, the latter group were found to be notably reticent about the kind of changes examined in previous chapters. They could be observed as acting more as foot-draggers rather than active change agents.

Figure 7.1   A crucial fusion

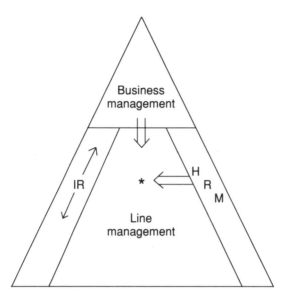

There was sufficient commonality in the evidence collected from the case studies to enable a broad-brush picture to be drawn. What seems to have been happening is the coming together of two relatively separate developments to create what might be termed a 'crucial fusion'. This is depicted in figure 7.1.

The directional arrow from the apex downwards indicates the general tendency towards devolved management. This has been occurring in a range of ways and for a variety of reasons, many of them evidently without people-management issues being their prime concern, but carrying implications in this sphere nonetheless. Corporate headquarters have been cut back: sometimes on a massive scale. A related feature of devolved management has been the creation of cost and profit centres at lower levels within organizations. Strategic business units (SBUs) have been set up in place of large centralized industrial bureaucracies. Lucas Industries for example, recast itself in the 1980s into 130 separate businesses each with its own competitiveness achievement plan and profit and loss accounts. In these types of devolved forms, business unit managers, whether they be managing directors or general managers, became increasingly responsible for the total array of resources at their disposal. In accord with this logic, the way in which they wanted to deploy and utilize the human resource was increasingly seen as necessitating a loosening of uniform central rules. One indicator of this process was the dismantling of company-level bargaining machinery and its dispersal to divisions and constituent businesses. But that is not even half of the story. Other moves impacting on the way human resources were managed were simultaneously being made.

Another feature of change signalled in figure 7.1 concerns what was happening within the industrial relations and human resource management specialisms. The bifurcating tendency within personnel was discussed in the previous chapter. The arrow from the HRM area denotes how the non-proceduralized approach, characteristic of human resource management as opposed to personnel, operates primarily through the actions of line managers. This is witnessed particularly in the realms of direct communications with employees, participation and involvement, management style and on-the-job coaching and development.

It has to be stressed that a figure of this nature is a heuristic device. It graphically points up certain vital aspects but necessarily in a very incomplete way. The key point about figure 7.1 is that two developments (devolved management and human resource management) were occurring simultaneously. Together, they presented line managers with a tremendous new opportunity; there was a crucial fusion of forces.

This broad-brush depiction should not, of course, be taken to suggest that this model was played-out in practice in a straightforward way. On the contrary, there were, in reality, clearly many false starts and many exceptions. Perhaps most significant is the observation that the forces were not always quite so mutually reinforcing as the simplified model implies.

But, in any case, figure 7.1 is not about whether the approach to managing people has become 'more strategic' in the sense of deriving from a high-level plan at a corporate centre. Rather, the issue it portrays is that line and general managers heading up key operational units have been exposed to new opportunities in shaping how the human resource will be managed and that these opportunities have come from dual but reinforcing sources. The issue therefore is what these line and general managers have done in response to these possibilities.

Figure 7.2 Types of line manager

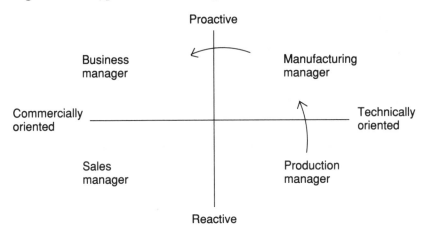

It was in relation to this question that the case research revealed one of its clearest messages. It was found that there was a discernible trend towards a new type of role for the middle-level line manager. Indeed, it was this development which was found repeated in some three-quarters of the cases, which persuaded me, more than anything else, that at least some of the postulated changes in the management of human resources had a substantive base. In order to make the key aspects of that development manifest it is useful to portray it in simple diagrammatic form. The role of line manager can be, and is, played out in many different ways. It is possible to capture the essence of these differences by contrasting the main alternatives along two key dimensions. The first dimension reflects the extent to which a manager is commercially oriented as opposed to being technically-oriented. The second dimension measures the degree to which a manager takes a predominantly proactive or reactive stance. These two dimensions are the basis for the 2 × 2 matrix shown in figure 7.2.

Mapped out on this figure are four 'types' of line managers. These types represent different ways in which the line manager may enact the role. 'Production manager' is the traditional, circumscribed, interpretation of the role. In this mode the manager responds to instructions, concentrates effort on meeting the designated schedules and finds most satisfaction in keeping the technology running according to plan. A predominant trend, observable in a range of companies from many different sectors, has been to recast that traditional production manager role into a new one: that of 'manufacturing manager'. In this mode, line managers actively seek to find new ways of reducing costs, of improving quality and of deploying labour, materials and plant in new configurations which will add-value to the processes in hand. Manufacturing managers thus have a wider remit. They are more generalist, they have greater responsibilities and they undertake a wider range of tasks. To allow them to do these things reorganization is normal, so that hitherto distinct lines of reporting associated with 'support' functions such as engineering, maintenance, quality, materials-flow and the like become subordinated to this all-embracing 'boss' of manufacturing operations.

A few organizations have sought to take this one step further, that is to transform the manufacturing manager into an even more rounded 'business manager'. Such a person has to develop an awareness of the total organization and how it fits within its wider environment. This role implies gaining a more holistic view from which vantage point a strategy can be devised. The business manager will thus be competent in SWOT analysis, planning, target setting, finance, marketing and the management of change. Whilst he or she will not be expected to exercise these capabilities at a corporate level it will be expected that they will lead to an understanding of his or her subsystem as an integral part of the whole rather than a mere fragmented slice.

Just to complete the picture from figure 7.2 a fourth type is conceptually possible, designated here as the 'Sales Manager', but, in practice, this type was not encountered to any significant degree. At a conceptual level, it suggests a middle manager who continues to operate in a reactive manner but shifts orientation from the technical aspects of production to the commercial aspects. This market and customer awareness will usually be welcomed by senior managers but where it merely translates into behaviour in direct response to customer demands this 'sales' type role is unlikely to be encouraged.

The basic trend has been for a transformation in the middle-level line manager's role from the production manager model, through the manufacturing manager type, and, for a few (but as an aspiration for the many) a further transition to the business manager type. We can draw upon the findings from the case studies in order to explore what this has meant in practice.

What was found first of all was a near universal practice of redesignating 'production managers' as 'manufacturing managers'. The significance of this change was that instead of having a series of separate and independent hierarchies or 'functional chimneys' such as process engineering, production engineering, quality control, and so on, these reported directly to the manufacturing manager. The span of control of manufacturing managers thus increased as they became responsible for a wider mix of employees.

Middle-level line managers had also become more generalist in that they had assumed a wider range of responsibilities. They were acutely aware of budgets and costs. The management accounting practice of allocating costs (both variable costs and a proportion of fixed costs) to zones of production has become widespread. Managers heading up these 'cost centres' were expected not merely to ensure a regular smooth operation but, additionally, to find imaginative ways of reducing costs.

But the expanded role of line managers extended beyond budgets and accounting. The business orientation also embraced a sensitivity to, and greater understanding of, customer needs. Some departmental heads talked of ensuring that they and their direct reports made a definite commitment to get out and meet customers at least once a month. One such head pointed out that when he arrived at the company he found that most of his team had never actually met a customer. This reorientation of the team became a top priority.

A related feature was the search for continuous improvement as distinct from simply meeting planned schedules. In these and other ways therefore, they had embraced the concept of the 'business manager'. When asked whether their roles had changed at all the typical response was to emphasize the drastic nature of the change and to reference the additional responsibilities they now had for quality, efficiency, costs, people, and for managing change.

A senior line manager at Austin Rover, Longbridge put the point succinctly:

> Yes, there has been a massive shift! Fundamentally, we have moved
> from how a production man would run it to how a businessman

would ... that is, it is no longer just a question of meeting schedules, we do that now with monotonous regularity. . . .
(Austin Rover: plant director, Power Train)

The form in which these changes came had the appearance of
being decidedly non-HR in character. Examples of far-reaching
initiatives of this nature would include:

- total quality management (TQM)

- materials requirements planning (MRP)

- just-in-time (JIT)

- organizational redesign which placed operatives in teams or
created 'cells'

- computer-aided manufacture (CAM).

A good case can be made for saying that, especially when ag-
gregated, changes of this sort have had a far more profound impact
on the way human resources are currently deployed, utilized and
managed than any or all of the initiatives deriving from the
personnel camp. If this is so, then one implication is that most
of the studies which have tried to track and measure change in
IR and personnel over the past decade have been looking at
dimensions which are peripheral to the fundamentals of the
relationships between management and employees. The survival
of IR institutional machinery may not be the most significant of
factors.

   This point deserves emphasizing. The changes to operational
and organizational systems and practice carried important implications for the way the human resource is used and the
conditions under which it operates. Reporting and authority
relationships have been upturned, and task responsibilities have
been altered radically – often without prior collective negotiation.
This is not to say that these changes have been smoothly and
coherently introduced. On the contrary, one of the most notable
limitations may turn out to be that the full complexities of personnel and industrial relations have not been properly taken into
account. But meanwhile, some large pebbles were lobbed into
the water and the ripples were felt far and wide.

For example, in one of the process companies, a complex web of change had been introduced comprising, at various times, total quality, MRPII and reorganization. A departmental manager reflected on the implications for his role and for the way labour was managed:

> This used to be a union-dominated site: the stewards had their fingers into everything. As a result, overtime was running at very high levels, job demarcation was ridiculous and we were the most antiquated part of the company. Personnel had tried negotiating us out of trouble on numerous occasions but we never seemed to get anywhere. But since [Mr Y, the manufacturing director] got a grip of things, the amount of change we have achieved is just incredible. I no longer have supervisors and section heads reporting to me, I directly manage the teams, the teams are cross-functional, the shift patterns have been changed, the teams get their work schedules direct from the computer terminal in their area, and so on and so on. . . . As I said, just about everything is different. I don't see that personnel helped us in this!

In response to a question about how his own role had changed in consequence, he replied:

> Oh, quite significantly. The old progress chasing game has gone, I am much clearer about what my contribution is. I look outwards to the customer but I also get involved with the motivation of the teams. In a sense what is new is that employee relations now have to be seen to make sense in a market context.

This was just one instance of the message received from a number of the companies. The picture built up from the case organizations was that there were relatively many more 'general manager' positions which had been created, and that line managers had seen their roles greatly expanded so that they had come to resemble 'general manager' positions. Organizational devolution tends to increase the number of general manager posts. The shift from monolithic, pyramidal structures to a multiplicity of semi-autonomous business units tends to have this consequence. Another reason and another source of the proliferation of general manager positions is the purposeful creation of arrangements, whereby one of the production line managers comes to be designated as a critical decision point. In the NHS, for example, the long-standing system of 'consensus management' loosely coordinated by an administrator was replaced under the Griffiths reform by designated 'general managers' who were given the authority to make key decisions and given responsibility for the unit budget. This formal subordination of hitherto competing specialisms finds echo in manufacturing industry with the trend towards the subjugation of engineering and other 'support' functions to the 'manufacturing manager'. The Peugeot Talbot example of the 'Manufacturing Manager as King' which was referred to earlier, is again relevant here.

The expanded and changing role of line managers carries many ramifications. These include implications for the handling of human resources; line managers' role in initiatives such as TQM and MRPII; and implications for the recruitment and selection of these post holders, their training and their attitudes and behaviour. This last set of issues arise in part by virtue of the consequences these will carry for the handling of the human resource in general, but they also arise because line managers are often the object as well as the devisers and implementers of HR initiatives. This can be seen clearly for example with regard to changes to managers' own payment systems, their appraisal, their style, and with regard to managerial union derecognition. Each of these action points is associated, in consequence, with uncertainty and ambiguity which may be expected to carry through into the way the variegated human resource is 'managed'. We need to look at each of these points in turn.

IMPLICATIONS FOR HUMAN RESOURCE MANAGEMENT

At senior levels, the change seemed to involve a more active role for line and general managers in setting the direction for HR policy. Conventional wisdom still follows studies by Winkler (1974) and Fidler (1981) which depict top managers as having little or no interest in labour relations. But these sources were describing board directors and, in any case, the ambit of concerns embraced by terms such as 'labour relations', 'industrial relations', 'human resource management' and the like has expanded considerably during the intervening period.

The evidence from the present study points to a rather different picture. If one attends to managers at very senior (i.e. submain board level) then the case studies suggest that human resource management issues enjoy quite a high profile in their deliberations. Examples were found in the cases of Smith & Nephew, Ford, Bradford Council and Peugeot. The significance of this finding is that it is at this level that the link between a 'strategic' human resource policy and corporate strategy is to be expected if such a link is ever made. The first piece of evidence comes from the most senior group of executives in Ford of Europe. In an interview with one of their number, the following observation was made:

> Every month the Executive Committee of Ford of Europe (i.e. the vice president's board of directors) moves, in the afternoon, from the board room to a more relaxed atmosphere to discuss the 'people' issues of involvement, appraisal, employee relations etc. . . . . In total it adds up to a very considerable proportion of the board's time. . . . (director, Ford of Europe)

In other case companies, the engagement with human resource strategy by senior executives was evident in the increasing practice of holding six-monthly meetings for the 'Top 100' or 'Top 300'. At these gatherings corporate strategy would be presented and opened up to debate.

In Peugeot-Talbot, the Managing Director, Geoffrey Whalen, and the Assistant Managing Director, Dick Parham, were found to be engaged in an active consideration of the interlink between the company's business strategy and its human resource management practices. For example, issues of employee communications, supervisors' spans of control, and employee involvement were all frequently discussed at the weekly executive committee and occasionally at the quarterly UK board. But the latter is really more of a formality as Peugeot UK is a wholly owned subsidiary and all the major decisions have 'to be confirmed in France'. The French decisions relate to investment, disinvestment and product; but operational matters are entirely left to UK management. All IR issues – for example a proposal say, to switch to a single union agreement – would be left to the UK executive. This, as Parham pointed out, is entirely different from the days when the company was owned by Chrysler. Then, the Americans wanted to know production figures day by day, sometimes even hour by hour and they would seek also to intervene in industrial disputes.

A policy on the nature of an appropriate 'man management' style was adopted by the Peugeot UK executive and so too were ways to 'positively influence the attitudes of employees'. Underlining the point, the director of manufacturing claimed that one of the biggest changes in the company had been that personnel policy itself had been taken over by the executive:

> The central personnel function is now basically a coordinating activity. The personnel director leads for us in the formal negotiations with the trade unions. But on the major policy shifts in areas such as communications, man-management, quality, team building, problem-solving teams and the like, these are matters for the executive.

And the assistant managing director confirmed that general managers are now expected to 'incorporate the activities of personnel management into their own role'.

But tracing, in any direct sense, the vaunted link between corporate strategy and human resource management through the actions of the senior players is an exercise fraught with difficulty. In part this reflects the problem of pinning down strategy formulation *per se*, and in part it stems from the subtlety of human resource issues, for, as has been pointed out in this chapter, some of the most important decisions affecting labour do not necessarily present themselves as 'labour issues'. The subject of senior, non-specialists' involvement in linking corporate strategy and human resource strategy is one requiring of study in its own right. What can be done is to infer strategic choice from the pattern of commercial moves and decisions and then to track the compatibility of practices in the human resource management sphere. That was the approach adopted in this study most especially with regard to middle-level line managers.

At middle management levels, the line manager's changing (and usually expanding) role could be seen to carry many HR implications. They were subject to, and far more involved in, new practices in selection, direct communications, target setting, appraisal, motivation, training and development. In what follows, illustrations on the changing role of middle managers are provided – most particularly with regard to selection, communication, training and development and the impacts on attitudes and behaviour.

Selection

The role changes so far described carried implications for the selection of the incumbents. Selection methods for middle managers had been made more systematic. The fact that there were fewer of them operating in flatter organizations made this task more feasible. There had been an increased usage of formal testing (including a dramatic increase in the use of psychometric tests) and a more frequent resort to assessment centres. Selection for the expanded role occurred not only for new entrants but also in the sense of deselection of present role occupants. For example, even within the pragmatic Smith & Nephew organization, when a senior manager was asked about changes to the managerial role he replied:

> Oh yes! There has been a definite weeding-out of managers who do not or cannot act in accordance with our new ways. Quite a number have been displaced or transferred.

The new requirements for middle managers were cogently described as:

> A management which is more positive, more effective, able to define clearly what it is they wish to do and to be able to ensure that their employees are moving in the same direction. Hence they have to be able to inform them better, train them better, allocate tasks to them better, define priorities better. In total, to be a more thinking and effective manager.
> (corporate level manager, Smith & Nephew)

In some cases the very act of organizational redesign with its implicit reallocation of influence and power is intimately related to the selection and promotion of certain kinds of people. Hence, in British Rail when the business sectors were created and superimposed over the traditional engineering and production functions, the choice of those who would be marked-out to staff these new roles was regarded as critical by all concerned. These roles were of the 'business manager type' *par excellence*. A regional finance and planning manager summarized what has happening:

> The business side is being filled with younger, very good people. They are enthusiastic to make change happen. In contrast, the production people are older and more established, long on experience but reluctant to change. There is a struggle going on and one side will eventually come out on top. In my view it will be the business lot.
> (regional finance and planning manager, British Rail, 1987)

Communication

Enhanced communications were a characteristic feature of the new role for line managers. As part of their expanded remit they could expect to receive more information themselves and as part of their clearer responsibility for managing the people in their area they were also expected to be key transmitters of information. We have already described the extensive and interlocking patterns of communications adopted at Jaguar and Peugeot. What needs to be stressed at this point is the role of the line manager in such initiatives.

In most of the 15 cases, line managers were designated a part in the now familiar 'cascade' system of communication. They had to filter and retranslate information coming to them from top levels, add their own 'local content' and ensure direct personal delivery of the messages to their own reporting staff. In addition, as we saw clearly from the example of the Ford case, some line managers were crucially engaged in another form of direct communication. When a key decision had been made about changes to working practices, shift arrangements, technology and the like, these line managers could be found directly addressing large groups of employees to get the message over to them without the mediation of elected representatives. The impact of this appeared to be very considerable.

This enhanced role for the line manager did not, however, always proceed unproblematically. British Rail managers complained that their task was made difficult because:

The information we are given as the basis for our team briefing is often outdated and is not particularly accurate either. On a number of occasions I have been embarrassed by giving out a statement which has been challenged by a union representative who has more precise and more recent information. Occasions such as that undermine our credibility and they are not easily forgotten.

Managers at Jaguar also ran into difficulties. The company had tried to bypass the unions by seeking information about employee views directly through an 'attitude survey'. The trade unions' attempt to prevent this had failed at the form-completion stage but they did manage effectively to boycott the subsequent shopfloor feedback sessions.

In other cases, senior managers claimed that problems encountered with direct communications by line managers were 'teething troubles' which were eventually overcome. In some instances this claim seemed to be borne out by the case work at lower levels. For example, at Peugeot the early days of direct communcation were not a success. But with training and persistence the situation did appear to have been transformed. By 1987 the area managers interviewed and observed during this study appeared comfortable with the shopfloor communication system and expressed considerable satisfaction with it.

But in a host of other companies, the practice of direct communication by line managers appeared to be operating in a very desultory way. This was especially so with regard to the supposed 'two-way' feature which, in the abstract, is so critical. From a wide range of possible examples it is most telling to pick out Whitbread because this company had, in general, made more progress than most in its new human resource initiatives. Yet, even here, the actual practice of direct communication by line managers was evidently problematical. Despite 'audits' of the briefing record books which all line managers had to maintain, it was very clear that the amount of 'upward' communication from the shopfloor was negligible and of little significance even where it had, occasionally, been teased out. As one middle-level manager observed:

Yes, I do the briefings but I normally feel as if I am just going through the motions. I can't remember the last time I had anything worth writing in the log as a result of reactions to the brief. . . . Sure, these log books are supposed to be monitored but if there's nothing to record then there's nothing to record is there? What can I do about it?

The latter question posed by the Whitbread line manager is starkly indicative of the limits to change in the line manager's role in some of the cases, and in particular to the limited shift relating to the human resource aspects of their changing role. It raises questions about the training which the line managers have had, or not had, as the case may be, to equip them to undertake the projected enhanced role.

Training and development

As we observed earlier, according to the clutch of reports published in the mid-1980s, the provision of management education, training and development in Britain compared poorly with that of her major international competitors. If this was to prove to be an accurate picture and if it was persisting, then how could line managers take on and perform effectively the kind of expanded roles discussed above?

In fact in the 15 case organizations which were the subject of this study a good deal had begun to happen in the management development field by 1988. In the first place, there was a heightened consciousness of the importance of management development as an area for concern. To some extent, the massive publicity given to the earlier reports and to the subsequent various declarations from the government, the CBI, the BIM, all culminating in the launch of the Management Charter Initiative (MCI), probably helped to stimulate this. But this was not the only pressure, as was evident from the fact that even where there had been no awareness of the MCI and its antecedents, these organizations had begun to take action.

The steps which they had begun to take were of variable quality. The more notable initiatives moved forward across three fronts: the launch of a suite of training programmes; an emphasis upon each manager being held accountable for the development of his or her subordinates; the encouragement and support of self-development.

On the first of these, training, it has to be recognized that most of the organizations were building up from a very low base. The reason for this is that even where the organizations might previously have enjoyed a proud reputation for training, the provision had almost invariably been drastically reduced in the early to mid-1980s. However, most of the 15 case companies had begun once more to place considerable emphasis upon training, they had resourced it and new programmes had been launched. A fairly typical approach was to design a package of units which, taken together, would constitute a 'core programme' of 'essential skills' which all persons occupying managerial posts in these organizations would be expected to have attained. The packages were frequently grouped into stages so that on first managerial appointment a junior management development (JMD) course would be offered which would teach basic management skills; on promotion to a grade where a person was managing other managers, an advanced management development programme (AMDP) would be triggered; and for those taking up senior posts with strategic responsibilities an executive development programme (EDP) would complete the suite of programmes. In addition to this core group of programmes designed to meet critical 'life-stages', the training and development functions, which appeared to have become more sophisticated, would, not untypically, also offer services designed to meet particular identified needs and in some instances they also offered internal consultancy OD-type services.

Not quite so integrated as this, but illustrative of the targeted advance towards training for 'managerial leadership' for line managers, is the case of Whitbread. Here, the departmental managers, at the Samlesbury and Magor 'superbreweries' had attended no less than three management leadership courses: 'Action Centred Leadership', 'Coverdale', and a 'Management Leadership Programme'. Each of these were built around one week full-time residential courses. The emphasis is upon skills-acquisition. Small group 'task teams' are typically formed and the Whitbread managers described how the challenges they faced were designed to get the 'adrenalin flowing'.

At Peugeot-Talbot, the whole production and manufacturing band of managers attended a Leadership Trust course. This programme included outdoor activities and emphasized problem-solving techniques using group methods with an open style of management. All the area managers had attended the course along with the manufacturing manager, and the manufacturing director. In Massey Ferguson, where the expanded role for middle-level line managers was particularly evident, the main thrust on the training front had been the encouragement of self-development. In these instances one was struck by the powerful reinforcement between simultaneous learning and role change. At the very least, the outcome from this interaction was the tremendous enthusiasm and optimism which these line managers were bringing to their expanding roles. Whether these qualities would be translated into meaningful behavioural and attitudinal changes among their subordinates (i.e. among supervisors, cell leaders and shopfloor workers) was more difficult to discern.

Running in parallel with these developments and adding a further fillip to the momentum already underway, were the attempts to identify critical 'managerial competencies'. The resultant competency tests were used in selection, appraisal, assessment centres, training and in personal development plans.

There were exceptions to this groundswell of activity on the management training front. In a few of the cases the training provision even for managers was extremely desultory – Smith & Nephew was a case in point. Also noteworthy is that even in the most sophisticated of cases where the training function was riding high and perhaps even enjoying a reputation extending beyond the organization's boundaries, there were typically large segments of the organization's managers who remained largely untouched by the paper provision. The legacy of neglect was such that there was a massive remedial job to be done. But perhaps the central point – and the one which flies in the face of most previous reports on management training in Britain – is that the job had at least begun.

A further front on which movement was occurring related to attempts to hold managers responsible for the development of their direct reports and indeed of their subordinates more generally. In part, this was done through listing 'development' as one of the mandatory items in the appraisal system. Another way was to try to establish the expectations that development was part of the culture of the place. In Lucas, development of the human resource is now a 'measurable' which is audited as part of the Competitiveness Achievement Plan system (see chapter 3).

Self-development forms the third side of the triangle. A number of the organizations were offering open-learning facilities and/or central 'libraries' of video and learning packages for extended hire. Less concrete, but nonetheless potentially important was the general encouragement and respect for self-development that was sometimes established. There was also an increasing use of 'personal development plans' accompanied by personal 'work-books' in which the individual manager logged his or her training needs analysis, strengths and weaknesses, targets, priorities and action plans on a rolling one-year cycle. Some of the more memorable self-development examples from a research-visit point of view were found, quite simply, in those instances where managers were struggling valiantly, on an individual basis, to master subjects such as accountancy or marketing in their spare time. Many of the newly appointed unit general managers in the health service were found engaged in this and their desks were often festooned with books on management accountancy. A similar rash of study had broken out at Massey Ferguson among the greatly reduced complement of general and line managers who, consequent to successive waves of redundancies, were coping with greatly expanded portfolios.

Attitudes and behaviour

One of the most impressive features of most of the line managers encountered (in contrast to staff and technical specialists) was the evident degree of confidence that they displayed. This con-trasted with the general state of disillusionment I had encoun-tered in a previous extensive study of managers conducted in the 1970s (Storey, 1980; 1983). The enduring impression in 1988 was of a stock of line managers who had a belief in, and a passion for, what they were doing. A plethora of examples spring to mind in relation to each of the 15 companies. There is space here to illustrate the point with just two examples.

The first person in question was an area manager of body-in-white in one of the car companies. He had left school at 15 years of age and joined the company as a trainee machine operator. He had taken up an apprenticeship and studied for City and Guilds on a one-day-a-week release scheme. He joined the toolroom and was engaged in designing jigs and tools. He then got involved in computer aided design and eventually in process supervision. On his present position as area manager he commented:

I love the motor industry and all that comes with it – the pressure, the demands and the crises. There's always something going on. I didn't like my period in design – there wasn't enough challenge or excitement, it was like working at the bottom of your garden. Production management is totally different. You need the right attitude to manage production, nothing gets me flapping, I have a common sense approach to managing people. I've been running body-in-white for five years now and I'd like eventually to run the plant.

A second memorable enthusiast was responsible for the paint shop in another of the car plants. The atmosphere was fairly hectic and problems concerning blemishes came thick and fast. But the manager in charge of the shop pointed out:

I know it may look pretty rough and I suppose it is. A few years ago I said to myself 'Sod this I need a quieter life' and so I tried setting up as a painter and decorator. It nearly drove me barmy! It was too quiet!

The importance of general attitude and shared meanings should not be underestimated. The 'interpretation of the lived experience' (Schutz, 1972) is achieved through a process of ordering experiences in social settings. The deeper level of social exchange between those in like positions can therefore not only be revealing, it also functions to shape the meaning of events. Instances of 'out of hours' dialogue revealed telling aspects of line managers' systems of meaning with regard to changes in labour management. One very memorable event occurred with a group of line managers from the car industry. It suggested ambivalence about the new programmes in their company.

The incident occurred during an after-midnight discussion in a large bedroom of one of the delegates at a weekend planning conference. About a dozen managers had gathered to continue the discussion following the closure of the bar. A very assertive plant manager was holding court. He was known as a 'bit of a character' and few dared cross him. He tended to set not only the agenda for discussion and banter but also the tone. The talk turned to reminiscences about the good old days of conflictual labour relations that they had all shared. Notable shop stewards who had made their mark in one apparently outrageous fashion or another were brought to mind and stories about them were swapped with glee. Allowing for the power of nostalgia (and the alcohol which was free and plentiful!) it seemed clear that an implicit shared understanding among this (admittedly macho) crowd was that 'at least we knew where we stood' under that regime. In contrast, they appeared to be saying the present arrangements with talk of 'involvement' and the like are all very ambiguous and uncertain . . . and what do you guys really make of it all?

Such events are important in the generation and maintenance of shared meanings. As such they are likely to colour responses to new initiatives. What was surprising was not so much this incident but its absence in many of the other companies where, on the contrary, the unofficial accounts seemed to echo the official ones. Line managers in the study, although probed and prodded from different angles, emerged as a pretty satisfied lot. Moreover, they were generally upbeat with regard to the new developments, organizational redesign, their changing roles and the related aspects of human resource management.

There were, however, certain features associated with the line manager's role which seemed likely to limit the smooth delivery of new human resource policies. First, the problem of lack of development of the human resource tends to reproduce itself. Managers who have themselves received little education and training are less likely to recognize or approve the need for investment in the training of their subordinates. The impoverishment of training and development is also part of a vicious circle which locks too many industrial and service organizations in Britain into a low-cost, low-wage, low-investment, bottom-end-of-the-market predicament.

Second, the frequency of reorganization in many of these companies with the creation of divisions, of territories, areas, business units, and even divisions within divisions was the source of massive ambiguity concerning the appropriate level at which a 'general manager' should assume responsibility for human resource management. Corporate level typically sought to preserve some authority over issues such as pensions, executive remuneration and total reward packages, and the control over the top tier of managers who may be regarded as a 'company resource'. But this left extensive uncertainty about whether for instance, new graduates should be similarly regarded and if so, for how long. Further, it was often left unclear whether corporate levels were trying to provide broad frameworks on policies across a whole catalogue of human resource areas or whether these matters were being left to 'local' discretion. In the course of the study it became evident that divisional general managers and business general managers were adopting different, frequently contradictory, stances with regard to these questions. Some had taken corporate-level silence as the cue to devise local strategies. Others had interpreted it as a wait-and-see message.

CONCLUSIONS

The role of senior and middle line managers appears to have been undergoing considerable change. In large measure this derives from organizational responses to marked environmental upheaval. Initiatives to improve viability and effectiveness have involved structural alterations including devolved organization and new forms of flexibility; accompanying these have been cultural changes such as new management styles which give renewed emphasis to customer orientation, innovation and competitiveness.

These tendencies have typically carried implications for the way the human resource is deployed and managed. It was found in the study that steerage with regard to these matters has increasingly been taken-up by operational managers of the organization rather than personnel specialists.

The investigation revealed that, contrary to speculative reports about the *demise* of the middle manager, occupants of these roles were exercising authority across a greatly expanded territory. The core production managers' jobs in particular had become more generalist; they were responsible for a wider range of staff and carried a broader remit. There was evidence to suggest that in some organizations these core line managers had seen their roles recast: first into a wider 'manufacturing manager' role and second, they had felt pressures and seen opportunities to extend it even further into a general 'business manager' role.

It was found that some adjustment had been made to recruitment and selection practices in order to upgrade the capabilities of people entering these more demanding roles but that there was still some considerable way to go to establish these more systematic practices across a broad front. The same applied to the provision being made for the training and development of these managers. Despite these points, the level of enthusiasm and commitment found among a large proportion of this smaller number of managers with extended responsibilities was impressively high. This enthusiasm had, however, not been matched, as yet, with the kind of integrated and strategic approach to human resource management that some analysts have suggested will be necessary if the organizational and role restructurings are to be carried through into sustained competitive performance.

There is an important final conclusion to this chapter on the line manager's role. There was very considerable evidence of transformation with *line managers as the objects of change*; there was much less evidence that this had as yet been carried through into similar behavioural and attitudinal changes at shopfloor level. Nonetheless, managerial staff are themselves a crucial component in the human resource and so even this degree of change is of significance. The extent to which it might have percolated to junior management levels and to supervisors is an issue we attend to in the next chapter.

Notes

1 For example, even recent assessments of changes to IR in the 1980s (Batstone, 1988; MacInnes, 1987; Bassett, 1986) are silent on the subject.
2 The path-breaking study *Beyond the Workplace* by Marginson et al. (1988) was largely confined to managers with a designated responsibility for personnel and industrial relations – that is, mainly specialists from the personnel function.

8

The Part Played by First Line Managers in the Management of Human Resources

The range of developments discussed in the previous chapters has impacted on the supervisor's role in a very marked way. The case studies revealed a number of common themes which surfaced with surprising regularity despite differences in industrial sector and in technological circumstances. The most evident of these commonalities were:

- an attempt to bolster the supervisor's role so that he or she would shoulder more extensive responsibilities

- an attempt to embrace the supervisor more decisively within managerial ranks – this being done, *inter alia*, by enhancing their terms and conditions and redesignating the role as that of first line manager (FLM)

- initiatives which sought to establish 'teamworking' on the shopfloor and thus which aimed to install 'team leaders' in place of foremen and to have FLMs as 'coordinators' of a number of different teams.

Paradoxically, these moves to enhance the supervisor's role are occurring at a time when the role itself has come under special scrutiny. In nearly one-third of the cases there was bullish talk about simply eradicating the role completely. In yet others, internal studies were being conducted with an open agenda as to the future of the role – if any. Ford Motor Company had two major studies of this kind running in parallel with this research. One of these was on a European-wide scale and involved managers from other European countries besides Britain. While not usually on such a scale, most of the other core case companies and a number of the wider panel of organizations were also giving some considerable thought to the 'first line' role.

Company reviews of this kind are not entirely new. Periodically the 'future of the supervisor' becomes a topical issue. What gave the theme an extra boost this time around was the fact that developments in the human resource management arena and initiatives of a related kind in the realms of quality, production and operations methodology, and in flexible manufacturing systems, were serving to pose very fundamental questions about the supervisor. What training would supervisors need to handle their new responsibilities? Was the supervisory level the right one to allocate these responsibilities to in the first place? What kind of person specification would be needed for this role in the future – would it be a graduate position or at least a technical-craft position? If teamworking was to be successfully installed would supervisors be needed? On a rather less speculative and future-oriented level there were other relevant questions concerning the here and now. Most centrally, these addressed the questions: what changes had already occurred to the role and how were incumbents responding? Such questions are clearly seen as especially pertinent when it is remembered that a complex mix of initiatives have recently descended upon the heads of first line managers. As argued earlier, these initiatives comprise both explicitly 'people-oriented' approaches and production/operations management-driven changes. Both sets are alike in that they typically depend for their implementation upon the behaviour of first line managers. For example, direct communication using such techniques as team briefing rest crucially on the ability of supervisors to be able to deliver in this area. Similarly, initiatives concerning employee motivation, involvement and direct participation are likewise usually predicated upon a competent and willing first line manager contribution.

Running in parallel with these production and operations management initiatives are a range of others including:

- total quality management (TQM)
- statistical process control (SPC)
- material requirement planning (MRP)
- just-in-time (JIT).

All carry implications for the supervisor and usually depend, in no small part, upon his or her commitment and capability. Further, greater technological sophistication along with a need to produce a wider range of products, a renewed downward pressure on costs, higher expectations of reliability and similar such higher performance standards are also further factors which imply an enhanced role for the production supervisor. Each of these has a profound effect on the way human resources are managed at the sharp end.

Previous studies, some of them stretching back nearly 50 years, raised issues about supervisors which were never completely resolved (Roethlisberger, 1945; Gardner and Whyte, 1945). Increasing complexity in industrial production following the Second World War, the proliferation of technical specialists and the rise of shop stewards each prompted questions about the coping capacity of the supervisor. Out of these conditions four (recurring) themes soon came to dominate the literature in this area:

- the tension and ambiguity of being the 'man-in-the-middle' between management and labour (e.g. Roethlisberger, 1945; Gardner and Whyte 1945)
- the much-vaunted 'demise' of the role (Hall, 1986, Kerr, 1986, Page, 1977)
- a contingency approach as a way to understand the variation in supervisors' roles by relating them to particular contexts (Thurley and Hamblin, 1963; Thurley and Wirdenius, 1973; Child and Partridge, 1982)
- seeking to 'model' different 'types' of supervisors: most notably contrasting the 'traditionalist' supervisor with the 'modern manager' variety (Klein, 1986; Nichols and Beynon, 1977).

There is insufficient space to undertake a full review of this literature here but what can usefully be pulled out from this body of previous work is a set of interlocking issues which still have relevance upon which our own research can shed further light. The most central of these issues is the extent to which, and the way in which, the present-day supervisory role is changing towards a new mode. It may be fairly said, however, that the current body of literature shows signs of seriously lagging behind the magnitude of the changes to the supervisory role in wide swathes of British industry.

THE EMERGENCE OF THE NEW MODEL SUPERVISOR

There was sufficient evidence to be found among the divergent tendencies to suggest that the underlying thrust in most of the recent managerial initiatives spelled a shift in the character of the supervisor towards the 'mini-manager' model. The concept implies a wider set of responsibilities for supervisors; more authority; higher pay and status; better training; more careful selection of persons entering the role; and enhanced competencies being required. Many of these features are captured in the interview with Dick Parham, Assistant Managing Director of Peugeot-Talbot. He begins with the speculative, anything-is-possible aspect but soon focuses on what has happened in practice:

> We have questioned whether we need supervisors. But after debate we decided to commit ourselves to this role. One consequence is that we have moved from ratios of 1:25 to 1:20. Some of our manufacturing managers even argue we should go so far as to have a ratio as low as 1:15. An alternative would have been to go for a chargehand type role or for far fewer supervisors each having a wide span of control and with a number of hourly-paid team leaders reporting to him and handling their own team briefings etc. We are trying to encourage our supervisors and area managers in particular to regard themselves as mini-bosses. But we don't go so far as to designate profit centres for them – cost centres yes . . . we operate very distinctive cost centres. Profit centres are another matter I believe them to be disruptive, leading to arguments about notional pricing. They are not appropriate in an interwoven organization.

Even recognizing the point that there were clear variations in supervisory behaviour between the companies, between

Figure 8.1   Types of supervisor

Traditional foreman	First line manager
Older	Younger
Waged	Salaried
Ambivalent about allegiances	Part of management
Ambivalent about capabilities and function	Clear and confident about capabilities and function
Poorly trained	Extensively trained
Poorly selected	Carefully selected
Easily diverted into progress-chasing	Priorities well mapped
Uncomfortable with IT and statistical data	Adept at handling data in various forms
Follows orders/transmits orders	Plans ahead, seeks continuous improvement
Looks to precedents	Forward looking
Union member	Non-union
Career blocked	Expects promotion

departments in the same company, and indeed between supervisors on different shifts in the same departments, there were nonetheless sufficient pointers to warrant a broad depiction of the nature of these changes which Parham describes. This depiction of the emerging 'new model' supervisor (the first line manager) can be contrasted with an ideal-typical 'traditional foreman'. The contrasts are shown in summary form in figure 8.1.

The figure is of course a stereotypical representation of the two types of role, but it does help to clarify certain real tendencies. Moreover, it is without doubt the case that most of the sample organizations which were attempting to restructure the supervisors' role held the FLM model as a point to aspire towards. Numerous managers across a range of organizations referred to the idea of their supervisors becoming like 'mini managing directors'. By this they meant a person who would not only ensure conformance with rule, budget and schedule but someone who would inspire, would be alert to market and customer needs and would be adept at creating appropriate responses to those needs.

Examples of the 'traditional supervisor' were not hard to find in the case companies. Where organizations were consciously seeking to transform themselves these characters inevitably soon became very evident. One only has to recall the graphic example from the Rover 'Working With Pride' Programme:

> I spent every Friday afternoon for six months with a dozen fore-men at a time on WWP. Some said, 'Its a load of bollocks Ken. . . .' It's difficult for them when they have got used to kicking arses for the past ten years. (plant director, Power Train)

This is a problem well recognized in all of the other manufacturing companies including, most noticeably, the motor companies of Ford, Jaguar and Peugeot. Many supervisors in the late 1980s were products of the get tough policies of the early part of the decade. This was especially so at Austin Rover where the Michael Edwardes' era was still fresh in the memory. The journey 'Back from the Brink' (Edwardes, 1983) was seen as being made possible in no small measure due to the robust performance of supervisors appointed at, or surviving into, that time. The general tenor of the plant director's observations was reiterated by many other managers throughout the company. A plant IR manager makes the point in a slightly different way:

> Since 1983 we've tried the face-to-face communications approach. It works to a degree but we are not so good at the supervisory level . . . enthusiasm for WWP [the Working with Pride Programme] is proportionate to level in the hierarchy, for supervisors it's often just seen as a gimmick. . . .
> (plant IR manager: Manuals)

Supervisors were frequently identified as the weak point. But, as in the above quote, one sometimes detected a set of reservations on the speaker's behalf also. The supervisor's attitudes were often used as the main 'excuse' for lack of progress. An aspect of this was, however, also the underlying view that as representatives of management 'at the sharp end' it was they who really 'knew what was going on'. Implicit therefore was sometimes a criticism of starry-eyed senior managers safely distanced from the action. Supervisors were thus simultaneously scapegoats, heroes and realists.

What had companies done to create the conditions which might encourage the growth of the 'new model supervisor'? The answer to this question varied across the companies – not so much in the types of things done but more in the extent to which things had or had not been done. In certain cases the reality was that precious little in concrete terms had been undertaken: the 'mini-managing director' talk was mere rhetoric. But for the rest, a fairly common pattern was discernible.

The supervisors/first line manager's position had first of all been clarified by cutting out chargehands and general foremen. The remaining supervisors had then been given extra responsibilities: these included, for example, the task of recording and analysing production and quality data in computerized form. It also meant the removal of specialist supervisory positions such as quality control and the placing of these responsibilities in the hands of the relevant zone supervisor who thus assumed sole charge of his or her area.

It was normal to find that the upgraded position would be marked by a retitling such as 'head of shift operations' (HOSO), 'first line manager' (FLM) or 'module leader' (ML). Typically, there would be fierce competition for these posts: not so much because the terms and conditions were enhanced, but rather in consequence of the fact that as the supervisory positions were phased out the former supervisors were in danger of being returned to operator ranks. In one facility, for example, 60 supervisory posts were removed and the reorganisation gave rise to only 20 FLM positions. Not only that, competition for these new posts was also opened up to graduates and to the former chargehands (the chargehand level was at the same time eradicated).

The actual work activity of supervisors operating in the traditional mode often amounted to walking around, engaging in technical troubleshooting and chasing up shortfalls in materials and components. They were not perceived as being very good at managing people. In particular, they were criticized for evading responsibility for counselling and discipline. Restructuring often resulted in FLMs being clearly held accountable for administration and 'man management'. These changes were accompanied by up grading of the operator role. In manufacturing and process industries the essence of the shift was towards a wider set of responsibilities. A notable innovation was the creation of technical operators or operator technicians (op techs) who were retrained and given multi-skilled roles. Op techs were given problem-solving responsibilities whereas, in the former system, they rarely had to think as all problems were handled by chargehands. In future, op techs will operate in teams and are being trained to a level which allows up to 25 per cent of their function to be that of handling minor maintenance and repair. (In some locations the complementary move is to arrange for the craft maintenance crews reciprocally to spend up to 25 per cent of their time on operational duties.)

Another adjustment to the upgraded supervisor role is that they are now involved in 'managerial matters' such as attending review and action-planning meetings. In one plant it was found that whereas up to 1987 the supervisors had typically not been invited to any meetings, by 1988, following the introduction of FLMs, they were attending production, safety, planning and engineering meetings. A number of them were even engaged in making presentations.

Further steps were taken by devoting far more resources to the careful selection of new supervisors. Psychometric tests were often used and qualifications, 'leadership potential' and 'attitudes' were taken into account rather than relying on 'Buggins Turn' or simply promoting the most technically competent. The policy of seeking to install more graduates into supervisory posts was also being revamped following hiccups in the past with graduates who were found to be uncomfortable with on-line positions when they aspired rather more to staff posts in design and the like. In each of the engineering-type organizations a number of successful examplars of the 'tuned-in' graduates were proudly paraded as pointers to the future model.

But there were problems here. Typically, the traditional supervisors held no qualifications. In those process sites where they had successfully applied for the new posts of head of shift they could theoretically aspire to career advancement into further managerial grades. Under the prevailing system of shift payment and overtime supplements their earning levels exceeded, however, the initial graduate grades by some £3000 to £4000 per annum. In practice, therefore, the new grades were often not seen as part of a career path. In a number of cases, entitlements to overtime payments were removed upon the regrading. But even in these situations, the FLMs were not typically regarded by themselves or others as fully integrated into the management stream. While the revamped roles were described as 'very demanding' and involved responsibilities for planning, administration, counselling and disciplining, the extent to which FLMs and others of this rank would, in practice, fully embrace the spirit and letter of the new model remained an open question. Middle managers still tended to complain that these 'new' supervisors were continuing to show resistance in taking full responsibility for discipline. Oral and written warnings remained largely the province of those at departmental manager rank.

Hence, while the number of levels of management and supervision had typically been reduced and while, in consequence, first line manager roles had been expanded considerably and their selection, training and involvement in meetings had all been radically improved, the way in which they handled human resource management issues had, in the main, not altered to the same degree. Senior managers nonetheless appeared sanguine and even optimistic about this. The salary bill for supervisors had been considerably cut and the argument was propounded that the restructuring had put in place the conditions which would allow markedly different behaviour once the present generation of supervisors had passed through.

In addition, special training programmes for supervisors, designed explicitly to engender a culture change and to equip supervisors for the 'new model' role were a regular feature. At Rover, for example, the training schools at Longbridge and Cowley had been geared-up to process practically the whole supervisory stream using modules of full-time courses lasting as much as a week at a time. A further support was provided by adding 'line trainers' to the zones. These individuals who were paid a supplement for the training contribution helped to 'free-up' the supervisors from regular hands-on training thereby giving them the opportunity to think, to plan, to look for improvements: in sum, to manage.

Another element was the spread of formal performance appraisal systems into the supervisory ranks. Some two-thirds of the supervisors were being subject to managerial-style performance review and appraisal interviews. Derecognition of the unions representing these 'upgraded supervisors' was not always a feature, but there was a tendency to emphasize the 'managerial' status of the new positions. The reorganizations surrounding these moves also often led to a greater divide opening up between them and the shopfloor. For example, where the chargehand role had also been removed this meant that any demotion from FLM or head of shift operations would be viewed as taking, in effect, two steps down the ladder not just one.

IMPLEMENTING THE NEW MODEL

The actual implementation of the desired model naturally varied between the case companies. Each placed the emphasis rather differently and each encountered different levels of resistance. The purpose of the next section is to reveal how the first-line management tier was implicated in human resource management initiatives and to bring to the surface some of the problems encountered. For purposes of illustration, just four cases are picked out. In the first case, Birds Eye, the prime emphasis was in fact upon establishing teamworking but the so-called AMs ('assistant managers') were envisaged as playing a crucial part in the revamped organizational structure. At Whitbread Breweries, the old-style 'supervisor' was supposedly abolished and FLMs (first line managers) were established. At Eaton Corporation, by way of contrast, supervisors as such were retained but even here the aspiration was to relaunch the role in such a way as to approximate to the Birds Eye and Whitbread Models. Finally, at Ford Motor Company the less dramatic approach similar to that at Eaton was also followed but the steps taken to restructure the supervisor's role were nonetheless very evident.

Birds Eye

This company had set about an extensive restructuring. Facilities at Yarmouth and Acton had been closed in 1986 and production was concentrated in revamped premises at Lowestoft and Gloucester. At these locations the supervisors' jobs were radically altered as a consequence of large-scale and technologically-sophisticated capital investment accompanied by a root-and-branch re-examination of working methods and organization.

Through the 'Workstyle' programme the company looked for a high level of shopfloor commitment to quality and it sought functional flexibility across a range of jobs. In pursuit of these objectives teamworking was introduced. This naturally had repercussions on line management. Each team decided for itself which person would cover which particular job at any given time. The extent of the rotation was entirely given over to the team, and first line management withdrew from this type of allocative task. In addition, other responsibilities which were hitherto part of the remit of supervisors were also devolved to the team. These included the organization of work, quality, and the meeting of cost and tonnage targets. Each team was designed to be a largely self-managing entity.

There were no officially appointed team leaders. Managers said, 'We wanted each team to have its own identity; they could develop their own informal leadership.' But a key point is that each member of a team was expected to be fully flexible across the whole range of jobs and tasks covered by that team – and that included minor maintenance. Some managers now say they actually went further on this than was absolutely necessary because it was later realized that not every person needs to be able and willing to do every other job just so long as the majority are able and willing to.

The supervisors were taken out completely. The management hierarchy now shows a product manager (responsible for example, for frozen vegetables) who has reporting to him usually two assistant managers (AMs), one for each shift. Beneath the AM are the teams themselves.

The design of the AM's role was clearly crucial. Before teamworking there were traditional supervisors. The redefinition of the role recognized the group's responsibility for its own organization and allocation of work and achievement of objectives. The AM's responsibilities were also spelled out: they include final responsibility for health and safety, quality, auditing team performance, advising the production manager, planning, identifying training needs, and, in the final analysis, discipline.

Now this last, in particular, opens up the real possibility that AMs would revert to a supervisory role. As one senior manager argued, 'At the end of the day we have to have a single person to carry the can, someone has to have ultimate responsibility.' This, not unnaturally leads some of the AMs to be 'too interventionary' for the liking of senior managers. These AMs claim they have to 'keep on top' of the employees. Others have, however, 'backed-off too far'. In training sessions with senior management the AMs were inclined to look for a blueprint or at least formal guidance on how they were supposed to respond – when should they 'go in' to sort out a problem in one of the teams? They complained that they got no real answers to such questions from senior managers. As one AM put it:

> We get no proper support. We are supposed to let the teams look after themselves and allow them to learn from their own mistakes. Yet we carry the can if things go wrong. Under Workstyle we get criticized for being too interventionary and also criticized for standing back. If we ask to be told about the guidelines for intervention we are told, 'It's up to you. That's where your skills of judgement comes into play.' Fine words, but they don't solve my problem.

In British terms, the total package represents a radical change. But dilemmas still certainly remain. Management admit that they have not yet fully thought through the implications for the assistant managers. Some of the latter still revert to tasks which they feel comfortable with such as 'fetching cartons'; and the engineering equivalents find it difficult to resist 'getting their fingers in the grease'.

The latter problem is putting a brake on yet more radical scenarios with perhaps fully integrated production-engineering teams fully flexible with a technically-qualified AM 'assisting' a range of them. 'Would you then even need the production managers?' a senior manager asked. At the moment, while the TGWU and the production workers have 'bought into' Workstyle and teamworking, the AEU and the maintenance craftsmen have secured exemption – for the time being at least! The main result of this is that the aspiration for fully integrated teams with technically qualified assistant managers overseeing flexible operatives and maintenance technicians has been thwarted. As a result, the people-management methods cannot be yet said to have undergone a radical step-change. The teams are certainly operating in a way which is different from what went before, but the variabil-ity in the way the AMs play their roles indicates that retrogres-sion to the previous supervisor-operative relationship remains a possibility.

Whitbread

Whitbread, our second case example, bears many of the hall-marks of the previous case. It too has rationalized by closing marginal facilities and concentrating production in a few capital-intensive sites. This strategy has been accompanied by a thorough review of its human resource provision – with special attention paid to its managerial and supervisory structure.

In formal terms, supervisors were dispensed with in the early to mid-1980s. They were replaced by 'first line managers'. The FLMs, described by senior line management as marking a 'key departure' are officially regarded as unambiguously part of management. The former supervisory negotiating group was disbanded and FLMs in consequence now have no negotiating rights. As part of management they are also not paid overtime and, unlike the shopfloor, (or, as they are termed at Whitbread the 'managed group') they are subject to annual appraisal.

The basic organizational structure at brewery level is from production manager through departmental manager (e.g. head brewer or canning manager) and down immediately to FLM. Below this level there are sometimes 'senior operatives', also known as 'line leaders'. These last are in effect 'chargehands'. They are graded at E compared with the rest of the team who would be on grade D. The line leaders are operatives who co-ordinate breaks and who personally substitute for individuals during break periods.

The FLMs are thus supposed to be able to 'stand back' from the supervisory role. They have their own offices where they keep performance and employee records. Their role was described by one FLM as based on 'anticipation' and routine checking. Thus, one shift manager in the canning department said:

> I spend about 80 per cent of my time wandering around the line – checking that the beer is available, that cans are available, anticipating any potential people problems. Basically, a lot of the job is just checking that everything is running as it should. I might investigate, for example, a squeaking conveyor.

In this high-capitalization, high-throughput industry their span of control is remarkably generous averaging around 1:6. In the maintenance area the ratio was 1:12. Many of them said they had been on training courses to help them in their FLM role and they instanced three-day Coverdale courses and courses in Action Centred Leadership. A number of the FLMs were of graduate intake but these were not in the majority.

According to some senior line managers the FLM role is, in theory, a highly responsible one. While they admit there is still some 'legacy' from the supervisory role, new recruits to the FLM position are seen as potentially ready to act fully as a part of management:

> They are willing to be responsible for decisions and for the men on their shift; the traditional supervisors said to their men: 'It's not me, I've just been told to say . . .' they wanted to be Mr Nice Guy all the time but now our FLMs have to make decisions. They do the suspensions and they can even dismiss. Admittedly, they cannot authorize expenditure or make quality variances but otherwise they have full rein.

This departmental manager also claimed he consulted his FLMs on the annual budget: 'They see the budget for overtime etc., and they have control over budget sundries – they have to put things in priority order.'

Although the creation of the FLM role was a consciously planned move on the part of the company and although it was part of a wider programme of change, the degree to which the role really does depart significantly from that of the previously-existing supervisory position remains doubtful. There was mixed opinion among the FLMs interviewed at the two superbreweries (Samlesbury and Magor) as to whether they really were different from traditional supervisors. Indeed, a small majority tended towards the view that the position had drifted back to approximate the old supervisory role. A phrase a number of them used was 'a rose by any other name is still a rose'. The FLMs have their own separate salary structure and senior managers saw this as a problem. Some of the FLMs said that the main change so far had been simply that they were now no longer paid overtime! Nearly all FLMs were, however, still doing their weekly briefings and most were prepared to appraise the manuals – although this had so far been blocked by the unions.

There appeared also to be some contradiction between Whitbread's policy to move towards 'harmonization' and the policy to emphasize and clarify the distinction between managers and 'the managed group'.

At Magor, South Wales, the managed group is supposed to be involved in a teamwork arrangement – managing their own work allocation and job rotation and being fully flexible between operative jobs. The FLMs are also the only members of 'management' to be required to work shifts and they are often referred to in fact as 'shift managers'. Given the emphasis upon the FLM role it was a surprising oversight to find that their doors were still signposted with this title.

The FLMs on the engineering side manage electricians and fitters, welders and storemen, in addition to a few operatives who monitor equipment for them. These FLMs were still engaged in some 'hands-on' activities though they claimed it accounted for only between 5–10 per cent of their time. This, they claimed was really training – for example, teaching how to overhaul a pump. Though all of them added that if there was a major breakdown 'we all get involved'. The reaction from the fitters to the routine hands-on involvement by the FLMs was said to be tolerant and more in the nature of 'leg pulling rather than genuine aggro'.

Similarly, although the teams might be involved in self-allocation in the process areas, in engineering the FLM would typically hand out the jobs. Also, among the maintenance crews, fewer FLMs had experienced any people-management training.

The other key factor which tended to lead some FLMs in both engineering and production to say they were 'really just supervisors' was the perceived lack of opportunity for career development. For the non-graduates this seemed to be a fairly realistic assessment. Moreover, FLMs, although they used to be involved in making selection decisions for entrants into their sections, now report that this practice has been undermined by the number of internal transferees who are 'dumped on them'. This was one of a catalogue of complaints which fed on the gap between rhetoric of being 'integrated into management' and the perceived reality. Another example concerned the annual appraisal system. This supposedly could lead to extra percentage points in merit pay. But the system was regarded as at once both divisive and insignificant. A typical comment was, 'Last year I don't know whether I got anything above the average – how can that be motivating?'

Nevertheless, a significant minority of the FLMs – mainly the younger ones – did identify strongly with their managerial role. They had attended all the leadership courses and expressed enthusiasm about them; they had additionally got involved in further developmental activities both inside and outside the company. This group had clearly caught the 'managerial bug'. They exuded confidence in relation to their present role and in relation to future career prospects. As one expressed the point, 'We have the opportunity now to get more involved in management if we want to: it's really optional.'

Eaton Limited

The redesign in human resource management in this American-owned engineering company, manufacturing truck axles in Manchester, illustrates the importance of the change to the supervisor's role in such a scheme. The conscious philosophy-led shift in human resource management in this company, at all its sites, rested in large measure on moving responsibility from traditional IR and personnel specialists to the line managers. The expansion of the supervisor's role and the increase in responsibilities was a key element in this. Production foremen became heads of cost centres. They were given training to equip them to take on budgeting duties, quality responsibilities and, most centrally, they became more clearly responsible for managing their people. This involved helping to select, monitor, train, discipline, communicate with and motivate them in order to meet forecasts on a whole array of measures.

A quotation from such a cost-centre supervisor helps to set the scene. He describes the change in his role in recent years:

> In the early 1970s we each had 40 or so men to supervise. We now have about 16. At that time we had no special training for the role and the men were on PBR which meant that our role was even further diminished. We had no involvement in recruiting; we couldn't plan; we were there to be kicked. Now, we are very much involved in the selection of our operatives. We make an input into the scheduling plans for our cost centres and into the budgeting for our areas, including for example, the tooling budget. All this

carries through in the way we manage our people. We get more information from the top and we are able to pass that down in our fortnightly briefing sessions. We also are actively involved in employee counselling.

To complement this shift in emphasis, management was very consciously pulling-back the previously hands-on industrial relations manager. The interventionary trouble-shooting style was now considered defunct. In its place a new human resource manager had been appointed. He saw his role as that of distant adviser; an internal consultant. He made it abundantly clear that tackling disciplinary problems, controlling absence and other similar duties were, in future, to be the province of the supervisor and they were not to slough these off to personnel. If the 'Eaton Philosophy' (see chapter 3) was to be implemented it was crucial that line managers, and supervisors in particular, would take centre stage in handling people.

The reaction of the supervisors, as the quotation above indicated, was on the whole very positive. Yet the supervisors were prone to holding dual perspectives on the change. Even the individual cited above, whose tone indicated a receptive frame of mind, nonetheless also talked about 'extra duties', such as curbing lateness and absenteeism, being 'pushed on to us'. Doubts were expressed about whether they had been adequately rewarded for this role. These cost-centre managers also remained as union members, represented by what was then the ASTMS. They undoubtedly retained a collective consciousness. The talk was of 'the company attitude' as being one of 'getting what they can from you' and of the consequent need for supervisors to have their own union. Yet at the same time these supervisors were often highly critical of the shopfloor. As one said:

A key problem is lack of shopfloor responsibility – especially with regard to the sickness absence scheme. They get full pay for up to 12 weeks absence. A few spoil it for the many.

It is useful to look at the role from the vantage point of the next level up – that is production superintendent. These post holders tend to agree that the restructured supervisors are in a somewhat ambiguous position. The 'foremen' are regarded as not fully part of the management. Ideally, more information would be passed on so as to assist in co-opting them into management more emphatically. But the limits on so doing was explained by one superintendent:

> The MD says that its the line's role to decide, for example, whether to pay a guy who has been absent. But how can we (superintendents or supervisors) do this when we don't get accurate personnel records from the personnel department?

The supervisors at Eaton are almost entirely time-served craftsmen. The training they have had to equip them for the supervisory role had relied in the past mainly on the NEBSS courses (the National Examination Board for Supervisory Studies). But increasingly this was seen as inappropriate for the new role they were expected to play at Eaton. So far, the company had not settled on a pattern of training which it felt was fitted to its particular needs. Some of the supervisors who had embraced the new role most enthusiastically had embarked on external training courses with company support. Hence, a number were studying computing, finance and economics on the modules offered by the Institute of Industrial Managers.

At Eaton, the general picture was of a traditional work setting with a legacy of traditional attitudes. Many supervisors, despite the programmes associated with the Eaton Philosophy, still talked of 'a wall between management and shopfloor'. The composition of supervisors and indeed of superintendents was overwhelmingly time-served craftsmen many of whom had served as union representatives on their path to promotion. They were alert to 'double standards' applying to staff jobs and the shopfloor and cited the problem of exercising discipline on lateness and early leaving when the staff were seen to behave in this way. This type of problem was continually raised in justification of the reluctance to accept the responsibility for disciplining which they felt had been 'sidled-off onto us'. The supervisors thus welcomed certain aspects of their new role but resented others – in particular the 'personnel problems' of lateness, absence and the like. When these aspects to the job had to be activated, the supervisors tended to revert to their traditional personae; but when issues of planning, budgeting, progress chasing and similar activities were to the fore they tended to embrace the role more enthusiastically.

The company had tried graduate engineers in the supervisory positions but, according to the superintendents, without much success. They 'couldn't stand the pace' it was said. All of the supervisors interviewed for this study had been promoted from the shopfloor – either from within Eaton or recruited from other local engineering companies. Through their experiences they had been familiarized with the traditional supervisor role. The attributes of the new model (as depicted in the right hand column of figure 8.1) had been impressed upon them by the managing director. But the degree of training to equip them to make such a shift had been extremely deficient and the infrastructural underpinning to allow them to enact the preferred role was also inadequate. As a consequence, while there had been some changes to the supervisory or first-line-management role these fell considerably short of the expectations of senior managers. The discrepancies were a source of general dissatisfaction not only for managers but the current cohort of supervisors. Hence, the implications of human resource management for these supervisors were simultaneously perceived as both positive and negative.

Ford Motor Company

As part of its wider package of reform, Ford is addressing the role of the supervisor with particular concern. A not inconsiderable stimulus to this exercise is the potential cost savings which could be made from any rationalization. There are currently some 2400 on the salary role. In 1988 they were earning between £10,000 to £18,000 per annum. When superannuation contributions and the like are taken into account supervision represents an ongoing cost to Ford of Britain of approximately £48 million a year. But direct cost alone has not been the only issue which has prompted such scrutiny of the supervisory role at Ford.

A prime driver in the attention paid to recasting the role has been the desire to inject the tenets of 'leadership' into the factories. In the late 1980s two major studies were being conducted into the role of supervision and its future. One was a joint study agreed with Clive Jenkins and involving Ford and ASTMS in reviewing the implications for supervisors of changes such as the introduction of microelectronic control-technology into more and more production areas, the devolution of responsibility to the shopfloor and the developing role of 'group leader'. The basic question was: what would be the future role for the supervisor? (In some US locations, Ford plants were operating without them.) The second study was part of a Ford of Europe review sponsored by Manufacturing under the guidance of Stuart Hymer. This, known as the 'leadership study' was regarded as the more significant of the two. A number of line managers from Europe had been seconded to the team and they were seeking to construct 'images' and 'profiles' of the kind of 'leaders' who would be needed in factories of the future. The profiles would include capabilities, knowledge, responsibilities and even demeanour. From such a constructed image one practical outcome would be a more targeted plan for training. But the review went beyond that. There was wide-ranging questioning about whether plants would be moving to teamworking or perhaps more intensive supervision. A key question was whether supervisors would be needed at all.

Another line of enquiry was to follow the logic of particular contingencies, leading perhaps to very different arrangements in, say, a body shop with a highly automoted environment and no supervisors, in contrast to trim areas with teams and elected leaders. Part of the remit also was to consider, even if supervisors were not the chosen group, the critical levels in manufacturing at which 'managerial leadership' would in future be exercised. The implications for selection and for training were to be the key learning points here.

The backcloth to these major studies was formed by certain contemporary pressures. Product market competition was universally regarded as more severe; the area management concept had already been introduced; investment in new technology was increasing; there had been a 'blitz' on Statistical Process Control at superintendent level and the question of supervisory involvement was pressing; an age-profile analysis of the 2400 supervisors had revealed a skewing at the over 50 age-band; and, not least, the continuous-improvement policy on quality was increasingly seen as vital and, when measured against the requirements for this, too many foremen were seen as falling short.

The gap between future aspiration and present stock was made evident by the research for this project at Dagenham and Halewood. In the latter, interviews with supervisors and superintendents were supplemented by observational 'shadowing' of certain individuals as they went about their normal routines. The most remarkable feature to emerge was how the traditional model had survived intact despite the extensive changes made to surrounding working methods and the attempted shifts in culture. Part of this change was indicated for example, at Halewood, by the arrival of a new assistant plant manager from Holland who marked the changes to come by personally visiting every single supervisor at Halewood. He asked each one to list their main problems. He was perceived to be listening seriously to them and he consequently set up task forces of process engineers to tackle the problems identified. Supervisors were well paid, were on salary and enjoyed BUPA cover and similar managerial/staff status benefits.

And yet, as noted, the elements of the 'traditional supervisor' were very much in evidence. The working environment was described as 'unforgiving'. Supervisors said they were made to feel only as good as their last shift. Performance was closely monitored. Problems for the supervisor began each day at the very outset – that is between 7.30 to 8.00 a.m. with the task of ensuring an appropriate manning-up of the line for the shift. There was a strict model-mix (for example, at Halewood at the time of this research it was 10 vans, 6 Escorts and 24 Orions per hour down one of the lines or 1.5 minutes per vehicle for assembly). A three minute line stoppage meant two lost cars. The supervisor had to balance the model-mix with the appropriate manning (work study had calculated the number of people required for various build volumes and mixes). He also had to ensure that the stock and tool check was in accord with requirements; and during the shift he had to monitor quality standards.

The message had reached these foremen that 'in future' there was going to be less emphasis in the military-style overseeing and rather more on modern concepts of 'leadership'. But given the pressures of the everyday work situation – at least in the final assembly areas – one could only view these scenarios with scepticism. The pressures were self-evidently high. The trim-assembly areas were mainly staffed by boisterous youths; they maintained a banter with each other and with the supervisors. The atmosphere had a note of bravado and tension. This was fuelled to an extent by supervisors themselves who dramatized their roles by talking of adrenalin flow, of excitement, and of how previous incumbents of the role had 'been broken' by the pressures. One of the supervisors whom I shadowed rather revealingly referred to how he consciously recomposed himself when returning to his line. He had to 'slip into character' and 'put-on-a-face' to survive, he said.

Thus the 'new manager' model for supervisors faced a tough environment here. Adversarial relations were not far below the surface. A constant pressure on the foreman was the loss of schedule. If the critical man-up period before 8.00 a.m. was too slow it was not difficult to 'lose' 20 cars in the morning. The supervisor was held to account for these results. He needed the cooperation of a range of people – not least his line operatives and the stock suppliers to the line area.

Yet, in many regards, Halewood supervisors did meet the criteria of the first line manager model as represented in figure 8.1. A number of them were young (early to mid-30s), they were salaried and well paid, they appeared confident and capable and recent appointees had been carefully selected. But, conversely, they were not particularly well trained; their priorities were, of necessity, short term and they were not clear about how they slotted into management or whether they could expect promotion.

At one level higher up were the superintendents. Approximately a dozen supervisors reported to each of these. (In parts of the plant the 'senior foreman' role survived. These were described as the right-hand-men of the superintendent. But their numbers had been halved in the past few years and many of their functions had disappeared. The future of this tier was very much in doubt.) As for superintendents themselves they, more so than the supervisors, tended to represent the traditional legacy. Many of them had been promoted for the robust way in which they had handled labour relations in the 1970s and early 1980s. They were out of tune with the late 1980s talk of 'managerial leadership' and employee involvement. Indeed, they tended to reminisce about the classic conflicts of past years. The list of their training needs was extensive: method study, SPC, material handling, human resource management, preventive maintenance, time management, legislation, new technology, problem solving, continuous improvement and quality. This shopping list of needs had been drawn up by a member of management in conjunction with an ASTMS representative. Its length and breadth indicated the perceived gap between present capability of a number of superintendents and the desired state. The 'traditional supervisor' model was evidently a problem – arguably a bigger problem – at superintendent level. Perhaps it should not be a matter of surprise that, as we have recorded, in other settings this tier of line management has simply been removed.

DISCUSSION

Across the case companies there had been a declared intent, especially at senior management levels, to transform the supervisory role. The 'traditional supervisor' stereotype was held up as the point of the compass to steer away from. This chapter has used empirical data to point up what this has meant in practice.

The general picture – at least as a preferred model – was fairly uniform. The prevailing view was that a new first line management tier had to be introduced. Few of the existing supervisory stock were thought likely to be suitable candidates. This was not perceived as, in itself, a major cause for concern because it was envisaged that there would be far fewer FLM posts than the current headcount at the supervisory level. Enactments of the policy did not result, however, in a uniform trend with regard to the supervisor-to-worker ratio. Some companies, were found to be increasing the numbers of supervisors as was the case at Peugeot, and this had the effect of reducing the ratio from 1:25 to 1:20 in its Ryton plant. Others, taking advantage of teamworking arrangements and new technology, and responding in particular to the opportunities for cost savings, were moving in the reverse direction and were reducing the number of supervisors. Nonetheless, in both scenarios the declared intent was to upgrade the first-line role in terms of the responsibilities it would carry.

The switch between 'traditional supervisor' and 'first line manager' had been clearly attempted in a number of the mainstream cases. This does not mean they necessarily succeeded in attaining it in practice. Evidently there were instances such as at Whitbread and Birds Eye where whole tiers had been removed: most typically chargehands, supervisors and superintendents. In their place had been installed assistant managers, first line managers or heads of shift who were fewer in number, usually salaried, more carefully selected, younger, more extensively trained, privy to more managerial information and generally more fully integrated into managerial ranks. Their roles were expanded: they embraced aspects of planning, scheduling, agreeing budgets, being responsible for a cost centre, ensuring quality and being the main managerial representatives in human resource management. If operating in production environments they would also typically have an expanded remit in that, reflecting the manufacturing manager model (discussed in the preceding chapter), they would be responsible also for maintenance, quality, materials, people and general housekeeping in their 'zones'.

This mini-manager concept was, however, found to be compromised even in those instances where it had been pursued most vigorously. Typically, among the FLM stock were considerable numbers of former supervisors who continued to regard their 'new' role in the 'old' way. The supposed integration into management was usually highly partial. In most cases there was little expectation that this was the first step on a career ladder. Salary structures were an anomaly which exacerbated this problem. They occasionally entailed a significant reduction in earnings for anyone graduating from a supervisory/first line management position into the junior managerial tier. In British Rail there could be a reduction of as much as 40 per cent of total previous earnings arising from the loss of overtime payments and similar 'specials'. The nature and degree of training was usually too limited for the kind of expanded role envisaged by the planners. The opportunity to 'manage' and plan ahead was frequently undercut by everyday production demands – not infrequently this was, in any case, the preferred stance of the incumbents. There remained a lack of clarity about what the new model roles really entailed.

The expectation, or hope, of senior managers in these cases was that as a new generation of FLM comes through, (many of them possibly graduates) the full potential of the restructured role will be realized and that retrogression will be less likely. For the time being, the average FLM and supervisor spends most of his or her time attending to operational matters of a day-to-day kind, materials supply and machine performance. Supervisors in the study tended to view 'managing the human resource' as an attractive idea in the abstract but in practice they were chary about moving from a proceduralized system where they simply followed rules (however begrudgingly) to a state of affairs where they were expected to exercise judgement – and be accountable for that judgement. The anxiety which was felt on this count they expressed in terms of 'not being backed-up' by senior management or by personnel.

First line managers were, as the case studies demonstrated, usually at the front line of moves towards human resource management. They were expected to embrace and embody the new 'managerial styles'; they were the key channels in the open two-way communications; they were to be monitored for 'involving' employees and for 'developing' them. The obvious shortfalls between aspirations and delivery in these and similar regards led to renewed scrutiny of the role. The typical way forward was seen to be to have fewer, but higher quality, first line managers. Even where this type of restructuring had begun, there were many evident tensions which persisted as is shown in this chapter. Nonetheless, at the time of writing (1990–1), the type of model described here as being actively sought across a broad front in 1988, continues to be the objective for an even more extensive population of companies.

The biggest difference found between the case companies was between those which had sought to enact the model in a determined way and those which had merely mused about it. The sources of the variations stemmed from factors associated with the characteristic features of the different production processes and from factors related to social organization and the power of symbols.

To take the first of these, production processes, it seemed fairly evident that, for example, the sheer pressures of production as witnessed at Ford's Halewood and Dagenham assembly plants made the shopfloor realization of the new model role highly problematical. Despite the rhetoric, the production imperative to 'man-up' the line at the start of each shift and to avoid 'losing cars' at any point during the shift, was the paramount message which Ford's supervisors had internalized. The incessant pace of the assembly areas and the young workforce employed to match that pace, generated a climate which put a premium on the traditional 'gaffer' role. The contrast was immediately evident in the non-assembly buildings on the Ford sites. Machining areas were far more relaxed and the relationship between supervisors and operators very different.

The contrast was more marked still in the process technology settings as found at Whitbread and Birds Eye – two of the other cases extensively used in this chapter. In Whitbread in particular, a number of the newly designated first line managers had enthusiastically embraced the role. And yet even in these more favourable circumstances there was, as we saw, by no means a smooth take-up of the FLM model. To explain this, the second set of factors referred to will be found useful – that is factors concerning social organization and symbols.

The 'reluctant managers' in these favourable settings were, in the main, schooled in the lore of the traditional foreman. They were older and many had worked as supervisors for previous employers – in the case of Whitbread breweries a remarkable number had experience as marine engineers in the merchant navy. In consciously seeking to manage a change of culture, senior managers had manipulated some symbols to signify a new order but these were insufficient to counterbalance the range of signs which persuaded the sceptical that things were pretty much the same. Hence, the name change to 'first line manager' was not accorded very much significance by those who could glimpse little realistic future as a 'manager'. Without that glimpse even training courses on 'leadership' could make little impression. Those FLMs who had 'caught the management bug' had been receptive to the new set of symbols because they relished the planning and data-handling aspects of the role and they could envisage a future in a management career. It was these who had gone to the trouble of taking the old 'shift supervisor' name plates off their office doors. For the rest, the companies' paradigmatic shift (in Birds Eye, Whitbread and Eaton) had been too ambivalent to persuade most supervisors that they personally should buy into a new mode of operating. There were, on balance, simply too many contra-symbols (including middle and senior managers' general demeanour towards them) to overcome the power of inertia.

9

Trade Unions and Industrial Relations

The purpose of this chapter is to examine how managers in those organizations which were seeking to bring about a new approach to people management had acted with regard to trade unions and industrial relations. This is in the context of the mainstream companies which were all unionized and in many cases extensively so. Given that the new human resource initiatives carry, as we have seen, a considerable element of 'individualism' as opposed to 'collectivism' in their composition, there is clearly plenty of scope for tension between the two paradigms. How would this be worked through and accommodated? Four main scenarios seemed possible:

- the unions and the joint procedure arrangements might be directly attacked so as to leave an open field for the new approaches
- they might simply be ignored in a way which is tantamount to derecognition
- the established and the new approaches might be run in parallel
- the joint arrangements might be integrated into the overall new approach.

The evidence accumulated in this chapter will show that, broadly speaking, it was the third path which was followed by most of the case companies. In other words, the British mainstream organizations were operating *dual arrangements*. It is note-worthy, in addition, that elements of each of the other three possibilities were to one degree or another encountered in some of the 15 cases. Nonetheless, it was 'dualism' which best expresses what was largely happening.

In addition to exploring how the variations in approach to this issue might be explained, it is also intended in this chapter to give some feel for the dynamics of the relationship between human resource management initiatives and the ongoing collectivist arrangements.

There is practically no previous literature which tackles such issues. The HRM literature which has already been referred to in earlier chapters of this book has been almost totally silent on the subject of trade unions and industrial relations. Conversely, the industrial relations' reviews of the 1980s have had little to say about human resource management and its place alongside the traditional issues of institutional machinery, union recognition and industrial action. Those few industrial relations academics who have actually passed comment on the relationship between IR and HRM have typically viewed the latter as a threat to the former. Thus, one British commentator refers to the relationship as 'very awkward [and] essentially negative' (Beaumont, 1992/forthcoming). This assessment is based on the assumption that HR policies will 'threaten the position of collective bargaining as the traditional centrepiece of industrial relations research, teaching and practice'. Leaving aside the strong suspicion about a naked defence of vested interests here, the main point of note is that no evidence is brought forth to substantiate these expectations.

Attention to the crucial distinction between 'individualistic' and 'collectivistic' management 'styles' has been drawn by Purcell (1987). This has since been modified by Marchington and Parker (1990) though fundamentally we are left with the point that in seeking to interpret recent changes in employment management approaches, attention has to be directed both to policies and actions with regard to union relations, and policies and actions which impact on individual employees. It is the dynamic inter-action between these aspects which really needs to be explored.

The point is borne out by the findings of a study on the impact of flexibility agreements on British manufacturing productivity (Marsden and Thompson, 1990). They found that it was the changes to 'working methods' as a precursor to changes in 'working practices' which best explained changes to productivity. By working methods they meant aspects such as product redesign leading to easier methods of assembly. By working practices on the other hand, they are referring to jointly agreed rules about working, or 'informal rules' such as custom and practice which workers and managers have normally respected. 'Flexibility agreements' *per se* were directed at these latter – that is, working practices. But it was the changes in working methods which contributed most to rises in productivity. Moreover,

> there is an important relationship between the two types of arrangement. Sooner or later managers find that further changes in working methods require changes in working practices ... there comes a point, for example, when further reorganisation of an assembly line requires changes in maintenance methods, which in turn, may require alteration of craft demarcations.   (p. 85)

The dynamic can, in consequence, be seen as having multiple facets: market changes, technical redesign, collective renegotiation and human resource 'cultural' preparation.

The link between individualism (HRM) and collectivism (industrial relations) has been tackled most directly of all by Guest (1989b). He observes that the unitarist and individualistic character of HRM and 'the values underpinning' it, leave 'little scope for collective arrangements and assume little need for collective bargaining. HRM therefore poses a considerable challenge to traditional industrial relations and more particularly to trade unionism' (p. 43). Nonetheless, as an approach he argues, it is not *necessarily* anti-union. Key aspects of HRM such as strategic integration and quality are in no sense at odds with unionism. Likewise, the attribute of the flexible utilization of labour can quite easily be made a central point of collective negotiation. 'The main challenge' to unions, he suggests, is likely to stem from 'the pursuit of employee commitment' (p. 43).

These are then, the main contributions in the literature which have broken the overall silence on the relationship between managerial approaches to industrial relations and the wider span of ways in which human resources are managed. Pulling these strands together and placing them alongside the hypothetical scenarios outlined at the beginning of this chapter, they help to frame four key questions which need asking of the mainstream cases:

- What stance had managements taken with regard to trade unions (i.e. in terms of the grade of recognition or moves to derecognition and what action had been taken in relation to shop stewards)?

- Irrespective of the institutional security of trade unions and their representatives, what stance had these managers adopted concerning collective bargaining?

- To what extent were trade unions treated as partners in the process of managing change?

- What impact did the new management initiatives on direct employee communications, task-level involvement and the like, have on trade unions and industrial relations?

These four questions constitute the subjects of the four sections into which this chapter is divided.

The institutional integrity of trade unions under the change programmes

There had been few outright assaults in these case companies on trade unions *per se*. The highly publicized cases of complete or partial derecognition have in fact occurred in only a few specific areas most notably at GCHQ, parts of newspaper publishing and shipping. In general terms, personnel managers in the rest of the economy, especially in large established companies, tend to make reassuring noises with regard to official policies towards trade unions. There is little new in that. But behind the PR there is a rather more mixed picture.

In some cases this meant the targeting of particular groups or levels of management. Hence, in British Rail, the shift to individual contracts for certain management grades was accompanied by a simultaneous withdrawal from collective negotiations for these groups. In other cases, managers began to scrutinize membership levels among 'marginal' groups such as sales staff with a view to giving notice of withdrawal of bargaining rights.

Among the manufacturing group of cases covered by this research, one might have expected that, at the very least, the place of the manual and technical unions would probably be reasonably secure. But in fact there was one particular case (which for obvious reasons cannot be named) where, in a key constituent business, there was a definite plan to withdraw recognition from all the unions in the relevant cluster of sites. It is interesting to note that, in the case in question, membership levels were not very high (they were just over 50 per cent) and the unions appeared to offer little effective challenge. The variables at play appeared to be both sheer vulnerability and the fact that the personnel director happened to be using, as his prime reference point of 'relevant others' certain non-union sites (many of them American- and Japanese-owned) in the geographical vicinity. In this case then, the opportunity to build collaborative relations with the unions in the management of change had clearly been spurned. Plant representatives had been put on the defensive. Each issue had to be hard fought – including the question of the number of recognized stewards. Under constant pressure of this kind, the steward group in one of the sites in this business had difficulty in getting people to put themselves forward as representatives. As a result, in some areas of the factory there was no steward. The stop-gap arrangement was to have these areas covered by representatives who also covered other sections of the site. While this seemed to be an unnecessary and totally unconstructive point of conflict between managers and the steward committee, it did have the effect of demoralizing and distracting the latter group. The point that certain areas were apparently unable to produce a representative was constantly cited by management as indicative of the lack of demand for union coverage. The dispute about the number of shop stewards to be recognized eventually went to national level for talks between the EEF and CSEU.

A point worth noting about the case just quoted is that among the 15 it was the only one where a clear, unambiguous policy intent to derecognize the main unions both existed and was admitted to. More common was a generally more aggressive stance towards the unions but without any apparent agenda (hidden or otherwise) to displace them. Thus, at Massey Ferguson, for example, the new initiatives on direct communication, human resources and the Tom Peters' memos which were referred to earlier, were accompanied by an adamant managerial stance that the number of shop stewards had to be reduced. On this and a host of other issues, the company took the fight to the unions who found themselves, for the first time in some while, simply responding to management's agenda of issues.

In many of the other cases too, such as Lucas and Jaguar in particular, the state of relations with the trade unions during this period was by no means harmonious. On the contrary, they were generally conflictual. But what was especially notable was the fact that management, at this time, evidently had it as no part of their list of priorities to rectify that state of affairs. Rather, the aim was to keep up the pressure and wrest areas of control out of the hands of the stewards' committee. To what extent was this part and parcel of the new human resource set of policies and practices? The fact that there was an 'alternative' suite of measures might be thought of as contributory to the hard-line attitude. However, the balance of evidence was that such a linkage should be regarded as unlikely. First, this was because the managers responsible for the industrial relations approach were quite separate from the group sponsoring the human resource management initiatives, and not indeed only separate but, in some considerable measure, in conflict with each other. Second, given the straitened product market circumstances it seems highly probable that this fairly aggressive line with the stewards' organization would have been adopted irrespective of the existence or non-existence of a set of human resource management policies.

One of the more distinctive approaches to trade unions during this period was taken by Ford of Britain. As we witnessed in earlier chapters, Ford had departed somewhat from its traditional constitutionalist stance and had adopted certain innovative policies including, for example, employee involvement (EI). Despite this, there had been no attempt to attack or undermine the recognized trade unions. On the contrary, as John Hougham, the Personnel Director of Ford of Britain, explained:

We are engaged in a definite policy of 'relationship building' with the unions. I am taking time out to meet informally with all the main national officers for this purpose. It's something we have to do to run alongside the NJNC sessions which can be incredibly formal and stultifying. Part of this also is what our American colleagues call 'jointism' – that is, purposely seeking out key areas where we have a recognized common interest.

Broadly speaking then, the mainstream companies revealed that this period of innovation was not accompanied by a frontal attack on the trade unions. Apart from the instances cited, the characteristic tendency was a generally 'tougher', more assertive, stance by management but not a mindless 'macho' posture. There were variations to this central orientation – and Ford's 'relationship building' is a classic case. Another variant is to be found in the 'phased' approach as, for example, at Austin Rover and Whitbread. In these cases the early part of the 1980s was characterized by an extremely tough stand against the unions. This was followed a few years later by a different tack – one which stressed product quality and hence the need to elicit cooperation from the workforce. In place of a disciplinary face towards labour, management adopted a qualified partnership face. This did not directly involve the unions, but the markedly adversarial stance towards the union was replaced by an approach which essentially trivialized the unions' contribution. Trade unions were pushed to the margins of concern.

A senior representative at one of the Whitbread breweries described the new arrangements in a way which clearly illustrates the new order of things:

> We, as a union, [TGWU] now have little direct contact with Personnel. For example, we are briefed in exactly the same way as everyone else on site. As for any problems or grievances arising, these we have to progress through the Block consultative committees. If there is a failure to agree in the Block, the issue is referred to the site JNC. I think we have to recognize that many of the steps that have been taken here have been designed to delimit the role of the T&G.

In this instance, the new modes of direct communication clearly were having a direct effect on the standing of the trade unions. In other cases an amended version of this was more prevalent: while the main emphasis was clearly being given to direct communication with all employees, the trade union representatives were accorded the 'courtesy' of a separate parallel briefing, timed either to coincide with the 'main' briefing or perhaps just an hour or so before it. In a number of regards then, the general approach to trade unions could best be described not as a direct frontal assault but as a *marginalization* of their role. This leaves open the question of what was happening with regard to collective bargaining.

Policies and practices relating to collective bargaining

A widespread move was to decentralize collective bargaining. One prime rationale for this was to take advantage of local labour market conditions. Another important reason was that it was seen to fit with the idea of distinct profit centres and other appurtenances of devolved management.

A point that should be noted when comparing and contrasting cases is that even among unionized companies the variety of practices concerning collective bargaining was extensive. Thus, whereas in some cases plant representatives were meeting with management as frequently as twice a week for relatively formal talks about various disputes, grievances and procedural matters (e.g. at the Austin Rover Longbridge site in Birmingham), in other cases, collective meetings were held very rarely. An AEU steward at one of the Plessey sites reported:

As a group of stewards we only meet with management during the run up to the annual negotiations. Even then it is a normal tactic for them to question our credentials. They claim that we don't really represent our constituents. All this makes it fairly hard going. It's not surprising that not many people want to put themselves forward as representatives. I suspect that this may well be part of management's aim, to keep up the pressure on us so that we become less effective. I'd have to agree that if that is their intention then to a large extent their plan is working. If you look at my own case for example, I cannot say categorically what the extent of my constituency is. The issue drags on and on. It's quite demoralizing. But we keep the representation going. We have to.

When I talked subsequently to one of the first line managers the difficulties alluded to became clear. This manageress supervising some 20 female assemblers, observed:

No, I don't really have any dealings at all with the union. My girls are not interested in involving the union in any problems they might have. They come to me with their problems and if I can help I sort them out. A small minority are members but they only join for the insurance cover in case of industrial injury.

She then went on, however, to criticize the union representatives for not showing sufficient interest either to come and talk to 'the girls' to see if they had any problems or indeed to ask new starters if they would like to join the union. In addition, the motives of the union representatives were questioned; she very much doubted if they were wholeheartedly supportive of the company's future.

Overall, the most notable aspect with regard to collective bargaining was that there was now far less emphasis upon achieving productivity gains through the once ubiquitous mechanism of productivity bargaining. Ahlstrand (1990) has demonstrated the long-standing attachment to this device at the Fawley refinery even though, at the rational level, there was little evidence of any success with the method. Significantly, these mainstream companies, with a few notable exceptions, had seemingly begun to place their own faith less in the continued pursuit of detailed productivity agreements in the Esso mode, and rather more in the wide span of initiatives which extended beyond collective bargaining. To this extent at least, the balance between industrial relations and the 'new' human resource approaches had therefore shown signs of adjustment.

Trade unions as partners or outsiders in the process of change?

In the main, trade union leaders both at national and workplace level were left on the sidelines of most of the managerial initiatives during this period. Half-hearted attempts were sometimes made to involve them. As one senior personnel manager at Austin Rover was fond of saying:

The unions were invited to the party but they didn't seem to want to come. So, the party went ahead without them.

Equally, it must be remembered, that the internal politics of change were such that the people issuing the 'invitations' were in any case rarely the main drivers of change. As we noted in previous chapters, the major change programmes were frequently devised outside the specialist personnel and industrial relations function. In consequence, by the time this branch of management got a hold on the change package its shape was pretty well settled. As personnel were still widely regarded as the chief mediators with the unions, this inevitably meant late involvement by the unions. One of the Austin Rover shop stewards commented:

> Yes I've heard about this invitation to a 'party'. The trouble is it had already started and in any case it was not the kind of party which we wanted to go to. 'Working With Pride' is a nice fancy label but the reality is not so very different to what they have tried to serve up to us before. Basically, they want more work out of fewer men.

Because personnel were themselves often marginal to the change process, this branch of management was itself frequently ambivalent about the new initiatives. We saw earlier how the Austin Rover industrial relations managers were especially critical of the Working With Pride programme. This being the case, it was natural that the circumstances were inauspicious for the formation of a partnership in change.

A somewhat contrasting situation obtained at Ford Motor Company and in the local authority, Bradford Metropolitan City Council. Here, 'bargaining for change' was the chosen path. In consequence, both personnel managers and trade union representatives were much more centrally involved. The broad thrust and the fine detail were exhaustively discussed by the parties. The ground was carefully prepared in advance and union representatives were flown out, for example, to overseas locations to witness at first hand the kind of practices, in operation, which Ford wanted to introduce in Britain. This contrasting approach was not unassociated, however, with the fact that Ford had a rather more recognizably 'traditional' agenda than that conjured up by Austin Rover. Essentially, it was seen as a productivity bargaining package with above-average awards being offered for changes to working practices. As such, although far-reaching, Ford's plan was not seen as so fundamentally threatening by the unions.

The more novel features such as the Mission, Values and Guiding Principles package, the Employee Involvement plan, and the potentially radical shake up of supervision throughout Ford Europe, were all in the background. They were never tied together and presented as a coherent package with which to frighten or impress the unions. In consequence, the unions felt able to take each proposal in turn without feeling embroiled by an overarching plan. And, at various levels, the unions did indeed respond. Hence, as one of the Dagenham conveners said: 'Don't tell us about the different ways of working in Europe, show us.' He continued, 'and to be fair, that is precisely what this new management has done. . . .' Furthermore, the company for its part saw an advantage in getting the unions on board for most if not all of these changes. Hence, it invested time in building and maintaining constructive relations with the unions. This did not mean of course that it did not drive hard bargains on the separate issues, but it did mean that the unions perceived at least that they were faced by a company ready to do business with them – now and in the future.

In the local authority, the Labour group, when in power, made 'partnership' with the trade unions a central plank in its social strategy. The translation of this manifesto-cum-corporate-plan into a personnel strategy led to the absorption of many ingredients associated with human resource management borrowed from leading edge private sector companies. The attempted inclusion of trade unions into the fine tuning and implementation of this plan was a novel element. Unfortunately, the experiment did not last long enough to allow a judgement to be made about how this mix of new human resource approaches with quality and commitment to the fore, and unions participating as partners in change, might fare in practice.

When the talk is of trade unions as 'partners' in change, a key question concerns who we mean by 'the trade union', for, just as managers are riven by factionalism, so too are the unions. A major line of tension runs between plant representatives and officials above and beyond the plant. Given the increased use of interplant competition for investment, it is hardly surprising that criticism has been directed at those plant representatives who have been seen to cooperate rather too closely with their local managers. In effect, some stewards were being accused of collusion with their domestic management. This has led to conflict between different steward groups as they have sought to defend local jobs. As one convener observed:

> We have been criticized for making deals which undermine traditional understandings on matters such as job demarcation, shifts, training and flexibility. But this doesn't worry me too much because I know that much of it is hypocritical. The critics are quietly making their own local deals.

Another traditional line of tension relates to the relationship between the stewards and their own constituencies. Shop stewards, particularly senior stewards such as full-time conveners, have long been susceptible to the charge that they have forged too cosy a relationship with management. It might be expected that this issue would rear its head most clearly during a period when 'joint problem solving' and 'partnerships in the management of change' were to the fore. Unsurprisingly, the research in the case companies did tend to confirm a certain sensitivity to this charge by the senior stewards who were interviewed. They were usually quick to point out that they were subject to election at the annual general meeting. Insofar as a new mood of realism had led to a more cooperative set of arrangements, this was invariably explained as arising out of popular aspiration. Hence, as a deputy convener in one of the engineering plants where a bargaining for change approach had been adopted, said:

> The lads are fully aware of the size of the problems. They are far more reluctant to take action – too much so in my opinion. They tend to want to avoid problems, our stewards have had to learn to restrain themselves even when they are more aware of the wider picture and can see the need at times for a determined stand. On the new industrial relations you were asking about, well, yes I think there is a new approach; for us it means we have to keep people far more aware of what's going on, there's more openness. This extends in both directions. We tell the lads more, but equally we ourselves are kept better informed by the plant manager. Today we are involved in purchasing decisions on new machinery; we've argued for, and won, the right for certain of the hourly paid to visit the suppliers and test the equipment before delivery; on occasions this has involved them in trips to Spain and Germany

to work on new equipment. These are the sort of changes towards openness which we have to keep in step with.

As might be expected, the situation was very different in those cases where the unions had been confronted or marginalized by management. In one of these instances a senior shop steward observed:

> The management talk about change, and communication, and all the rest of it, but it's just talk. OK so you've asked me about trade union and management partnerships in change . . . but from where I sit, what I see is a wolf in sheep's clothing. Remember, I know these managers. They are just the same lot I have dealt with in the past. I've been a steward for 26 years and you might say I've seen it all before.

To a large extent, the contrast between these two cases appears to rest on the divergent approaches taken by the respective managers. There is, however, the interaction process to be taken into account. In the former case for example, the informant referred to the initial hostility between the parties when the first round of meetings was set up:

> There were plant meetings and departmental meetings. For the first nine months these were really quite abusive in nature. The female site personnel officers had to be excluded because of the language (sic). There were no minutes, and no agenda. The idea was to keep it informal and build trust. We have moved on a million miles from that state of affairs but it may not have materialized had it not been for the fact that it so happened that we got both a new plant manager and a new convener shortly after these meetings began. The personalities in these things are very important I believe.

In exploring the potential for the partnership idea it soon became evident that individuals held markedly ambivalent and possibly even contradictory attitudes in matters related to the notion. For example, one senior steward was particularly scathing about his union's national leadership. They had 'missed the boat' he alleged with regard to technology; the policies were outmoded, defensive and indefensible he suggested and, in consequence, not only had the technological lead long been lost but jobs had suffered too. He implied that a more flexible attitude relating to working practices would have helped. Yet, when talking about a recent productivity deal, which had resulted in an extra few per cent in exchange for a certain measure of job flexibility, he maintained that, 'the company will be looking for a buy-out of 50 per cent of the agreements we have reached over the past decades'. Evidently the 'not invented here' syndrome which tended to hamper the adoption of innovation among managers had its counterpart among the unions also.

The impact of HR policies and practices on trade unions and collective bargaining

It is difficult to disentangle the effects of human resource management type initiatives on trade unions and collective bargaining from the whole array of other changes which were occurring at this time. It has to be remembered that the unions were in an already weak position as a result of adverse political and economic conditions. But if these other factors are stripped away in order to focus on the battery of HR innovations relating to selection, appraisal, direct communication, task level participation, training, performance-related pay, culture change campaigns and other similar initiatives, then the impact, though mixed, can generally be said to be adverse from the unions' viewpoint.

The reasons for this were not always direct and obvious. In part, it resulted from the sheer distraction of management from union relations. For example, at Plessey Naval Systems, one of the personnel and industrial relations specialists observed:

If I look at my list of priorities now and compare them with the list I would have had say, five years ago, there is a significant difference which is observable. Now, I am tasked with installing a sophisticated and modern system of communications so that we can get the message across to all of our employees. I'm into management development in a big way and I'm monitoring change across the board – not just in this company but in others here and abroad. To be perfectly frank with you, the trade unions just do not figure in this list of priorities. But if I go back just a few years, say to the five year mark I mentioned a moment ago, then the situation could be reversed. In fact, then and for a period extending way back, because I was dealing so much with trade union issues, I had little time for anything else. We, like many other managers at the time were caught in the situation of simply reacting to their agenda. Today, we set the agenda and it is very different to the one we used to dance to.

To this extent then, the unions could be seen as crowded out by other managerial concerns.

Another factor was, however, also at play. Each of the main elements of the human resource initiatives such as more rigorous and systematic selection techniques, the extension of appraisal to all levels of the workforce, direct communication to all employees, and job level participation programmes, tended to be viewed suspiciously by trade union representatives. This did not come as a surprise to most managers. On the contrary, they normally anticipated a hostile reaction. Indeed, they also tended to plan for it and thus in a sense provoked it. Even in those few cases where approaches were made to the unions to give some endorsement to the new systems, these solicitations were usually very half-hearted and token. The shape of the initiatives were invariably drawn up before the unions were invited to join the deliberations. Opposition was expected and planned for. A convenor in one of the engineering companies expressed how he saw the invitation:

> Consultants were engaged by management a long time before we were asked for our views. Sure, some vague references were made in the lead-up period that a new programme was coming but when it happened the only notice I received was a circular describing the package and it was the same circular received by everyone else. I think I got it about two hours before most people. We were asked if we wanted to arrange a meeting to discuss the changes. There was no point really. Management had already decided what they wanted and there was no way we were going to change their minds nor did we intend helping them implement this lot. Anyway, we did eventually hold a special meeting. We tried to uncover what was really in their minds but they tried to brush us off with a whole lot of guffaw. It was clear to us that the whole thing was designed to circumvent the unions and we were not, and will not be, a party to signing our own death warrant.

But where unions had not become involved as partners in the change programmes they alternatively risked being relegated to engagements on relatively trivial issues. In order to test this proposition I examined a series of joint works committee minutes in companies where a more 'traditional' adversarial relationship had been maintained and compared these with situations where a 'partnership in change' stance had been adopted. The comparison was restricted to those joint committees which met regularly. This exercise revealed that the subject matter dealt with by such bodies was broadly similar in both types of case. According to the minutes, items discussed were remarkably mundane. The constantly recurring issues on the agenda were: canteens, locker room facilities, car parking and regulation of contract work. Commenting on this finding over lunch one day, a plant manager smiled to his colleague and said, 'Well I'd rather keep them busy on such matters than get us involved in anything too heavy!'

The overall impact of the new emphases on individualistic, human resource-style policies upon trade unions, collective bargaining and industrial relations was hard to gauge in precise terms. But what seemed reasonably clear was that the traditional struggles at pay review time had hardly been affected. Industrial action continued as a periodic phenomenon throughout this period, and indeed manifest conflict broke out in a number of these 15 main cases during the period of the research – most notably at Lucas, Jaguar, Ford, British Rail and Massey Ferguson. Any assumption that initiatives on direct communication and job-level involvement would translate into the dissipation of conflicts over pay rates would thus be evidently naive.

There did, however, appear to be a reduction in conflict during contract periods on non-wage issues. As a number of these organizations had moved over to two-year negotiation periods this was a not inconsiderable factor. Moreover, although the record of conflict hardly indicated a major impact of human resource initiatives when the crunch issues relating to pay and conditions came around, there was, nonetheless, a managerial and trade union expectation that the various campaigns might make some difference. The temptation to use human resource techniques as a 'softening up' device prior to annual negotiations was usually countered, however, by a realization that such a crude measure could risk the long-term viability of these approaches. It was not unusual, nonetheless, to hear personnel specialists suggesting that their recent innovations in communication and the like were already showing through in the measure of patience displayed by the shopfloor in the face of pay settlement delays.

To this extent at least, a number of managers clearly looked towards a definite interlink between human resource initiatives and the handling of collective bargaining.

DISCUSSION

Managerial approaches to trade unions and industrial relations in these organizations which were at once both traditional and yet also at the time of the research, at least partly experimental, reveal the dilemmas and uncertainties surrounding the whole enterprise of human resource management in the British context. Perhaps unsurprisingly, there was little evidence of any forthright move to abandon pluralism in favour of a wholehearted commitment to an individualistically based human resource programme. Instead, the general tendency was to maintain the previous machinery in a ticking-over mode while experimenting rather more enthusiastically with policies and approaches which signalled a departure towards new priorities.

This dual approach to the management of labour was embodied, in a number of these cases, in the operation of separate and distinct specialists (and even departments) responsible, respectively, for industrial relations and human resource management. Such arrangements were found, for example, at Massey Ferguson, Jaguar and Ford. In such cases, the human resource management type of approach could be seen as 'bolted on' to the pre-existing and very much ongoing, industrial relations/personnel departments. As such, the overall implication of the new developments for trade unions and industrial relations could be seen not so much as an outright abandonment, but rather a downplaying of their status and significance in the order of things. This dualistic posture, while not so starkly expressed in all the cases as to be manifested in the type of parallel institutional arrangements exemplified by Massey's, essentially expressed the underlying character of nearly all these mainstream cases.

The attitude of managers towards trade unions and industrial relations might then be described as one of general neglect. In some locations this seemed sufficiently conscious as to suggest an intent to allow trade unions and collective representation to wither on the vine. But even this is perhaps to attribute rather more order than was observable in practice. Within most of the organizations there were divergencies of view. There was a tendency for the chief exponents of pluralism to be found among the personnel and industrial relations specialists but even this was not uniformly so. These specialists displayed a marked ambivalence towards trade unions, collective bargaining and due procedure. Some adopted a stance which, in effect, was designed to safeguard at least a modicum of trade union representation and collective negotiation from the more rampant aspirations of their line and general manager colleagues. For their trouble, these specialists were often labelled as the 'custodians of procedure' and their vested interests were made suspect. But an alternative position was taken by at least an equal, if not indeed a greater proportion, of the personnel and IR specialists who were interviewed. This was to profess prime interest in the new initiatives and markedly to downplay the significance and even the legitimacy of trade union representation and collective relations. They argued that competitive pressures had made unavoidable an approach which valued flexibility, leanness, learning and commitment. Personnel was seen as central to bringing about this profile and this was to be achieved through initiatives on training, selection, appraisal, new reward systems and the like. Some went so far as to state that when measured against this agenda the 'old obsessions' with unions and contracts and grievance procedures were essentially 'irrelevant'.

Across the variety of approaches, one startling fact stood out: while the old-style industrial relations 'firefighting' was disavowed and even scorned, there was hardly an instance where anything approaching a 'strategic' stance towards unions and industrial relations could be readily discerned as having taken its place. It would appear that identifying clear managerial policies towards trade unions and collective bargaining is as difficult to do now, if not indeed more difficult, than it was 20–30 years ago when the lack of policy on such matters was frequently berated (Donovan, 1968; McCarthy and Ellis, 1973; CIR, 1973; Cuthbert, 1973; Hawkins, 1978).

In a key regard there was perhaps little that was entirely new in this. Flanders had complained much earlier that British managers 'preferred to have as little as possible to do with labour relations', which was looked upon as 'a nuisance, a disturbance diverting their energies away from what they regard as the more important aspects of their work' (1964: 251). In the intervening period, however, there had been very considerable attention paid to industrial relations as they became identified as the root cause of economic underperformance. Arguably, managers in the 1980s were therefore merely reverting to type. It is suggested here, however, that there was rather more to it than that – namely that the new neglect of trade unions and industrial relations was a studied neglect. It carried a symbolic message: managers are in the driving seat, unions and industrial relations have to be demonstrated as relatively secondary and incidental to meeting market priorities, and secondary also to the newly discovered alternative ways of managing the labour (human) resource.

One of the crucial limiting factors in the attainment of such a clear message, however, was the relatively undeveloped nature of the HR function. Even in those cases where it had a separate institutional presence, there was a tendency for the function to be skeletally staffed and for the unit's specialists to concentrate their efforts on the managerial grades. The extension of initiatives into the 'rest of the workforce' tended to be piecemeal and somewhat haphazard. The state of affairs was sometimes akin to having a HR department to handle 'the personnel management of managers', and an industrial relations/personnel department to look after the remainder. HR professionals were seen as an intellectual elite who enjoyed easy access to the higher reaches of corporate management but who lacked a certain shopfloor credibility. In consequence, the legitimacy of initiatives formulated in the one setting for extension into the domain of the other was a source of tension. This again served to hamper the implementation of a coherent HR/IR policy.

As indicated, there were of course variations in practice between the companies. The different stances which were adopted towards trade unions and industrial relations were broadly associated with the prevailing patterns of collective representation which had been inherited. Hence, by and large, the engineering companies which had predominantly a legacy of well-organized workforces tended to adopt a 'realistic' view which entailed a fairly prominent place for trade unions for some time to come.

The companies in the process 'sector' saw rather more opportunity for marginalizing unions even further. Particular levels of staff, or types of staff (such as sales teams) or certain geographical locations were targeted as candidates for decollectivization. Ironically therefore, it was usually those segments of the workforce which were least able to assert themselves collectively which became vulnerable to the derecognition treatment.

It was notable that across all the 15 main cases, the general picture was one of some measure of stability in that there had typically been no overt all-out assault on trade unions or the collective agreements and procedures. Nonetheless, in every case these systems were under some threat to a lesser or greater degree. One saw this fairly markedly, for example, at Plessey, Austin Rover, British Rail, Bradford Council, Jaguar and Lucas. In a milder form, trade unions and industrial relations were facing difficulties at ICI, Eaton, the NHS, Smith & Nephew and Whitbread. It seemed that a generally 'cool' if not outrightly hostile stance towards trade unions and industrial relations was characteristic in these mainstream organizations at this time. This was not necessarily a direct product of the human resource management alternative. It seems likely that, even without the new initiatives, trade unions would have experienced a hard time during this period. But the existence – or promise – of an 'alternative' (from a managerial viewpoint) rendered the situation rather more precarious. The marginalization of the unions took on a greater significance than it might otherwise have been seen to carry. Bypassing union channels appeared symptomatic of investment in, and commitment to, the human resource management paradigm. In reality, that commitment was frequently missing, but the possibility that it might in time come about, stoked-up union fears that lack of attention to industrial relations was symbolic of a new order. In too many cases this side-skirmishing and posturing is more aptly interpreted as a substitute for a coherent alternative rather than a new way *per se*.

In sum, with the marked exception of Ford Motor Company which had adopted the clearest policy of finding some place for the unions in its 'bargaining for change', the generalizable proposition that might deservedly be made with regard to most of these mainstream companies, at least during the period of late 1980s, is that marginalization of unions and industrial relations carried a powerful symbolic message about the new order. More pressing priorities were being signalled and there was at least an *implied viability* in the alternative devices of direct employee communication and job level participation, close appraisal and performance-related rewards. How much of this was bluff and how much stemmed from deep-seated belief (or even misconception) was hard to gauge. In any case, the half-hearted way in which the 'distancing' of the trade unions was being handled at least afforded a certain comfort to the parties involved, that a pragmatic reversal might be steered if changed circumstances should suggest such a need.

10

Conclusions

The aim of this chapter is to review the main findings from the study and to consider their implications. The discussion is structured into two main sections reflecting these themes.

MAIN ISSUES AND FINDINGS

The real challenge to British management, and to British unions, is how to effect change on existing sites – change which makes them competitive with new sites. (John Monks, Deputy General Secretary, TUC, reviewing P. Wickens' book on Nissan, 1989: 161)

Monks might also have noted a further challenge: that is, for the research community to respond to the nature and extent of change which is already underway in this arena. To date, systematic research on the topic has been extraordinarily limited. The purpose of this present study was to help correct for that neglect.

The backcloth to the study was a debate about the nature and extent of change in the management of labour in Britain. The school of thought which posited the idea of a sea-change in this area was found to be countered by another which propounded a thesis of continuity. Among a number of problems in trying to unravel this debate was the lack of methodological comparability. The 'change thesis' largely rested on a few clearly exceptional 'non-standard' cases such as Nissan and Toshiba. The 'continuity thesis', conversely, rested on large-scale questionnaire surveys. This study of 'mainstream organizations' adopted neither of these approaches: it tackled the heartland of British employment using comparative case methods.

The four main findings hinged around the central themes of the study which concerned:

- the nature and extent of change

- the role of line managers in shaping these changes

- the points of tension within the change processes

- the sources of variation between the cases.

The nature and extent of change: on the road to HRM?

The first finding is that the way in which management sought to manage labour had indeed undergone extensive change even if its secure achievement was more in doubt. This measure of change could be seen in a number of ways. Most notable perhaps was that the drive had evidently come from sources and along paths which were not conventionally regarded as part of industrial relations proper. The paradox is that British industrial relations have been refashioned out of initiatives which were not industrial relations 'reforms' in the normal understanding of that term following, say, Flanders, Donovan or McCarthy. The reworking has derived, in no small measure, from repercussions arising from redesign in production and operational methods, organizational restructuring, quality, and what can summarily be termed 'culture campaigns'. As a result, the boundaries of what is understood by 'labour management' or 'industrial relations' have become even more blurred than they were previously.

To what extent did the observed changes amount to a shift towards human resource management? The temptation is to seek to measure all change against this 'template'. And an associated danger is the reification of subtle and incomplete tendencies. Both of these divert attention away from extensive and far-reaching changes, which albeit not in themselves constituting HRM, are nonetheless of profound significance in shifting the terrain of labour management relations. What seems to have been occurring in the British mainstream is a whole clutch of different, but not divergent, initiatives which range across specialist boundaries. Analyses which attempt to confine themselves within the ambit of conventional frameworks therefore risk a blindness with respect to the changing patterns which emerge from these.

One influential body of scholars (Kochan, Katz, McKersie, 1990) argue that a firm's industrial relations strategies have to be internally consistent if they are to be economically effective. The corollary is that lack of fit will eventually be penalized and hence there will be a tendency to pull policies and approaches into alignment. The problem with this hypothesis is determining what time-scale is involved. If economic systems can tolerate lack of fit for a period of years then the proposition does not really help to adjudicate on the recent changes in the British case companies. A more modest proposition is required. The cumulative weight of evidence deriving from this collection of British cases suggests some movement beyond the opportunist 'pragmatism' of the 'standard moderns' judged, by Purcell and Sisson (1983), to be 'by far the largest' type. By the late 1980s, if the mainstream companies selected for this study can be broadly taken as representative of this band, then the conclusion must be that events and approaches had moved on considerably. The pragmatic flavour was, however, still very evident; this suggests that the famed pragmatism has moved to a new centre of gravity.

The indicators of this shift, as shown throughout this study, are numerous albeit not definitive. Labour relations 'firefighting' had been pushed to the very margins of concern. While it would be an exaggeration to say that there was a common set of values or assumptions held in any of the companies there was, nonetheless, a reasonably consistent set of aspirations and understandings of what 'management' should be doing and, as part of this, what people-management should look like. Part of this consistency in the accounts of the managers undoubtedly stemmed from the increase in the volume and frequency of messages coming down from senior levels. Not only were the communication media more sophisticated than at the beginning of the decade, the insistent nature of the messages had usually been reinforced by concrete measures such as site closures, demanning, delayering, more formal target-setting, closer monitoring and evaluation and moves towards linking rewards to approved performances.

The significance of non-personnel specialists

Because much of the reshaping has arisen exogenously to the industrial relations system, part and parcel of the change is that key authors of these transitions have been located outside the personnel and industrial relations specialisms. General managers, manufacturing directors, quality directors and others, have not been content to respect specialist boundaries when matters relating to the utilization of the human resource are involved. As noted at many points throughout the book, line and general managers have been central to the people-management changes in two senses – both as drivers/devisers of new patterns and as implementers/deliverers of the preferred approaches. This constituted a continuing theme throughout the analysis and the details deserve further comment.

Senior executives were found to be having a far more extensive exposure to, and involvement in, issues pertaining to labour matters than has so far been reflected in the literature. This was directed not so much to trade union issues *per se* but rather to aspects of 'corporate culture', 'managing change', 'employee commitment', 'quality of service', 'flexibility', 'core beliefs', 'vision' and the 'communication process'. These sorts of concerns were certainly found constituting the agenda of 'chairman's groups' and senior management workshops. To what extent the diagnoses and action plans actually filtrated into business strategy as it unfolded was more difficult to determine. But at the very least, senior executives were found to 'have a view' about desired people-management approaches and tended to share a broad sense of the direction in which their organization should be heading in employment matters.

At middle line-management level, contrary to speculative reports about the 'demise' of the middle manager or of 'malaise' here, this core group appeared to be expanding their spheres of influence. Production managers had become more generalist and a key component of this was recognized to be a clear acceptance of, and indeed a claim to, the responsibility for managing the human resource. Almost uniformly, the middle managers in the study depicted personnel's role as simply that of offering advice. Noteworthy here also is that in readily embracing the general 'business manager' role alongside their acceptance of the prime responsibility for people management, they were moving to a position where the much-hailed integration of these concerns was therefore becoming more technically feasible and achievable.

Meanwhile, at junior line-management level, compatible developments were discernible. Irrespective of whether companies were increasing or reducing the relative numbers at the first tier level, the unmistakable trend was towards the creation of a new model 'first line manager'. Through selection, deselection, training, revised reward packages, revised job remits, appraisal and other devices, there was a drive to shift from the 'traditional supervisor' model to the new 'head of section' or 'assistant manager' model. These line managers were likewise expected to take on an expanded set of responsibilities and to handle people management to a far greater degree than had been the case under the 'traditional supervisor' system. They were expected to embody the new managerial styles, to be key conduits in open two-way communication flows and they were to be monitored for 'involving' and 'developing' employees in their sections. As the case studies revealed, however, there was still some considerable ground to be covered between these aspirations and routinized behaviour. Nonetheless, at the time of the study at least, there was a fairly consistent pressure being applied to move things along in this direction.

Points of tension

The findings, taken together, have emphasized that, contrary to much other comment, the degree of change in managerial approaches to handling the labour resource has been considerable. The evidence for this is found in management's articulations of what it is seeking to do and secondly in the range of initiatives so far taken. But none of this is to suggest that the path of change is smooth. On the contrary, a lengthy list of problematical aspects could be constructed from the cases. Two key ones deserve special attention.

The first of these hinges on the nature of what has been done so far and what has not been done. Essentially, the raft of initiatives coming from management has been focused on the individual plane and has neglected the collective. New selection procedures have sought to identify appropriate individuals; new communication devices have tried to elicit the understanding and support of individuals: appraisals, performance-related pay, attitude surveys and a host of other similar initiatives clearly reveal this individualistic orientation. Notably, the originators, champions and delivery agents of these initiatives within the organizations were almost invariably institutionally separate from those departments or units charged with handling collective labour relations. As we have seen there was, in the main, no direct assault on collective machinery, but that aspect of management's approach was afforded only residual attention and there was often more than a hint that the hope was that 'the union problem' would, in the fullness of time, simply fade away. Industrial relations conducted through collective bargaining and works committees continued, but its sphere of influence was reduced. Crucially, the two strands of managerial action with regard to the labour interface (the individual and the collective) were rarely brought into alignment in most of these cases. Human resource managers and line managers pursued communication, involvement and other initiatives while the industrial relations managers faced-off to union representatives on an entirely different agenda. The one stressed the importance of open, two-way communication, the other continued to protect and withhold information in accord with normal bargaining tactics.

This 'institutional separation' was a very notable feature in these companies. How long this approach would be seen as viable is a valid question. Arguably, the 'easy bit' had been done by these organizations. They had held their awareness-training programmes for all levels of managers; workbooks had been constructed and distributed; the frameworks and mechanisms such as quality circles and team briefing sessions had been at least partially installed. In the jargon of these companies, progammes were being 'rolled out'. But the difficult bits were to come: making these approaches stick, consolidating them, and building beyond them. Whether the attitude and behavioural changes necessary in the workforce to achieve this next phase could be attained without reaching some decision on the collective front seemed to be a very moot point indeed.

The second problematic hinges on the distinction, referred to earlier between 'managerial approaches/styles' and 'patterns of relations'. It can be seen that this point is related to the previous one. Essentially the issue is that even if, and when, management do succeed in building a consistency in their approach to managing people (this across all levels between different functions and even satisfying the individual-collective split noted above) this will not necessarily translate into a revised *pattern of relations*. Management style might change, but this may not be sufficient to transform attitudes and behaviours of other parties in the system.

Sources of variation between the cases

So far, these concluding observations have focused on the general pattern of the findings. As noted, there were some remarkable commonalities which extended across diverse sectoral and other divides. Nonetheless, there were also certain significant differences in approaches to labour management which survived this period of general change and which were indeed created during this period. The explanations for the different patterns found have been pointed up in each of the separate substantive chapters and it is not intended that these should be repeated here, but it is worth summarizing the key points.

Essentially, the differences derived from structural and political sources. The structural factors of note were the sector differences, organizational structure differences, and ownership. Sectoral variation was especially apparent between the engineering companies and the rest. The former, as in the cases of Massey Ferguson, Jaguar, Eaton, Rolls-Royce, Peugeot and Austin Rover, were pre-eminently struggling to install a viable alternative to the well-entrenched collective and proceduralized *modus operandi*. It was accordingly, in these cases that the dual system phenomenon was most in evidence. Human resource management type initiatives had been 'bolted on' to the embedded system. In the process companies by contrast, such as ICI, Smith & Nephew and Whitbread, the industrial relations cultures were less to the fore. The attempts to install participative working, involvement and other initiatives were less a struggle with a collectivist alternative and rather more a contest with work cultures and job designs which, while not part of the Coventry engineering model were nonetheless at odds with the implicit unitarist message of the new initiatives.

Differences in organizational structure, irrespective of sector, were also important. Those organizations with multiple products and multiple divisions were far less likely to launch, and even far less likely to succeed in establishing, coherent change programmes. Hence, Lucas, the NHS and Smith & Nephew could only draft guiding principles whereas Eaton and Jaguar were able to detail their philosophy and their preferred methods. The fashion for restructuring into distinct businesses, as for example, at British Rail, proved to be an important issue in the installation of human resource management methods. Devolving responsibility for the handling of various resources, including the human one, to business unit managers had divergent consequences for HRM. In some respects it made the introduction of strategic HR policies and practices more problematical. Many unit managers, pressured to show bottom-line results quickly, were loath to divert investment into the human resource. On the other hand, freed from central regulation, unit managers were prompted to make a fresh and total reappraisal of current practices and in this way experimentation with new approaches to the management of labour was stimulated by devolved structures.

The ownership factor was also discernible. The American-owned companies (Ford and the Eaton Corporation) made use of their overseas presence both as sources of ideas and as sources of discipline through the manifest fact of inter-plant competition for work and investment. Massey Ferguson was Canadian owned and it was noted in the study that the human resource director, newly installed in the UK, was a North American and he set about testing out the transferability of American ideas on HR into the British context. The role of a similar senior figure in Ford of Britain was also noted in the study. In all three cases (Ford, Eaton, Massey Ferguson) the attempt to transplant certain 'American ideas' into the British employment scene during this period was evident, though in none could it be said that the endeavour at the time of the study had scored any marked successes.

Ownership was also an issue in the public sector and private sector selection of cases. The Local Authority, British Rail and the NHS were the most notable public sector cases though Austin Rover and Rolls-Royce had both been publicly owned at the commencement of the study. These last two had, however, been temporarily 'rescued' from financial crises and were less imbued with public sector characteristics than the former group of three. Looking solely at this former group the enduring impression was that the Whitley legacy was powerful and enduring. Centrally devised structures remained the foremost point of reference though in each case a surprising degree of experimentation was uncovered. Indeed, just about every new initiative found among the leading private sector companies had been tried somewhere or other in these public bureaucracies but the weight of the extant systems were such that the new initiatives were pushed to the fringes. Typically they carried the mantle of being 'experimental' (therefore probably temporary) add-ons.

Another source of variation, in addition to these structural factors, was traceable to the 'political' dimension. In the public sector cases, change management was first and foremost triggered by a political imperative. But a far more pervasive manifestation of the 'political' was evident in the degree of intra-management competition which ran through all of the cases. Rival 'recipes' for managing the labour problem occupied a central place in this. As a form of 'symbolic action', HRM was such a recipe and a peculiarly powerful one in some of these cases – but not in others. Why? To answer this question regard has to be paid to the interplay between the nature of HRM and the circumstances of its unfolding.

As we saw, HRM is a chimerical phenomenon yet paradoxically it promises to bring coherence, form and direction, to a cluster of different personnel interventions. As such, it carries the potential to make available a whole new approach: complete with techniques and underpinning philosophy. In those cases where pre-existing policies had been perceived as exhausted, discredited, or simply ill fitted to new environmental demands, this aspect constituted a powerful appeal. But even in these cases this switch in recipe required someone (or some group) to champion the new way at an appropriate time. The take-up of the 'Working With Pride' package in Austin Rover, championed by the Manufacturing Director at a time when the Michael Edwardes' punitive style was seen increasingly as ill-suited to the emerging business strategy of concentrating on upmarket quality cars, was a case in point. At the opposite extreme, by way of contrast, Smith & Nephew continued throughout the 1980s with a successful business and product strategy; healthy profits were returned each year. The pragmatic approach to labour management was recognized within the company as unadventurous but still highly serviceable. In this setting, anyone broaching a change to the 'formulae' was usually quickly constrained or even sacked. (This happened to one of the innovative general managers during the course of the study.)

The other face of the chimerical quality in HRM was its very lack of firm boundaries. It was not necessary to commit in entirety, and at once, to a package in order to be seen to be keeping abreast of new possibilities. Various elements could be 'drawn down' from human resource management without abandoning the main planks of the extant approach to which still influential segments of the present management team have associated themselves. Ford of Britain exemplified this and so too Peugeot-Talbot.

The variation in the application of human resource management across these cases can, in part then, be interpreted as a result of the micro-political manipulation of symbols. As Weick observed: 'Managerial work can be viewed as managing myth, symbols, and labels . . . because managers traffic so often in images, the appropriate role for the manager may be the evangelist rather than the accountant' (1979: 42).

Manipulating symbols is a distinctly 'political' act. As we saw in chapter 1, symbols carry meanings which extend beyond and beneath their surface, 'apparent' purposes. Merton noted long ago (1936) that social action carries both manifest and latent consequences. Among the latter, as Trice and Beyer (1984) point out, are 'expressive' social consequences such as reaffirming group solidarity or enhancing the prestige of some individual or group. Using this insight they show how OD can be interpreted as a 'rite of renewal' in organizations which carries a range of such consequences. HRM can be seen in a very similar light. It:

- reassures significant others that something is being done about problems

- it disguises the nature of some of the more difficult of these problems

- it focuses attention on some problems and diverts it away from others

- it legitimates and reinforces the power of those able to manipulate these symbols.

HRM is peculiarly rich in symbolism. It conjures images, as we saw, of a people management '*strategy*'; it suggests that this is, moreover, integrated with core business needs; it promises a path towards employee commitment and away from conflict; and it puts management firmly in the driving seat. But which managers will drive is subject to micro-political struggle. The significant place which HR reserves for general and line managers is part of its powerful appeal. Even if it were within the gift of personnel specialists to take control over this form of management they would therefore be unwise to try to monopolize or appropriate it. Part of the expressive message has to continue to be 'all managers are responsible for this . . .'. But, as has been emphasized throughout this book, personnel are not the undisputed keepers or manipulators of these symbols. In those cases where HR had made little headway this had resulted from a number of political factors:

- the power of an entrenched personnel and IR department to fend off this challenge to the 'recipe' they had long safeguarded

- the power of organized labour to make its tenets appear unrealistic

- the failure of any individual or group to pick up this new recipe as a viable way forward in place of the status quo.

Each of these types of circumstance existed in one degree or another in the cases. The variation in managed change across the cases, despite the overall tendency to make some measure of departure from a total reliance on the 'proceduralist' paradigm, can be attributed to this interplay between structural and political factors.

IMPLICATIONS

In this section, the implications of the analysis for practitioners, policy makers and future researchers are considered.

For managerial practitioners, the book carries lessons which are perhaps both encouraging and discouraging. The former aspects arises from the very considerable changes which have been wrought even in what some might consider as the unpromising terrain of Britain's industrial heartland – after all, many of the companies involved in the study were operating with classic 'brownfield' locations. Further encouragement can also be derived from the positive attitudes of the majority of the line managers interviewed during the course of this work.

Discouragement may, however, result from the account herein of how difficult it really is to effect significant and lasting changes in industrial relations. This has been no evangelical work. The book has not carried the flavour of those management-of-change-merchants who imply that if a check-list of simplistic nostrums is followed then the 'management of a culture change' is relatively straightforward. The analysis has been too much of a warts-and-all review to allow for such complacency.

For personnel specialists in particular, the developments examined in this study must give cause for a rethink. The conventional notion that human resource management is something they may have to 'give away' in order to maintain their role, would appear to be somewhat fanciful. The developments recorded in this book represent not so much a new departure within personnel (*pace* Torrington) as a set of movements from outside it. These are sufficiently far reaching as to call for some response from, and possible repositioning by, personnel specialists.

This is especially needful at the most senior levels. Here, the specific advisory service required by line managers at middle and junior levels on matters such as legal requirements and questions of 'consistency', is not really the main point at issue. Rather, the question turns on the kind of contribution of a strategic nature which might be offered in circumstances where the senior team now have fairly firm ideas of their own about managing human resources. The axiom that 'business needs' must have primacy when devising people-management policies and practices, was found to enjoy near universal support. This presented personnel directors with a dilemma. If, in order to win business credibility on the board they suppressed traditional personnel perspectives, the whole question of the distinctive nature of their contribution would be open to question. Almost by definition, personnel specialists are less capable of competing effectively on issues of marketing, finance and corporate strategy, than colleagues raised and practised within these spheres. If on the other hand, the personnel director seeks to give a higher profile to the distinctive attributes of a 'personnel view' this may court the danger of being seen to renege on the 'business primacy' axiom which, as we have noted, is (or at any rate was at the time of the study) peculiarly powerful. The 'deviant innovator' bolt hole based on a plea to consider the merits of social values and to ponder the value of an independent 'professional stance' appeared to be offering a less secure refuge. General managers were themselves already espousing the aphoristic 'people are our greatest asset' statements. The hard question was, what could personnel offer which would help to deliver on this? Interest in personnel's claim to mediate or interpret shopfloor and union perspectives and values had waned. Senior teams were now more interested in what might be 'moved towards' rather than the sober pragmatism what 'was'. Hence, there was fresh regard for the process issues of 'managing culture change' and enactment of vision. Insofar as this implied that personnel directors were pressurized towards embracing an OD-style mantle and a training and development profile, then, what might be discerned in many cases was not so much personnel 'giving human resource management away' as, on the contrary, trying resolutely to acquire a slice of the action.

Trade union representatives are faced with even starker messages. Some trade union leaders when confronted by the catalogue of developments contained herein, in effect, refused to accept that things can have changed that much. It was sometimes difficult to unravel whether in these instances their certitude emanated from wishful thinking or from a sagacious long-term 'feel'. However, a significant minority of union leaders have begun to take a different view. They have recognized the transitions and have started to think through and plan an appropriate response. One example is the way in which some full-time officials have opted to embrace the total quality concept and to use it as a lever which will serve union needs. This is done in part through seeking union representation on the quality councils which are typically the senior watchdogs over TQM. It is also done by using the quality theme as a platform to argue for more adequate facilities, manning levels and working environments.

But the size and nature of the problem which some union leaders face should not be underestimated. Managerial initiatives in the human resource sphere have often been implacably regarded by union representatives as barely-disguised anti-union moves and they have therefore wanted no truck with these measures. As noted above, the bulk of the initiatives have been on the individualistic plane. But this in itself does not necessarily mean the moves are quintessentially anti-union and in certain instances unions could have strengthened their position by taking a more active approach. In a few cases however, the suspicion that derecognition was an agenda item did seem to be justified. Oddly, in the couple of instances where a prime managerial aim was to withdraw bargaining and even representational rights from shop stewards, the circumstances were such that unionism was presenting very little challenge in any case. Part of the explanation seemed to be that these instances occurred in situations where non-union plants were operating geographically close by and the 'model' had enticed certain individual managers.

In a wider frame, there has additionally been some sense in which a number of the new initiatives are to be seen as a 'spillover' of practices from non-union companies. This naturally fuels suspicion. A practice which stopped short of union derecognition but, nonetheless, served to weaken union involvement in negotiating over changes to working practices, was the 'project-team' approach. A number of the case companies had set up joint working parties comprising departmental managers and individuals from the shopfloor who were not necessarily union representatives. The 'joint plans' for changes to working practices – often involving 'teamworking' and 'flexibility' – were then already well fleshed out and carried a 'shopfloor seal of approval' by the time they came to the works committees for discussion.

This type of case is, in a sense, just one instance of the larger phenomenon that seems now obvious but needs noting, – that is, the fact that in recent years the vast majority of initiatives have come from management. Managers in industrial relations have become far less reactive; indeed it has been sometimes a conscious tactic literally to keep the run of the ball. Proposals for change – especially those built on well-researched projects and cases, have put many a union representative on the defensive. Overwhelmed, and lacking a coherent framework for a response, many initiatives have been imposed and pushed through by default.

A key lever in management's hands in enforcing this pace has been the practice of fostering inter-plant competition. Union acquiescence, if not cooperation, has frequently been gained by the threat of withholding investment from plants which do not accept proposed working methods. Today's shorter product life cycles mean that those periods when new investment in plant, products and tooling is urgently required, come round with increasing frequency.

What have unions done in the face of these factors and what might they do? Two different stances have been taken. In the first, the defensive posture, unions have tried to snuff out the installation of intiatives by withholding cooperation and by seeking to boycott, for example, team briefings, attitude-survey feedback sessions and the like. The effectiveness of such oppositional tactics is often difficult to gauge because, while management have usually persisted and have, in consequence, normally claimed victory in such circumstances, to measure the difference between what transpired and what might have transpired is an extremely hazardous venture. Much clearer is the point that the invitations to unions to cooperate in many human resource initiatives have been frequently lacklustre and token. In consequence, many of the initiatives, with some very notable exceptions as described in the body of the book, have simply gone ahead, with unions not so much on the sidelines as out of the frame altogether.

What would happen if trade unions adopted a different stance and sought to play a part in some of these ventures? This question can be answered to an extent by looking at those cases where representatives have sought a new role. The mutuality reported from the USA in such ventures as the GM-UAW Saturn agreement has no parallel so far in Britain but there are cases of dialogue in the 'new' areas of total quality, two-way communications, teamworking, new forms of work organization and performance-related reward. The joint study between MSF and Ford on the future role of the supervisor is but one example of attempted 'jointism'. In other instances, joint problem-solving committees have tackled issues such as alcoholism, training and involvement: that is, topics seen as outside the centre ground of conflicting interests.

Ford's Employee Development and Assistance Programme, a joint union-management initiative, stands as a classic example. What is essentially noteworthy is the degree to which a number of full-time officers have begun to question the simple 'failure-to-agree' tactic. In certain unions, strategic 'reassessment' papers have begun to circulate. These invariably point out the extent of change and the union's lack of 'voice' in that change. Proposals for action tend to hinge around entering into dialogue on quality, on investment and on training. Sometimes even new structural arrangements are floated, such as forms of representation at various levels within the total quality infrastructure. In general though, it has to be said that the extent to which fresh thinking has occurred at these policy levels has been slight. But at least the situation has moved on from the simple tactic of threatening to withdraw from the quality circle programme if the response to the annual wage claim is not expedited and improved.

For the policy maker the messages emanating from the study may appear less than obvious. Past attempts at industrial relations 'reform' in Britain have floundered both when pursued through legislative means and through exhortation and voluntaristic means. While there has been a considerable change recorded in the more recent period, the study also notes the limits to that change. As described, there has been no 'transformation' in these British cases. The comment about the extent of change is in large measure a relative phenomenon – that is when compared with the periods of change in past decades. The factors which help explain those limits to change are deep-seated and structural (Storey and Sisson, 1990). If policy makers are to contribute to moving relationships forward they will need to attend in particular to the problem areas identified in this study – most especially the persistence in the lack of integration between human resource initiatives and the collective aspects which have trodden water, and the related issue of the seeming lack of integration between these practices (individual and collective) and wider business strategy issues. In both regards, policy makers will find themselves in need of further research.

Finally, there is the issue of research implications for the future. Here I want to raise points bearing upon research methods and research perspectives. On the question of methods, it seems clear that further progress will require techniques which go beyond survey questionnaires and interviews into more observational-style approaches. This will be necessary not only for the examination of high-level policy-formulation processes but also for the aspect relating to implementation and response. Employee behaviours have, to an extent, been reshaped by the sheer weight of new demands and constraints – for example, where headcounts have been drastically reduced and yet work throughput has remained the same or increased. But the more nebulous aspects of working in a 'quality way', of offering commitment rather than mere compliance, and of securing an 'attitude' change to work, to management, to organization and to trade union – all require further investigation. In particular, what would next constitute a very fruitful line of research would be an ethnographic study, Donald Roy or Michael Burawoy style, in mainstream workplaces which had already gone some way in transforming their managerial approaches and where initial signals suggested some shopfloor response. The organizations reported upon in this present study would constitute an excellent start-point for such a venture.

Appendix: Research Methods

The research for this book was conducted over the two-year period 1986–88. During this time, data gathering was undertaken as a full-time occupation. Some 350 interviews with managers at all levels were conducted. These managers were located primarily in the 15 core case organizations. Further information was drawn from an additional 'panel' of 20 companies. The distinction between these two sources is explained below.

The main research method was an extensive programme of semi-structured interviews which were conducted, in the majority of cases, in the respondents own place of work. This entailed a great deal of travelling time. I recorded 30,000 car miles on study business plus an unmeasured number of miles travelled by train (usually on the London trips). Meetings were held in places as far flung as Dumfries in Scotland (ICI), Newport in South Wales (Plessey) and Dagenham in Essex (Ford). The study was financed by the Economic and Social Research Council (ESRC).

The two-year period was given over almost wholly to site visits. As the network of contacts extended, the analysis and writing-up phase was pushed into 1989 and 1990.

The issue of which organizations to study was settled by choosing to concentrate on a 'core' group of major, mainstream employers in both the public and private sectors. A listing of these is given in chapter 1. These companies were, in a sense, the central 'test-bed'. They were all extensively unionized – usually on a multi-union basis – and they had elaborated procedures. They were large and complex employers occupying multiple sites and were typically divisionalized in one form or another. Many of them had experienced turbulent periods of industrial unrest. As a group they approximated well to Purcell and Sissons (1983: 112–17) category of 'pragmatic or opportunistic' and Fox's 'standard moderns', although one or two could be entered also under the 'constitutionalist' heading (e.g. Ford) and even the 'sophisticated moderns' (e.g. ICI). When one departs from the ideal-type categorizations and considers these cases, *qua* cases, the similarities are more pressing than the differences. There undoubtedly are differences in emphasis upon, for example, the importance of consultation or the degree of commitment to ne-gotiation and the procedure, but at least during the fluid situation of the 1980s, the commonalities presented the most striking feature.

The core cases were indeed largely settled on precisely because they were seen to be *mainstream* organizations which might be thought to epitomize the standard British approach to industrial relations. Contact was made with the companies almost invari-ably at corporate level and in a range of ways. In particular, Pro-fessors Keith Sisson, George Bain and Chris Voss (all then at the University of Warwick) were generous in their efforts to secure introductions. The detailed negotiation of access was then left to me. The sources were supplemented with my own contacts and also by organizations which volunteered themselves, having heard about the project either from their own networks or having read about the study in the *IRRU Newsletter, Personnel Management,* or *Training and Development.* It was indeed as a result of 'vol-unteers' that the number in the core group grew to fifteen when the original plan had been to think in terms of ten. On the other side of the balance sheet, three organizations which were ap-proached, declined to participate.

The extensiveness of work within the organizations once ac-cess had been negotiated was mainly governed by the available time of the researcher. As already noted, these were very large and complex organizations, the aim in each case was ambitious: it involved a number of interviews at corporate level with both personnel and non-personnel managers followed by an interview programme in selected divisions and at selected sites. Usually, the major sites in each case were included and so these involved, for example Dagenham and Halewood for Ford Motor Company; Longbridge and Cowley for Austin Rover; the Browns Lane and Radford sites for Jaguar; the two 'superbreweries' of Samlesbury (near Preston) and Magor (South Wales) for Whitbread.

Within the establishments, interviews were conducted with the general managers and down through a vertical slice of the main 'production line' managers (e.g. plant director, manufacturing manager, area manager, superintendent, supervisor). In addition, in some cases, interviews were also conducted with union convenors, shop stewards and employees.

Inevitably, with such an extensive and ambitious research approach there was, by the autumn of 1987, a shortage of time. Hence, there was by no means a uniformity of coverage across these organizations. In a number of them particular levels were either missed completely or only sketchily covered. This undoubtedly is a drawback. But, overall, the openness and indeed eagerness of participants to engage in extensive discussion and explanation of issues were overwhelming, and this helped to compensate for gaps in the coverage.

The interviews themselves were variable. They were semi-structured, indeed often discursive, and were accordingly usually rather lengthy. On average they were of between one-and-a-half to two hours in duration. Some lasted as long as three to four hours. Just under half were taped on a microcassette recorder which had a capacity of one hour's usage per side of tape. The tapes were all transcribed, though again with some variability. When transcribed by one of the IRRU secretaries, they were transcribed verbatim and many interviews ran to 20 to 30 pages of A4; but when transcribed by me using a word processor, the interviews were invariably edited.

The interviews were supplemented by the collection of as much relevant documentary material about these organizations as possible. In addition to annual reports, the *Textline* database was found to provide a useful method of accessing published reports on organizational and managerial issues pertaining to these companies. These sources could, however, only furnish backcloth material; the kind of subtle changes being examined meant that only close-up investigation would yield the sort of information which was wanted.

In addition to published sources, organizational members were most generous in collecting and collating the internal documents and statistics that I requested. The sheer bulk of material collected eventually became a problem.

As mentioned, the 15 core case studies were supplemented by a programme of visits to an additional 20 organizations. This latter group was different and was treated differently in two main respects. First they were organizations which had seemingly taken innovative steps of a 'HRM' nature in recent times and they were visited and selected for this precise reason. Second, they were not treated as rounded case studies in the full sense of that term. They were visited usually only once and a typical visit would last half a day and involve a couple of interviews with senior managers and, if it was a production site, a tour of the facilities would normally be included.

There was another distinctive (though unplanned) feature of the supplementary group: unlike the core cases they were almost invariably medium-sized companies of between 1000 to 6000 employees.

Overall, the whole programme of visits and interviews was conducted in a complex and parallel fashion. That is, instead of neatly concluding one case at a time, an attempt was made to keep track of developments in the core cases by periodic revisits, sometimes to the same informants, more typically to new ones. The idea was to back track on developing ideas encountered elsewhere and to test these out in the main cases. This element in the method was undoubtedly an attractive feature for participating organizations for it opened-up a channel for them into a changing world of ideas. Most managers were sceptical of the simple nostrums of Peters and Waterman and were far more interested to discuss developments in Britain and in organizations which they saw as more closely approximating to their own situation and difficulties than the almost fairy tale 'models' of Hewlett Packard and IBM. The parallel approach was also beneficial to me in that aspects I simply had omitted to raise the first time around could be addressed on the follow-up visits. On the other hand, however, it was messy and was very costly in terms of time. It did allow a gestation period so that ideas could be followed through and claims checked through different informants in a way that I found to be extremely difficult, if not simply impossible, during a more concentrated period of two to three days interviewing *en bloc*.

The research methods adopted were then, in fact, an amalgam of approaches which had resonance in some large measure with the detailed studies in the Warwick IRRU tradition. There was, however, one innovation. A series of workshops was instituted where key representative participants of the core cases could receive feedback from the research as it was in progress. These workshops were one-day events held at the University of Warwick. Following a presentation, there was ample time to discuss and debate developments. This in turn generated an additional set of data.

The Warwick workshops were pitched at the policy level. But in addition, there were also a number of operational workshops for managers at 'site' or plant level. The focus of these events was typically a set of interrelated issues turning on the implications of corporate level initiatives. In some cases these top-down 'initiatives' simply took the form of 'enabling' messages or 'encouragement to experiment'. The issues which loomed large were usually the changing roles of middle line managers; the debate about supervisors and work teams; and the appropriate role for personnel specialists. These operational workshops took place on-site and occasionally involved senior stewards.

Overall, the research methods obviously had their strengths and their limitations. On the latter it has to be noted that, first, this was by no means a representative sample in the statistical sense. Second, there is further work to be done on making a closer study of the impact of the change initiatives on shopfloor employees; for example, there was no attempt in the confines of this study to make a systematic analysis of attitudinal change as a result of open-learning programmes or of quality circle participation and the like. Examples were encountered where 'team briefing' and similar innovations had been initially boycotted but eventually 'lived with' or even 'accepted'. But what real impact this 'acceptance' involved could not be fully gauged. Third, although, as noted, a series of parallel visits and re-interviews was arranged, this study, within a two-year time-frame could not really be considered 'longitudinal' and, given the nature of the issues being investigated, this is what could really help. While I avoided the 'snapshot' approach, there were naturally a whole range of instances where initiatives were being launched and it was difficult to see what would eventually happen to them. Fourth, on some aspects of the investigations a research approach based rather less on interviewing and rather more on observation would clearly be beneficial. On those occasions in the course of this study when observational techniques were exercised, as for example, at managerial 'efficiencies' meetings or when managers addressed the shopfloor to convince them of the need to accept some change, or where supervisors were 'shadowed' the occasions proved to be very illuminating. Although such events comprised only a small part of the overall package – which was certainly weighted towards interviewing – these occasions helped to inform the way information imparted in interviews was received. They also helped indeed, to shape the way future interviews were conducted.

Bibliography

Abernathy, W. J. (1983) *Industrial Renaissance.* New York: Basic Books.
ACAS/LBS (1986) *Participation and Communication: A Survey of Company Reports.* London: Advisory, Conciliation and Arbitration Service in association with London Business School.
Aglietta, M. (1979) *A Theory of Capitalist Regulation.* London: New Left Books.
Ahlstrand, B. (1990) *The Quest for Productivity: A Case Study of Fawley After Flanders.* Cambridge: Cambridge University Press.
Altshuler, A. and Appel, H. (1984) *The Future of the Automobile.* Boston, Mass.: MIT Press.
Anthony, P. D. (1977) *The Ideology of Work.* London: Tavistock.
Armstrong, P. (1984) Management control strategies and inter-professional competition: the case of accounting and personnel management. Paper presented in the UMIST/Aston *Second Annual Labour Process Conference,* University of Aston 28–30 March.
Armstrong, P. (1988) Labour and monopoly capital. In R. Hyman and W. Streeck (eds), *New Technology and Industrial Relations.* Oxford: Blackwell.
Armstrong, P. (1989) Limits and possibilities for HRM in an age of management accountancy. In J. Storey (ed.) *New Perspectives on Human Resource Management.* London: Routledge.
Atkinson, J. (1984) Manning for uncertainty – some emerging UK work patterns. *Institute for Manpower Studies.*
Atkinson, J. (1985) Flexibility: planning for an uncertain future. *Manpower Policy and Practice* 1, summer, 25–30.
Atkinson, J. and Gregory, D. (1986) A flexible future: Britain's dual labour force. *Marxism Today,* April.

Atkinson, J. and Meager, N. (1986) Is flexibility just a flash in the pan? *Personnel Management*, September.

Audit Commission (1988) The competitive council. *Management Papers*, no. 1, The Audit Commission for Local Authorities in England and Wales, March.

Bain, G. S. (ed.) (1983) *Industrial Relations in Britain*. Oxford: Blackwell.

Bassett, P. (1986) *Strike Free*. London: Macmillan.

Batstone, E. (1984) *Working Order*. Oxford: Blackwell.

Batstone, E. (1988) *The Reform of Workplace Industrial Relations*. Oxford: Clarendon.

Beaumont, P. (1992/forthcoming) *The US Human Resource Management Literature – A Review*. OU B884 'HR Strategies' (offprint), Milton Keynes: Open University.

Beckhard, R. (1987) Strategies for large system change. In E. H. Schein, (ed.), *The Art of Managing Human Resources*. Oxford: Oxford University Press.

Beckhard, R. and Harris, R. (1977) *Organisational Transitions: Managing Complex Change*. Reading, Mass.: Addison Wesley.

Beer, M., Eisenstat, R. and Spector, B. (1990) *The Critical Path to Corporate Renewal*. Boston: Harvard Business School Press.

Beer, M., Spector, B., Lawrence, P., Mills, D. and Walton, R. (1985) *Human Resources Management: A General Manager's Perspective*. New York: Free Press.

Belasco, J. A. and Alutto, J. A. (1969) Line and staff conflicts: some empirical insights. *Academy of Management Journal*, 12, December, 469–77.

Benjamin, A. and Benson, N. (1986) Why ignore the value of people? *Accountancy*, February.

Blackburn, P., Coombs, R. and Green, K. (1985) *Technology, Economic Growth and the Labour Process*. Basingstoke: Macmillan.

Bolman, L. and Deal, T. (1984) *Modern Approaches to Understanding and Managing Organisations*. San Francisco: Jossey-Bass.

Bradford, D. L. and Cohen, A. R. (1984) *Managing for Excellence: The Guide to Developing High Performance in Contemporary Organisations*. New York: Wiley.

Braverman, H. (1974) *Labor and Monopoly Capital*. New York: Monthly Review Press.

Browne, P. J. and Golembiewski, R. T. (1974) The line-staff concept revisited: and empirical study of organizational images. *Academy of Management Journal*, September, 406–17.

Brown, W. (1981) *The Changing Contours of British Industrial Relations: A Survey of Manufacturing Industry*. Oxford, Blackwell.

Buchanan, D. and McCalman, J. (1988) Competence, visibility &

pressure: the effects of shared information in computer aided hotel management. *New Technology, Work & Employment*, 3.

Chandler, A. D. (1962) *Strategy and Structure.* Cambridge, Mass: MIT Press.

Channon, D. (1982) Industrial structure. *Long Range Planning*, vol. 15, no. 5.

Child, J. and Partridge, Bruce (1982) *Lost Managers: Supervisors in Industry and Society.* Cambridge University Press.

Coch, L. and French, J. R. Overcoming resistance to change. *Human Relations*, vol. 1, 512–32.

Commission on Industrial Relations (1973) Report No 34, *The Role of Management in Industrial Relations.*

Constable, J. and McCormick, R. (1987) *The Making of British Managers.* London: British Institute of Management.

Cowan, N. (1986) The future role of the personnel manager. *Warwick Papers in Industrial Relations*, University of Warwick, Paper No. 4.

Cuthbert, N. H. (1973) Industrial relations and the development of company policies. In N H Cuthbert and K H Hawkins (eds) *Company Industrial Relations Policies.* London: Longman.

Daly, A., Hitchens, D. M. W. N. and Wagner, K. (1985) Productivity, machinery and skills in a sample of British and German manufacturing plants. *National Institute Economic Review*, February.

Dandridge, T. C., Mitroff, I. and Joyce, W. F. (1980) Organizational Symbolism: a topic to expand organizational analysis. *Academy of Management Review*, 5, 1: 77–82.

Deutschmann, C. (1987) Debureaucratization of enterprise organisation, work groups and industrial relations. Paper presented at the Second European Regional Congress of the *International Industrial Relations Association*, Tel Aviv, December.

Devanna, M. A., Fombrun, C. J. and Tichy, N. M. (1984) A framework for strategic human resource management. In C. J. Fombrun et al., *op.cit.*

Dickson, J. (1977) Plight of the middle manager. *Management Today*, December.

Donovan (1968) Royal Commission on Trade Unions and Employers' Associations (1968), *Report*, cmnd no 3623, HMSO, London.

Dopson, S. and Stewart, R. (1990) What is happening to middle management? *British Journal of Management*, 1, 1.

Drucker. P. F. (1988) The coming of the New Organization. *Harvard Business Review*, Jan/Feb.

Dyer, L. (1984) Studying Human resource strategy: an approach and an agenda. *Industrial Relations*, vol. 23, no. 2.

Dyer, L. and Holder, G. (1988) A strategic perspective of human resource management. In L Dyer (ed.) *Human Resource Management: Evolving Roles and Responsibilities*. Washington DC, BNA.

Edwards, R. C. (1979) *Contested Terrain: The Transformation of the Workplace in the Twentieth Century*. London: Heinemann.

Edwards, P. K. (1987) *Managing the Factory*. Oxford: Blackwell.

Edwardes, M. (1983) *Back from the Brink*. London: Collins.

Eliade, M. (1963) *Myth and Reality*. New York: Harper and Row.

Fidler, J. (1981) *The British Business Elite: Its Attitudes to Class Status and Power*. London: Routledge.

Flamholz, E. (1974) *Human Resource Accounting*. Encino, Calif.: Dickenson Publishing Co.

Flanders, A. (1964) *The Fawley Productivity Agreements*. London: Faber and Faber.

Fombrun, C., Tichy, N. M. and Devanna, M. A. (1984) *Strategic Human Resource Management*. New York: Wiley.

Fox, A. (1966) Managerial Ideology and Labour Relations. *British Journal of Industrial Relations*, vol. 4.

Fox, A. (1974) *Beyond Contract: Work, Power and Trust Relations*. London: Faber.

Friedman, D. (1983) Beyond the age of Fordism: the strategic basis of Japanese success in automobiles. In J. Zysman and L. Tyson (eds) *American Industry in International Competition*. Ithaca: Cornell University Press.

Gabriel, Y. (1987) *Working Lives in Catering*. London: Routledge.

Gardner, B. and Whyte, W. F. (1945) The man in the middle: position and problems of the foreman. *Applied Anthropology*, 4, 2.

Giles, W. J. and Robinson, D. F. (1972) *Human Asset Accounting*. London: Institute of Personnel Management and Institute of Cost and Management Accountants.

Goffee, F. and Scase, R. (1986) Are the rewards worth the effort? Changing managerial values in the 1980s. *Personnel Review*, 15.

Goold, M. and Campbell, A. (1986) *Strategies and Styles: The Role of the Centre in Managing Diversified Corporations*. Oxford: Blackwell.

Gowler, D. and Legge, K. (1983) The meaning of management and the management of meaning. In M. Earl (ed.) *Perspectives on Management*, Oxford: OUP.

Guest, D. (1987) Human resource management and industrial relations. *Journal of Management Studies*, 24, 5.

Guest, D. (1989a) Personnel and HRM: can you tell the difference? *Personnel Management*, January.

Guest, D. (1989b) Human resource management: its implications for industrial relations and trade unions. In J. Storey (ed.) *New Perspectives on Human Resource Management*, London: Routledge.

Guest, D. (1990) Human resource management and the American Dream. *Journal of Management Studies*, 27, 4.

Guest, R. H. (1962) *Organisational Change*. Homewood, Ill.: Dorsey Press.

Hackman, J. R., Oldham, G, Janson, R. and Purdy, K. (1975) A new strategy for job enrichment. *California Management Review*, 17, 4: 57–71.

Haimann, T., Scott, W. G. and Connor, P. E. (1978) *Managing the Modern Organization*. Boston: Houghton Mifflin.

Hall, A. (1986) Automation could make the factory foreman extinct. *Business Week*, March 31.

Hampden-Turner, C. (1990) *Charting the Corporate Mind*. Oxford: Basil Blackwell.

Hampden-Turner, C. (1990) *Corporate Culture: From Vicious to Vitrtuous Circles*. London: Hutchinson.

Handy, C. (1987) *The Making of Managers: a Report on Management Education, Training and Development in the United States, West Germany, France, Japan, and the UK*. London: National Economic Development Office.

Hawkins, K. (1978) *The Management of Industrial Relations*. Harmondsworth: Penguin.

Hayes, R. H. and Abernathy, W. J. (1982) Managing our way to economic decline. In M. L. Tushman and W. L. Moore (eds) *Readings in the Management of Innovation*. Cambridge, Mass.: Pitman.

Hopper, T., Storey, J. and Willmott, H. (1987) Accounting for accounting: towards the development of a dialectical view. *Accounting Organisations and Society*, 12, 5.

Hughes, J. (1976) *Sociological Analysis: Methods of Discovery*. Sunbury-on-Thames: Nelson.

Hunt, J. (1986) Alienation among managers – the new epidemic or the social scientists' invention? *Personnel Review*.

Hyman, R. (1988) 'Flexible specialization: miracle or myth? In R. Hyman and W. Streeck (eds) *New Technology and Industrial Relations*, Oxford: Blackwell.

Incomes Data Services (1986) *Flexibility at Work*. Study 360, April. London: IDS.

Industrial Relations Review and Report (1984) Flexibility agreements: the end of who does what? March, 316.

Industrial Relations Review and Report (1984) Merit pay for manual workers. May, 319.

Industrial Relations Review and Report (1986) Nissan: a catalyst for change. November, 379.

Jacques, E. (1952) *The Changing Culture of a Factory*. London: Tavistock.

Jauch, R. and Skigen, M. (1977) Human resource accounting: a critical evaluation. In Benston, G. J. (ed.) *Contemporary Cost Accounting and Control*, Boston: CBI Publishing Co.

Johnson, G. (1990) Managing strategic change: the role of symbolic action. *British Journal of Management*, 1, 4.

Kanter, R. (1984) *The Change Masters*. London: Allen & Unwin.

Kanter, R. M. (1986) The reshaping of middle management. *Management Review*, January.

Katz, H. (1985) *Shifting Gears*. Cambridge, Mass.: MIT Press

Keep, E. (1989) Corporate training strategies: the vital component? In J. Storey (ed.) *New Perspectives on Human Resource Management*. London: Routledge.

Kerr, S. (1986) The first-line supervisor: phasing out or here to stay? *Academy of Management Review*, 11, 1.

Klein, J. (1984) Why supervisors resist employee involvement. *Harvard Business Review*, September–October.

Klein, J. (1986) The changing role of first line supervision and middle management. Harvard Business School, *mimeo*.

Kochan, T. A., Katz, H., and McKersie, R. B. (1986) *The Transformation of American Industrial Relations*. New York: Basic Books.

Kochan, T. A., Katz, H., and McKersie, R. B. (1990) Strategic choice and industrial relations theory: an elaboration. Paper presented to Second Bargaining Group Conference, Cornell University, May 6–7.

Legge, K. (1978) *Power, Innovation and Problem Solving*. In *Personnel Management*, New York: McGraw Hill.

Legge, K. (1988) Personnel management in recession and recovery: a comparative analysis of what the surveys say. *Personnel Review*, 17, 2.

Legge, K. (1989) Human Resource Management: A Critical Analysis, In J. Storey (ed.) *New Perspectives on Human Resource Management*. London: Routledge.

Littler, C. and Salaman, G. (1982) Bravermania and beyond: recent theories of the labour process. *Sociology*, 16, 2.

Logan, H. H. (1966) Line and staff: an obsolete concept? *Personnel*, January/Feb, 26–33.

Long, P. (1986) *Performance Appraisal Revisited*. London: Institute of Personnel Management.

MacInnes, J. (1987) *Thatcherism at Work*. Milton Keynes: Open University Press.

Mackay, L. and Torrington, D. (1986) *The Changing Nature of Personnel Management*. London: Institute of Personnel Management.

McCarthy, W. E. J. and Ellis, N. D. (1973) *Management by Agreement*. London: Hutchinson.

McKinsey & Co./NEDO (1988) *Performance and Competitive Success:*

Strengthening Competitiveness in UK Electronics. A report prepared by McKinsey & Co. London.

Malinowski, B. (1955) *Myth in Primitive Psychology.* New York: Harper and Row.

Manpower Services Commission/National Economic Development Office (1986) *Challenge to Complacency.* Sheffield: MSC.

Marchington, M. and Parker, P. (1990) *Changing Patterns of Employee Relations.* Hemel Hempstead: Harvester Wheatsheaf.

Marginson, P., Sisson, K., Martin, R. and Edwards, P. (1988) *Beyond the Workplace.* Oxford: Blackwell.

Marsden, D. & Thompson, M. (1990) Flexibility agreements in Britain and their significance in the increase in productivity in British manufacturing since 1980. *Work, Employment & Society,* June.

Marsh, A. I. and Gillies, J. T. (1983) The involvement of line and staff managers in industrial relations. In K. Thurley and S. Wood (eds) *Industrial Relations & Management Strategy,* Cambridge University Press.

Merton, R. K. (1936) The unanticipated consequences of purposive social action. *American Sociological Review,* 11: 894–904.

Millman, Z. and Hartwick, J. (1987) The impact of automated office systems on middle managers and their work. *MIS Quarterly,* 11.

Millward, N. and Stevens, M. (1986) *British Workplace Industrial Relations 1980–84,* Aldershot: Gower.

Mitchell, C. (1983) Case and situation analysis. *The Sociological Review,* 31, 2: 187–210.

Monks, J. (1989) Review of Peter Wickens' *The Road to Nissan.* In *British Journal of Industrial Relations,* March, XXVII, 1.

Morgan, G. (1988) *Riding the Waves of Change: Developing Managerial Competences for a Turbulent World.* London: Jossey-Bass.

NEDO (1987) *Education and Training in Lucas Industries.* London: NEDO/MSC/DTI.

NEDO (1989) *Diffusing the Demographic Timebomb.* London: NEDO in association with the Training Agency.

NEDO/Manpower Services Commission (1984) *Competence and Competition.* London: NEDO.

Nichols, T., and Beynon, H. (1977) *Living with Capitalism.* London: Routledge and Kegan Paul.

Nolan, P. (1989) Walking on water? Performance and industrial relations under Thatcher. *Industrial Relations Journal,* 20, 2.

Nonaka, I. (1988) Towards middle up/down management: accelerating information creation. *Sloan Management Review,* spring, 29.

Odiorne, G. S. (1985) *Strategic Management of Human Resources: A Portfolio Approach.* San Francisco: Jossey-Bass.

Palloix, C. (1976) The labour process: from Fordism to Neo-Fordism. In Conference of Socialist Economists (eds) *The Labour Process and Class Strategies*, London: Stage One.

Parnaby, J. (1987a) The need for fundamental change in UK manufacturing systems engineering. Paper to Advanced Manufacturing Summit, 12–14 May, Birmingham: NEC.

Parnaby, J. (1987b) Competitiveness via total quality of performance. *Mimeo*, Birmingham: Lucas Industries.

Pascale, T. T. (1990) *Managing on the Edge: How Successful Companies Use Conflict to Stay Ahead*. London: Viking Penguin.

Peschanski, V. V. (1985) Middle managers in contemporary capitalism. Institute of Economy and Politics (IMEMO), Moscow, *Acta Sociologica*, 28.

Peters, T. J. (1978) Symbols, patterns and settings. *Organizational Dynamics*, 7, 2: 3–22.

Peters, T. J. (1987) *Thriving on Chaos: Handbook for the Managerial Revolution*. London: Macmillan.

Peters, T. J. (1988) *Thriving on Chaos*. New York: Random House.

Peters, T. and Austin, N. (1985) *A Passion for Excellence: the Leadership Difference*. Collins.

Peters, T. and Waterman, R. (1982) *In Search of Excellence*. New York: Harper and Row.

Peters, Tom (1989) *The Tom Peters Experience: The Customer Revolution*. BBC Enterprises.

Pettigrew, A. M. (1985) *The Awakening Giant*. Oxford: Blackwell.

Pettigrew, A. M. (ed.) (1988) *The Management of Strategic Change*. Oxford: Blackwell.

Pettigrew, A. M. and Whipp, R. (1991) *Managing Change for Competitive Success*. Oxford: Blackwell.

Pfeffer, J. (1981) Management as symbolic action: the creation and maintenance of organizational paradigms. In Cummings, L. L. and Straw, B. M. (eds) *Research in Organizational Behaviour*, 3, Greenwich, Conn: JAI Press: 1–52.

Piore, M. J. and Sabel, C. F. (1984) *The Second Industrial Divide: Possibilities for Prosperity*. New York: Basic Books.

Plant, R. (1987) *Managing Change and Making it Stick*. London: Fontana.

Pondy, L. R. et al. (1983) *Organizational Symbolism*. London: JAI Press.

Purcell, J. (1987) Mapping management styles in employee relations. *Journal of Management*. 24, 5.

Purcell, J. (1989) The impact of corporate strategy on human resource management. In J. Storey (ed.) *New Perspectives in Human Resource Management*.

Purcell, J. and Gray, A. (1986) Corporate personnel departments and the management of industrial relations. Two case studies in ambiguity, *Journal of Management Studies*, 23, 2, 205–23.

Purcell, J. and Sisson, K. (1983) Strategies and practice in the management of industrial relations. In G. Bain (ed.) *Industrial Relations in Britain*. Oxford: Blackwell.

Roethlisberger, F. J. (1945) The foreman: master and victim of double-talk. *Harvard Business Review*, spring.

Sabel, C. F. (1982) *Work and Politics*. Cambridge: Cambridge University Press.

Salaman, G. (1979) *Work Organizations: Resistance and Control*. London: Longman.

Scase, R. and Goffee, R. (1989) *Reluctant Managers: Their Work and Lifestyles*. London: Unwin.

Schein, E. (1977) Increasing organisational effectiveness through better human resource planning and development. In Schein (ed.) *The Art of Managing Human Resources*, Oxford: Oxford University Press.

Schein, E. (1987) *The Art of Managing Human Resources*. New York: Oxford University Press.

Schuler, R. (1988) Human resource management practice choices. In R. S. Schuler, S. A. Youngblood and V. L. Huber (eds) *Readings in Management*, 3rd edn, St Paul, Minn.: West Publishing.

Schuler, R. S. and Jackson, S. E. (1987) Linking competitive strategies with human resource management practices. *Academy of Management Executive*, 1, 3.

Schuller, T. (1989) Financial participation. In J. Storey (ed.) *New Perspective on Human Resource Management*. London: Routledge.

Schutz, A. (1972) *The Phenomenology of the Social World*. London: Heinemann.

Sisson, K. (1989) Personnel management in transition? In K. Sisson (ed.) *Personnel Management in Britain*. Oxford: Blackwell.

Sisson, K. and Scullion, H. (1985) Putting the corporate personnel department in its place. *Personnel Management*, December.

Smircich, l. and Stubbart, C. (1985) Strategic management in an enacted world. *Academy of Management Review*, 10, 4: 724–36.

Smith, C. and Child, J. (1987) The context and process of organisational transformation – Cadbury Ltd in its sector. *Journal of Management Studies*, 24, 6.

Steedman, H. and Wagner, K. (1987) A second look at productivity, machinery and skills in Britain and Germany. *National Institute Economic Review*, November.

Stewart, R. (1963) *The Reality of Management*. London: Pan.

Storey, J. (1980) *The Challenge to Management Control*. London: Kogan Page.

Storey, J. (1983) *Managerial Prerogative and the Question of Control*. London: Routledge and Kegan Paul.

Storey, J. (1985) The means of management control. *Sociology*, May.

Storey, J. (1987) Developments in the management of human resources: an interim report. *Warwick Papers in Industrial Relations* no. 17, IRRU, School of Industrial and Business Studies, University of Warwick, November.

Storey, J. (1989) Human Resource Management in the Public Sector. *Public Money and Management*, 9, 3.

Storey, J. (ed.) (1989) *New Perspectives on Human Resource Management*. London: Routledge.

Storey, J. and Fenwick, N. (1989) Bradford's two revolutions: political, organisational and human resource management change in a large Local Authority. *Journal of Organisational Change Management*, 1, 2.

Storey, J. and Fenwick, N. (1990) The changing face of employment management in local government. *Journal of General Management*, Autumn.

Storey, J. and Sisson, K. (1990) Limits to transformation: human resource management in the British context. *Industrial Relations Journal*, 21, 1.

Streeck, W. (1986) *Industrial Relations and Industrial Change in the Motor Industry: An International View*. Coventry: University of Warwick.

Thackeray, J. (1988) Tightening the White Collar. *Management Today*, July.

Thurley, K. and Hamblin, A. C. (1963) *The Supervisor and his Job*. Department of Scientific & Industrial Research, Problems of Progress in Industry, 13, HMSO.

Thurley, K. and Wirdenius, H. (1973) *Supervision: a reappraisal*. London: Heinemann.

Tolliday, S. and Zeitlin, J. (eds.) (1987) Introduction in New York: Berg Publishing. *Between Fordism and Flexibility*.

Torrington, D. (1989) Human resource management and the personnal function. In J. Storey (ed.) *New Perspectives on Human Resource Management*.

Torrington, D. and Mackay, L. (1986) Will consultants take over the personnel function? *Personnel Management*, February.

Torrington, D. and Hall, L. (1987) *Personnel Management: A New Approach*. London: Prentice Hall.

Trevor, M. (1988) *Toshiba's New British Company: Competitiveness Through Innovation in Industry*. London: Policy Studies Institute.

Trice, H. M. and Beyer, J. (1984) Studying organizational cultures through rites and ceremonials. *Academy of Management Review*, 9, 4.

Tse, K. (1985) *Marks & Spencer*, Oxford: Pergamon.

Turrill, T. (1986) *Change and Innovation: A challenge for the NHS.* London: Institute of Health Services Management.

Turner, B. A. (ed.) (1990) *Organizational Symbolism.* New York: de Gruyter.

Tyson, S. and Fell, A. (1986) *Evaluating the Personnel Function.* London: Hutchinson.

Walton, R. E. (1985) From control to commitment in the workplace. *Harvard Business Review*, March/April, 2: 77–9.

Walton, R. E. (1987) *Innovating to Compete: Lessons for Diffusing and Managing Change in the Workplace.* San Francisco: Jossey-Bass.

Walton, R. E. and Lawrence, R. R. (eds) (1985) *Human Resource Management: Trends and Challenges.* Boston: Harvard Business School Press.

Weber, M. (1949) *The Methodology of the Social Sciences.* New York: Free Press.

Weick, K. E. (1979) Cognitive processes in organizations. In B. M. Staw (ed.) *Research in Organizations*, I. Greenwich, Conn.: JAI Press.

White, M. and Trevor, M. (1983) *Under Japanese Management: The Experience of British Workers.* London: Heinemann.

Wickens, P. (1987) *The Road to Nissan.* London: Macmillan.

Winkler, J. (1974) The ghost at the bargaining table: directors and industrial relations. *British Journal of Industrial Relations*, 12, 2.

Wood, S. (1988) Between Fordism and flexibility? The US car industry. In R. Hyman and W. Streeck (eds) *New Technology and Industrial Relations.* Oxford: Blackwell.

Index

ACAS, 117
Ahlstrand, B., 4–5, 250
Alutto, J. A., 190
Anthony, P. D., 25
anthropology, 4–5
appraisal, 14–15, 107–8, 224, 230
Armstrong, Geoff, 151
Armstrong, M., 163
Armstrong, P., 39
attitude surveys, 60
Audit Commission, 63, 126
Austin Rover, 16, 50, 52–4, 269, 270, 271
  deployment and utilization in, 90
  line management in, 194, 199–200
  management of change in, 125, 150, 151–2
  personnel specialists in, 171, 176
  quality circles in, 110
  supervisors in, 221, 224
  trade unions in, 248, 250–1, 261
  training in, 224

BP, 120
banks, 12
Barclays Bank, 117
Barr, Andy, 52
Bassett, P., 16
Beaumont, P., 243
Beckhard, R., 119, 120, 143
Beer, M., 25, 40, 43, 189
behaviours
  explanations of, 3
  managers', 211–14
Belasco, J. A., 190
Benyon, H., 218
Beyer, J., 5, 272
biodata screening, 54, 79, 99
Birds Eye Walls, 20
  deployment and utilization in, 87–9
  management of change in, 148–9
  supervisors in, 225–7, 241
Bradford Metropolitan Council, 50, 63–4, 79, 270
  management of change in, 125–7, 153
  trade unions in, 251, 252, 261
briefing meetings, 14, 70, 101, 106

British Airways, 15, 43, 120, 153
British Rail, 12, 16, 50, 61–2,
    78–9, 270
  communications in, 106, 206–7
  deployment and utilization in,
    90–1
  line management in, 205–7
  management of change in, 126,
    153
  pay in, 108–9
  personnel specialists in, 172–4,
    178–9
  recruitment and selection in,
    205–6
  supervisors in, 239
  trade unions in, 245, 257, 261
British Telecom, 43, 120
Brown, W., 193
Browne, P. J., 190
business orientation, 24
business policy movement, 28–9

Cadbury, 16, 39
car industry, 12
  see also individual companies
career break schemes, 98
career development, 98, 223
Challenge to Complacency
    (MSC/NEDO), 14
change, organizational, 4, 9–10,
    118–22
  case studies of, 125–33,
    134–41, 143–9
  diffusion of, 149–56, 161
  framework for analysis of,
    122–5, 130, 133–4, 142, 160
  nature and extent of, 264–5
  selling of, 156–9
  trade unions and, 245–9,
    (outsider role for, 250–1,
    254; partner role for, 251–5)
Child, J., 39, 218
Chrysler, 120

Clarke, Kenneth, 147
Coch, L., 120
cognitive shifts, 4
collective bargaining *see* trade
    unions
communication with employees,
    14, 28, 101–6, 156–9, 206–8,
    248
Competence and Competition
    (NEDO/MSC), 14
computer aided manufacture, 200
computerized human resource
    planning, 85
conceptual models, 30, 32–4
concession bargaining, 133
confidence, 211–14
Connor, P. E., 190
Constable, J., 14, 112
consultants, 37, 99, 135, 155–6
corporate strategy movement,
    28–9
cost centres, 199, 231
Council of the Management
    Charter Initiative, 14
Council for Management
    Educational Development,
    14
crises, response to, 44–5, 150–1
Crosby, Philip, 75
culture, organizational, 13–14, 31
  see also change
Cuthbert, N. H., 25

Dandridge, T. C., 4
decentralization, 42
demographic change, 12, 84
deployment and utilization of
    employees, 87–97
descriptive models, 30, 31–2
Devanna, M. A., 24
development *see* training and
    development
diversification, 42

domain demand mapping, 161
Dopson, S., 191

Eaton Ltd., 44, 51, 64–6, 269,
  270
management of change in, 140,
  150–1
personnel specialists in, 175
quality circles in, 111
supervisors in, 231–4, 241
trade unions in, 261
education *see* training and
  development
Edwardes, Michael, 52, 221, 271
Edwards, P. K., 193
Edwards, R. C., 45
Egan, John, 59, 151
Eliade, M., 4
Employment Act (1982), 117
enterprise culture, 15
excellence literature, 32

Fell, A., 167
Fidler, J., 202
first line managers *see*
  supervisors
Flanders, A., 91, 259–60
flexibility, notion of, 15, 89
  see also change
Fombrun, C. J., 24
Ford Motor Co., 16, 39, 50, 54–7,
  270, 272
communications in, 106, 158–9,
  206
deployment and utilization in,
  90, 91–5
line management in, 194, 203,
  206
management of change in,
  139–41, 153, 155, 158–9, 179
personnel specialists in, 170–2,
  179–80, 184
and quality circles, 110

supervisors in, 217, 234–8, 240
trade unions in, 36, 247–8,
  251–2, 257, 258, 261–2,
  277–8
foremen *see* supervisors
Fox, A., 2, 281
French, J. R., 120
functionalism, 3

Gardner, B., 218
GEC, 90, 175
Gillies, J. T., 191
globalization trends, 12
goal setting, 107
Golden Wonder, 20
human resources planning in,
  85–6, 89
Golembiewski, R. T., 190
graduates, 98, 223, 234
Griffiths Report, 61, 143
Guest, D., 26, 32, 34, 244
Guest, R., 120

Haimann, T., 190
Hall, A., 218
Hall, L., 162
Hamblin, A. C., 218
Hampden-Turner, C., 22
Handy, C., 14, 112
Harris, R., 120
Harvey-Jones, Sir John, 143
Hewlett Packard, 16
Honda, 150
Hougham, John, 171, 247–8
Hughes, J., 32
human asset accountancy, 29–30
human capital theory, 29
human relations movement, 28
human resource management
  (HRM)
conclusions on, 263–73
conditions for development of,
  41–5, 46

as 'continuity', 7, 11, 263
explanations of, 3–10
implications of, 273–9
intellectual antecedents of, 28–30
meanings of, 23–8, 45–6
models of, 16–17, 30–41
as new paradigm, 1–3, 6
as 'transformation', 7, 10–17, 263
human resource planning, 84–6, 87, 89
Hymer, Stuart, 235

IBM, 15
ICI, 51, 74–5, 78, 117, 269
management of change in, 120, 134–8, 150
personnel specialists in, 179
trade unions in, 261
ideal types, 34
Industrial Society, 106
initiatives, numbers and impact of, 7, 43–4
interpretive analysis, 3
interviewing, 99–100
involvement of employees, 14, 109–11, 117

Jacques, E., 120
Jaguar, 50, 59–60, 78, 269, 270
communications in, 104–5, 207
deployment and utilization in, 90
line management in, 207
management of change in, 125, 151
quality circles in, 110
recruitment and selection in, 99
trade unions in, 247, 257, 258, 261
training in, 112

Japan, 12, 150
Jenkins, Clive, 234
Johnson, G., 4
Johnson and Johnson, 43
just-in-time, 115, 200, 218

Kanter, R. M., 120
Katz, H., 55, 139, 265
Keep, E., 112
Kerr, S., 218
Klein, J., 218
Kochan, T. A., 1, 36, 55, 139, 265

language, use of, 6, 154
Lawson, Nigel, 108
leadership, 100–1, 158
Legge, K., 30–1, 167
Lever Brothers, 16
line management, 18, 31, 58–9, 60, 274
and human resources management, 189–93, 202–15, 266–7, (case studies of, 193–202)
personnel specialists' attitudes to, 164–5, 167, 170–83 *passim*
see also supervisors
Logan, H. H., 190
Long, P., 107
Lucas, 51, 66–7, 270
line management in, 195–6, 210
management of change in, 150
pay in, 109
personnel specialists in, 179
trade unions in, 247, 257, 261
training in, 113–16, 210
Lunn, Terry, 166–7

McCormick, R., 14, 112
MacInnes, J., 11

McKersie, R. B., 139, 265
Malinowski, B., 4
Management Charter Initiative, 14, 208
management consultants, 37, 99, 135, 155–6
manpower (human resources) planning, 84–6
Manpower Services Commission (MSC), 14
manufacturing requirements planning (MRP II), 201
Marchington, M., 243
Marginson, P., 181
market orientation, 12
Marks and Spencer, 16
Marsden, D., 243–4
Marsh, A. I., 191
Marshall, Colin, 153
Massey Ferguson, 51, 67–9, 78, 269, 270
  line management in, 194, 210, 211
  management of change in, 120, 130–1, 154
  personnel specialists in, 175
  trade unions in, 246–7, 257, 258
  training in, 210, 211
material requirements planning, 200, 218
MBA programmes, 119
meaning systems, 6, 212–13
Merton, R. K., 272
Metal Box, 20
methodology, 19–21, 280–5
micro-politics, 3
middle management *see* line management
Millward, N., 139, 191–2
mission statements, 56, 57, 144, 153
Monks, John, 263

Morgan, G., 120
motivation, 100–1
myth and ritual, 4–5, 272

National Economic Development Office (NEDO), 14, 84, 112, 161
National Health Service, 16, 50, 61, 78–9, 270
  human resource planning in, 84
  line management in, 202
  management of change in, 120, 126, 143–8, 153
  pay in, 108
  trade unions in, 261
National Society of Quality Circles, 117
networking, 155
Nichols, T., 218
Nissan, 15, 100
normative models, 30–1
no-strike agreements, 86

objective setting, 107
Odiorne, G. S., 29–30
open learning, 112, 211
organizational development, 120, 154
  see also change
overseas visits, 150

Parham, Dick, 203, 219
Parker, P., 243
Parnaby, Dr John, 67, 113–15
participation *see* involvement
Partridge, B., 218
Pascale, R., 22
payment and reward systems, 109
  performance related, 14, 107, 108

Peach, L., 143, 153
performance appraisal, 14–15, 107–8, 224, 230
performance related pay, 14, 107, 108
personnel management, 24, 30–1, 274–5
and human resource management, 162–8, 185–8 (advisor role, 168, 170–2; changemaker role, 169, 180–5, 186–7; handmaiden role, 168, 172–5; regulator role, 168–9, 175–80, 187)
Peters, T., 101, 120, 121, 126, 130
Pettigrew, A. M., 119, 120
Peugeot-Talbot, 50, 58–9, 269, 272
communication in, 101–3, 156, 207
deployment and utilization in, 90, 95–7
line management in, 194, 202, 203–4, 207, 209–10
quality circles in, 110
recruitment and selection in, 99
training in, 209–10
Pfeffer, J., 4
phenomenology, 3
planning *see* human resource planning
Plant, R., 119
Plessey, 51, 71–2
appraisal in, 108
communication in, 106
deployment and utilization in, 90
quality circles in, 111
trade unions in, 249–50, 255–6, 261
pluralism, 177, 258–9
Pondy, L. R., 4, 5
portfolio planning techniques, 42

prescriptive models, 16–17, 30–1, 40
proceduralism, 6, 178
productivity bargaining, 4–5, 91
psychology, 4
psychometry tests, 14, 54, 99, 205, 223
Purcell, J., 2, 20, 42, 74, 243, 265, 281

quality management, 14, 60, 61, 109–11, 200, 201, 218, 275

Ramsey, Bob, 170
Rank Xerox, 15
rationalism, 3
recruitment and selection, 14, 97–100, 205–6, 223
research needs, 278–9
reward *see* payment
ritual and myth, 4–5, 272
Roethlisberger, F. J., 218
Rolls-Royce, 51, 69–71, 78, 175, 269, 270
Roots, Paul, 170, 171
Rowntrees, 16, 117

Saville and Holdsworth, 99
scepticism, 5, 7–8
Schuler, R., 22
Schutz, A., 212
Scott, W. G., 190
Scullion, H., 41
selection *see* recruitment
self-development, 112, 210–11
senior management, 12, 43, 266, 274
see also line management
Sisson, K., 2, 10, 16, 41, 74, 111, 187, 188, 265, 278, 281
Smith, C., 39
Smith and Nephew, 51, 75–7, 78, 269, 270, 271

appraisal in, 107–8
employee involvement in, 111
line management in, 205, 210
management of change in,
  131–3
personnel specialists in, 174
recruitment and selection in,
  100, 205
trade unions in, 261
training in, 112–13, 210
social psychology, 4
social sciences, 3, 32–3, 34
Stanton, 155
statistical process control, 218
Stevens, M., 139, 191–2
Stewart, John, 55
Stewart, R., 190, 191
Storey, J., 10, 26, 211, 278
strategic business units, 42, 195
strategic change management, 4
strategic human resource
  management, 24, 29
structuralism, 3
succession planning, 84
supervisors (first line managers),
  216–25, 238–41, 267
case studies of, 225–38
SWOT matrix, 12–13
symbolism, 3–6, 39, 43, 272–3

task forces, 67, 114–15
team briefings, 14, 70, 101, 106
team working, 61, 87–9, 95,
  144–5, 200, 216, 226
technological control, 45
testing of employees, 14, 54,
  98–9, 205, 223
'Thatcherism', 2, 11
Thompson, M., 243–4
Thurley, K., 218
Tichy, N. M., 24
Tioxide, 117
Torrington, D., 162, 163–4

Toshiba, 15
total quality management, 200,
  201, 218
Toyota, 12
trade unions, 11, 36, 44, 232,
  242–5
  impact of HR policies on,
    255–62, 267–8, 275–8
  policies and practices of,
    249–50
  and programmes for change,
    245–9, (outsider role for,
    250–51, 254; partner role
    for, 251–5)
  and quality circles, 111, 275
Training Agency, 161
training and development, 14, 98,
  99, 111–16, 121, 208–11, 213,
  224
traumas (crises), 44–5, 150–1
Trevor, M., 16, 100
Trice, H. M., 5, 272
Tse, K., 16
Turrill, T., 143
Tyson, S., 167

unions *see* trade unions
utilization *see* deployment

visioning, 161

Walters, Colin, 58, 97, 171
Walton, R. E., 1, 25, 33, 36, 139
Weber, M., 34
Wedgwood, 16
Weick, K. E., 272
Weitzman, Professor, 108
welfare provision, 174
Whalen, Geoffrey, 203
Whitbread, Sam, 74
Whitbread Breweries, 51, 72–4,
  78, 269
  appraisal in, 108, 230

communication in, 207–8, 248
line management in, 207–8,
209
management of change in,
127–30, 151
personnel specialists in, 174
supervisors in, 228–31, 241

trade unions in, 248, 261
training in, 209
White, M., 100
Whyte, W. F., 218
Wickens, P., 16, 100, 263
Winkler, J., 24, 202
Wirdenius, H., 218

Index compiled by Michael Heary